M000191896

Walkabout to Wisdom is a modern- [...]
the World Trade Center and the sh[...]
math, to his seeking refuge in the Australian Outback, a life challenged becomes a life regained. We follow Lachlan on his journey across the Australian continent and connect with its unique places. We meet its Aboriginal people, Australian explorers and adventurers, and travellers from around the world. We see its wildlife and share his campfires under the great dome of the night sky. And we follow the evolution of his thinking about what makes us Australian, what really matters in life, and how we need to change our lives if we are to have lives worth living.

Darrell Lewis
Author – Beyond the Big Run

This is a personal journey, physical and spiritual, searching for what makes Australia and how Australia makes Australians. It explores our most powerful and persistent traditions, the bush and Anzac. A foundation story well told, it will interest every Australian.

Bill Gammage
Author – The Broken Years

Lachlan Hughson has a unique way of looking at Australia's landscape, people, and history. His storytelling draws you in like a campfire on a chilly bush night.

Jeff Maynard
Author – The Unseen Anzac

From the debris of the World Trade Center and a young man's shattered aspirations comes a story of 'liberation' and the power of going walkabout. From the sandy deserts, wrinkled plains, and ancient ranges of Outback Australia, Lachlan's insightful journey captures the monumental tectonic wanderings of the Australian continent and the many secrets its antiquity holds. Lachlan's realisation that our traditional view of humanity as a pinnacle of evolution, and the glittering star atop a

'Christmas tree of life', is just a load of anthropocentric nonsense, came to him as mine did – after a similar journey during which time I changed my view of life and reassessed my place within the planet's biota. I highly recommend *Walkabout to Wisdom* for this insight alone.

Reg Morrison
Author – Australia: Land Beyond Time

Walkabout to Wisdom by Lachlan Hughson arrived in a particularly busy part of my year.

With my new album completed and awaiting release, and a promotional and performance tour being pieced together, I was feeling that even the margins of my day were packed with high priority to-dos.

And yet, I said yes to the request for a review. There was something in the title of this work by, to me, an unknown author, that drew me in.

Upon receipt of the manuscript, I skimmed a few chapters and discovered thought pathways that I have been ambling down myself over the last months – and how my travelling life songwriting, recording, and performing was akin to Lachlan's 'walkabout' but with one major difference – I know these places he tells us about – I have travelled over, through, and around them en route to many destinations and audiences, but rarely have I paused, listened, lay on the ground, and communed with Nature in the way he has…

Needless to say, I ended up finding an extra half hour at the close of each day to follow his 'walkabout' – confirming how timely it was for me to receive this wisdom.

So, thanks to Lachlan, I am now committed to and am planning my own adventure that reconnects me to the great mystery and wisdom of this magnificent force we call Nature.

See you on the road – or maybe not – I'll be where Nature leads me and three could well be a crowd.

Graeme Connors
Australian Country Music Songwriter, Recording and Performing Artist

Walkabout
to Wisdom

Awakening to Nature's Teaching
in the Australian Outback

Trust in Nature!
Lachlan Hughson

Lachlan Hughson

First published in Australia by Aurora House
www.aurorahouse.com.au

This edition published 2019
Copyright © Lachlan Hughson 2019
www.lachlanhughson.com

Book interior and e-book design: Amit Dey
Cover design: Simon Critchell
Map design: Watermark Advertising

ISBN number: 978-0-6483292-2-0 (paperback)

A catalogue record for this book is available from the National Library of Australia

Lightning Source has received Chain of Custody (CoC) certification from:
The Forest Stewardship Council® (FSC®)
Programme for the Endorsement of Forest Certification® (PEFC®)
The Sustainable Forestry Initiative® (SFI®)

Distributed by:
Ingram Content:
www.ingramcontent.com
Australia: phone +613 9765 4800 | email lsiaustralia@ingramcontent.com
Milton Keynes UK: phone +44 (0)845 121 4567 | email enquiries@ingramcontent.com
La Vergne, TN USA: phone +1 800 509 4156 | email inquiry@lightningsource.com

Gardners UK:
www.gardners.com
phone +44 (0)132 352 1555 | email sales@gardners.com

Bertrams UK:
www.bertrams.com/BertWeb/index.jsp
phone +44 (0)160 364 8400 | email sales@bertrams.com

To Ken,

It has been a pleasure getting to know you. I hope you appreciated the connection to the land + its

To the Australian Outback in all your glory—
May we learn to live in harmony within your realm.

people, both European + Aboriginal. I look forward to continuing our conversation + friendship about both the Scots + Australia. And to enjoying some more Scottish connection while in Denver.

Lachlan
9·11·2020

About the Author

Lachlan Hughson, the son of a mining engineer and teacher, was born in Broken Hill. Growing up in remote mining and cattle towns across the continent, Lachlan connected with the Australian bush at a young age. It was the experiences and insights gained from his childhood walkabout, in conjunction with an unexpected career interruption 20 years later, which inspired the writing of his first book: *Walkabout to Wisdom*.

Following his experience in the mining industry, combined with university holidays spent working on several Central Queensland cattle stations, Lachlan's fascination with corporate finance manifested as a natural resources investment banking career in Sydney and New York. It was from New York, following his 'liberation' after the September 11, 2001 attacks, he returned to Australia to relearn the life wisdom he had unwittingly lost to the demands and dis-ease of the modern world.

While his most important life lessons have come from the natural world, Lachlan is equally at ease in the investment banking and business worlds. He holds a Master of Business degree from the University of Technology Sydney, a Master of Business Administration degree from the Kellogg School of Management, Northwestern University, and a Master of Science degree (with Distinction) from Imperial College London. He is both an Australian and British citizen.

Lachlan's desire to give the natural world a voice, in this time of profound cultural, technological, and environmental change, was the catalyst for putting his career on hold in 2018 to publish this book following its slow evolution in the 15 years since completing his journey. He remains on walkabout, personally and professionally, seeking other paths to connect with Nature's teaching and wisdom.

Acknowledgements

To my life guides Will H. Ogilvie, John McDouall Stuart, Ernest Giles, Robert O'Hara Burke and John Wills, Captain Charles Sturt, Essington Lewis, Patsy Durack, Captain Charles Bean, Sir Hubert Wilkins, Nat 'Bluey' Buchanan, Sir Augustus Gregory, and John Eyre, thank you for your magnificent journeys of adventure and exploration across the Australian frontier. It is the adventurers and explorers throughout human history who provide inspiring examples of what we are truly capable when adversity strikes. Thank you for blazing your unique paths across the Australian continent of yesterday such that we are able to follow our own today.

While my life guides are the foundation of this story, the adventurous lives of other men and women have equally inspired me over the years. Accordingly, it is fitting they too be recognised. To Robert the Bruce, Sir William Wallace, Captain James Cook, Captain Matthew Flinders, Sir Alexander Mackenzie, Sir Ernest Shackleton, Roald Amundson, David Livingstone, Alexander von Humboldt, Major General Sir Neville Howse, Major General Harold 'Pompey' Elliott, and General Sir Harry Chauvel, thank you for being such unique wellsprings of inspiration and action in, and for, the natural world. Thank you also to 'Rabbie' Burns, Robert Louis Stevenson, 'Banjo' Paterson, Ernestine Hill, Elyne Mitchell, and Slim Dusty for the wisdom and inspiration of your works. Without them, I would never have followed the path of walkabout.

To Jack Tarrant, Charles Bingham, Ernest Guest, and the men and women of the First Australian Imperial Force who took the time to share their experiences of Gallipoli, France and Flanders, and Palestine over the years, this book is a result of those many conversations. I will never forget the sacrifice of the best years of your life in the service of your country.

While the final form of this book is quite different to that we initially envisaged, I think you will be happy with the direction it took. I did not forget my promise to you.

To my parents Robert and Carol Hughson, thank you for allowing me the freedom to indulge my connection with the natural world and fascination for walkabout. I also recognise and thank my Scottish and Nordic ancestors for their education, enterprise, and courage. In particular, I acknowledge my grandfather, Sergeant John Hughson of the 70th Siege Battery, Royal Garrison Artillery, who enlisted in 1914 and served from 1916-18 on the Western Front, and his only brother, Signaller Robert Hughson of the 8th Battalion Seaforth Highlanders, killed in action 26 August 1917 near Passchendaele, Belgium.

To the Australian bands of my youth including Redgum, Midnight Oil, Cold Chisel, INXS, The Church, Hunters & Collectors, Icehouse, Dragon, Mondo Rock, Australian Crawl, Mental As Anything, Skyhooks, Men At Work, AC/DC, The Angels, Rose Tattoo, Party Boys, Goanna, Yothu Yindi, Mop & The Dropouts, Warumpi Band, Fitzroy Xpress, and Coloured Stone, thank you for music that inspired and cajoled, beguiled and resonated, educated and motivated. And thank you to The Royal Scots Dragoon Guards whose music called to the depths of my soul.

To the Australian singers and songwriters of my youth including John Schumann, Graeme Connors, Shane Howard, Neil Murray, Paul Kelly, Bon Scott, Richard Clapton, Eric Bogle, John Williamson, and Archie Roach, thank you for telling your stories of Australia in a manner that reflected all facets of our culture.

To Batt and Laura Humphreys, Adam Redman, Albert and Dorès Klinger, Lyne Cossins, Robert and Raye O'Sullivan, Sam and Bruce Cobb, Tim and Emily Holt, Lars Rekemeyer, Takashita, and the many other travellers who made my walkabout such an incredible and life-changing experience, thank you for your friendship, the warmth of your fires, and the many laughs we shared on the track.

To Sylvaine Hughson, Sally Hughson, Angus and Abigail Hughson, Glen McLaren, Darrell Lewis, Bill Gammage, Jeff Maynard, Andrew and

Merri Hoholt, James and Karen Sleeman, Stuart and Alexandra Pearce, Ejvind and Margie Hoholt, John and Pam Sleeman, Rob and Jenny Wild, John Tankard, Kevin Zalanskas, Ann Holt, Kerry Monaghan, Eli Dempsey, Nathan Teegarden, Brynn Asarch, and my many other supporters, thank you for your encouragement, ideas, and enthusiasm through the challenging and exciting process of writing and publishing this book.

To Catherine Reid, Will H. Ogilvie's great-granddaughter, who graciously permitted me to use his inspiring poetry throughout this book, I hope you find this story a fitting tribute to his memory and the inspiration of his works.

To Rob Curtis, Stuart Smith, and Reg Morrison who checked the Australian geology sections, thank you for helping me to share the fascinating and beguiling geological history of the Australian continent in a simple, concise, and educational manner.

To Heathe Cooper, Cameron Burns, and Miranda Coleman who helped create the maps I could never have conceived myself, thank you for your ideas and attention to detail that awed me at every turn.

To Tammy Bennett and Sarah Power who painstakingly converted several hundred 15-year-old 35mm negatives to the photos throughout this book, thank you for ensuring we captured the splendour of Outback Australia in a manner that reflects its exquisite and timeless beauty.

To my beautiful feline companions Shadow, Yoshi, and Ardoise who sat and rested beside me as I wrote and rewrote this book over 15 years, and Peppy, Kynan, and Sheba whose memory still makes me smile, your presence and elegance remind me every day why it is so important to give the natural world a voice.

To my majestic equine companions Anna, Banjo, Can-Can, Papa, Mousaka, Connor, Forrester, and the other horses in my life whether playing polocrosse, packhorse trekking, mustering cattle, or working in the dressage arena, I owe you an equal debt of gratitude. For it was your beauty, power, and elegance that helped me to connect with Nature's teaching most of all.

To Linda Lycett and her remarkable team at Aurora House, including Josie Dietrich, Amit Dey, Melissa Aliling, and Simon Critchell, without whom this book would never have seen the light of day, I give the biggest 'thank you' of all. It was your professionalism, insight, and desire to convert the initial manuscript into a story worthy of the lives woven through its pages that made it all possible. I could never have conceived, let alone achieved, what we have with this book without your passion for the Outback and the telling of a walkabout tale. From start to finish, you were a joy to work with. I hope this book serves as an inspiring example of what a truly collaborative effort can achieve.

Finally, to the Australian Outback itself, whose rugged grandeur, tender touch, and enchanting magnificence have beguiled and fascinated since my first memory. I will remain forever grateful to have simply been the medium through which one of your inspiring and evocative stories could be told. I trust I have done it the justice it deserves.

Contents

Chapters

9. —■—■—
10. —|—|—
11. ·—·—·
12. □□□□□
13. — — — —
14. ·············

Katherine

Darwin

Manning Gorge

Kununurra

Cape Leveque

Broome

Cape Range

Bungle Bungles

WA.

Dales Gorge

Tom Price

Ormiston Gorge

Monkey Mia

Coober Pedy

SA.

Light Horse Memorial

Perth

Albany

Port Augusta

N
W   E
S

Walkabout Map
2003
Seisia
Normanton
Cairns
NT.
Lawn Hill
Gorge
Porcupine
Gorge
Brisbane
QLD.
Alice Springs
Last Camp
Bourke
NSW.
Sydney
VIC.
Adelaide
Melbourne
TAS.
Hobart

Walkabout Mentors

Will H. Ogilvie

John McDouall Stuart

Ernest Giles

Robert O'Hara Burke and John Wills   Captain Charles Sturt

Essington Lewis

Patsy Durack

Captain Charles Bean

Sir Hubert Wilkins

Nat 'Bluey' Buchanan

Sir Augustus Gregory

John Eyre

Foreword

John Schumann
Singer-Songwriter

I think it was June 1972. I was in the second year of my undergraduate degree at Flinders University, majoring in English and Philosophy. I was sick of study and distinctly less than engaged by the Restoration Plays. The sky was a translucent blue, the air was crisp and clean, and the Outback called me by my name.

Two mates and a bull terrier rejoicing in the name of 'Magi' piled into a 1963 Ford Thames van and headed up the unsealed Stuart Highway. We were away for two or three months, just knocking around the bush like three characters in a Lawson story. Call it my 'gap year' – but it didn't look too good on my academic statement of record. Nonetheless, in many ways I learned more on that trip than I would have in six months of lectures and tutorials. I even wrote a song about it.*

> *"There's a corrugated highway leaning north from Port Augusta*
> *lined with ratted cars that didn't rate a tow...*
> *... someone mentioned walkabout and kiss your job goodbye*
> *just to see the country shimmer through the windscreen..."*

In the four decades that have followed, our world has changed almost beyond recognition.

Our planet is screaming at us to stop exploiting it like there's no tomorrow. Because it knows, even if we don't, that it is entirely possible there will be no tomorrow.

Meanwhile, people who were elected to conduct our national affairs caress lumps of coal in our parliament. Noisy archconservatives thrash around like fish in a bucket at the mere mention of renewable energy.

Too few of us ever stop to consider that the unimaginable wealth and comfort we enjoy in Australia today is built on the dispossession and the misery of the people who were here first.

Too many of us would rather consign our grandchildren to extinction than change our behaviour.

Too many of us spend more time punching text messages into smart phones than we do actually talking to each other under the open sky.

When we download our engagement with the universe from the internet, we can't hear it whisper to us in the breeze or rumble at us in the ocean breakers. Worse, in our eternal struggle to produce and consume, we forget that our happiness and health are inextricably tied to the happiness and health of the planet on which we all depend.

All this is to say that Lachlan Hughson's *Walkabout to Wisdom* will speak to all of us who have lain in a swag under the desert sky at night and looked into the universe.

It will speak to all of us who've ever wondered why we're here.

And it will speak to all of us who've thanked whatever gods there may be that we live in Australia.

* The Last Frontier
(John Schumann – Universal Music Publishing)

*   *   *

Dr Glen McLaren
Research Historian

When first requested to write a foreword for Lachlan's manuscript, being exceptionally busy with a particularly large manuscript of my own, I agreed cautiously. To my delight, though separated by a generation, half a world, and dramatically different styles, the more I read, the more I realised how closely we share an unending love of the Australian Outback specifically and nature generally.

My awakening came in January 1984 when I was asked to re-educate a horse which, after jumping from the race day barriers, was turning left and crashing into the inside running rail. The retraining was proceeding well when, with no reason and no warning, on the third jump out it turned outwards and galloped into the outside fence, springing the pipe rails open at a joint and scooping half my right foot off. Although I recovered remarkably quickly and was back breaking in 11 weeks later, over the next three years I came to realise I had lost a degree of my previous resilience. Instead of bouncing back day after day, month after gruelling month, by about June or July of each year I had become very tired and wanted a break.

I yearned instinctively to see the red Pindan country and ranges of the north, so built a canopy for my ute and purchased the necessary camping equipment. While initially my friend and I had no skills or system, within a day or so we had become proficient and revelled in the peace and solitude. Within 10-15 minutes of selecting a secluded campsite and pulling up, we would have the table set up, a fire going, and a billy boiling for a cup of tea. We had no itinerary and sometimes liked our lunchtime campsite so much we stayed there for the afternoon and evening. Occasionally we walked down creek beds, marvelling over and collecting the multi-coloured stones of the region; other times we took the dogs for walks and drank in the vivid colours of the sky, the ranges, and the bush. We sat in our fold-up chairs and read or chatted, topping up our mugs of tea from the billy simmering quietly on the coals at the edge of the fire. The evenings were especially beautiful as we sat reading by the quiet hiss of our gas lamp, occasionally stoking the fire before sitting and staring into the flames or at the stars that shone so clearly in the crystal clear air of the inland.

Only after a few such days did we realise how bone-tired we were and how much we needed to rest. In summer we generally stayed near the coast where we swam, fossicked in rock pools, and snorkelled along reefs as we had done while children. And that was how we were. We didn't have the money to go to expensive tourist resorts, but, even if we had, we wanted nothing more than being able to choose where we camped, peace and solitude, and being extremely close to nature where we could recover physically and psychologically. They were peaceful, restorative days that I treasure still.

And that is the message Lachlan Hughson provides in abundance in his intensely evocative work: *Walkabout to Wisdom.* Being immersed in and communing with nature provides physical and psychological succour beyond value. Quintessentially, we are primal beings with but an extremely thin veneer of civilisation, and are 'hot-wired' to live within nature. As Lachlan points out on numerous occasions, we came from nature and we draw comfort, strength, and wellbeing from nature.

Indeed, we share identical beliefs on how nature provides to those willing to draw from its unbounded gifts. My awakening to this joie de vivre, this exultation of spirit, occurred at the age of 14 when I was staying at a family friend's farm at Mount Barker, in the southwest of Western Australia. On the morning in question, the farmer and I were walking down through his orchard shortly after sunrise to commence picking apples. Everywhere I looked, my eyes were taken by flashing jewels of light as the rising sun struggled through the mist, refracting through the beads of moisture on the apple tree leaves, the grass... even the fence wire. Indescribable beauty surrounded me with glorious gradations of green, misty white, orange, blue, and yellow. I said to my friend how stunning it was, to which he replied, *"It's a pleasure to be alive."* Simple sentiments and simple words, yet how profound, and I have never forgotten them, still employing them over half a century later when moved by the beauty of nature. How can one not be one with nature?

In short, for me, Lachlan has covered the essence of living in harmony with nature. Both he and I realise that nature and the Australian Outback are in our souls. We will always remain true to them and, no matter where we finish our lives, our spirits will return to the red dust and blue skies of our true home.

I truly commend Lachlan's heartfelt work.

*   *   *

Prologue

Ormiston Gorge, one of the most inspiring jewels in the majestic crown of the Australian Outback, lies tucked away within the spectacular, rugged beauty of the West MacDonnell Ranges. Embraced by its nurturing realm in the twilight of a winter's day, while gazing over the natural amphitheatre patiently and dramatically created by Nature's hand, was a moment of transcendent bliss. Enthralled by the serenity of this ancient land, enchanted by its surrounding grandeur, I felt I had discovered Nature's Cathedral.

In that unique moment, I felt part of the natural world in a profound way. I felt it had granted me a privileged insight into its soul. Nature now spoke a language that resonated not only with its first beguiling call to a child on the Australian frontier over 30 years before, but also with its all-encompassing presence at that moment. A language that connected with my mind and body, heart and soul. A language that made me acutely aware of how much Nature will teach those of us who seek its wisdom, and how much we could learn if only we would listen.

From the moment of its first siren call, I have felt a deep and intimate connection with the Australian bush and the natural world. The bush has held me willingly in its thrall since that moment much as the sun holds the Earth naturally and firmly in its orbit. Like the Earth's relationship with the sun, I look to the Australian bush and the natural world for energy and understanding my place in the Universe. It is the power that supports and sustains my whole being. My early memories revolve almost entirely around the natural world and the opportunity it bestowed on a child to understand the elements to a life well lived. It is my guide and my sustenance. I cannot put it any more succinctly than that.

Tragically, however, since that first siren call, humanity's rapacious and wasteful ways have further despoiled the nurturing splendour of the Australian bush, and the environment globally. From human-induced climate change to the increasing destruction of the oceans and forests, from the ongoing poisoning of our food and health systems to the sixth mass extinction now underway, humanity is slowly destroying the very habitat that gives us life.

Moreover, as we destroy the natural world so we destroy ourselves as reflected in the increasing incidence of self-inflicted dis-ease through much of society today. For when the hallowed lands of our youth are irrevocably destroyed, when its creeks and waterholes are nothing but cracked mud and dried mussel shells, when the tall, welcoming stands of timber remembered are nothing but dried grass and scarring gullies, how can we possibly believe we have not inflicted the same destruction on ourselves and our society?

How can we expect to live as inspired and healthy human beings if we consciously and subconsciously destroy the very thing that gives us life? As I came to learn, the only true cure for humanity's increasingly intractable issues is living in a manner that balances our society with the natural rhythms of the Earth: our ultimate creator. For, as is Nature's way, it will nourish us in every respect, much as it has humanity since the dawn of human history, if only we reciprocate that respect.

How do I know this? Because life gave me the unique opportunity to reconnect with Nature's teaching in the Australian Outback. In October 2001, after the September 11 attacks, I was 'liberated' from my investment banking career in New York. After 15 years spent faithfully following the education and career path to that position, suddenly it was gone in an instant. Yet, at the moment of 'liberation', I knew exactly what my future held. I would return home, back to the bush, to follow Nature's siren call to walkabout and the wisdom it would surely teach.

On returning home, I quickly rolled my swag and headed off to where my heart truly belongs – the wild, rugged, inspiring vastness of the Australian Outback. Apart from my swag, the only other items required were a 4WD, two spare tyres, a fuel jerrycan, basic cooking gear, a shovel and bucket, a duffle bag of clothes, my quart-pot, and my camera. I spent two years and 50,000 kilometres travelling Australia's vastness, primarily alone, following in the tracks of its explorers and adventurers, working horses and cattle, exploring its many remote and captivating places, and connecting with the land and its intrinsic wisdom.

Fortuitously, as I trusted at that unique moment of 'liberation', the rousing voice whispering it was time for the road less travelled did not disappoint. For I discovered far more than I ever thought possible. Not only did I regain my health and sense of adventure, returning to the levels of vitality, stamina, and strength remembered as a younger man, I learnt a wisdom that will help me maintain this capacity for the rest of my life. I learnt, once again, that we will feel most alive, be most alive, when connected to and supported by the natural world.

I learnt that Nature will not only provide us with every nourishment necessary to live in harmony within its realm, but that its wisdom and teaching are the key elements required to achieve the life of health, happiness, and adventure human beings seek.

This is the story of that journey.

1

Liberation

'So, see that the bit that holds you straight
Is wrought of a stainless steel,
And the spur of ambition that rules your gait
Is hung on a careful heel.
And then through the stockyard's open rails,
Where the waiting world lies wide,
Like a peerless knight of the ancient tales,
Ride out as the best men ride!'

Will Ogilvie – Life's Ride

Being 'liberated' from your career, or being 'let go' as society euphemistically describes it, is an experience that can have a profound impact on your life. It can either destroy your world or make it your oyster; the end result often hinging precariously on your attitude and the vicissitudes of fate. It is never easy, that is for sure. Until I fully experienced the harsh reality of joining the ranks of the unemployed, it was difficult to appreciate how exciting or soul destroying it could be. As I discovered, it was a confusing yet intoxicating mix of both. The trick was to have the courage to follow my heart, to turn it into an opportunity for adventure, to look all my fears in the face and laugh at their impotence. It can be the start of a new life, a chance to rediscover lost dreams, an opportunity to slow down long enough for our soul to point us in the right direction. Being 'liberated' can be one of the truly great gifts we receive as a human being. However, what gives me the right to be so philosophical? Because, in October 2001, I was 'liberated' for what would turn out to be three years. Three years without employment, three years without a salary. In fact, three of the best years of my life!

September 11, 2001 in New York started out as a very normal day. The economy was a little slow as was work. Like many others, I was appreciating what I hoped would be a brief respite from the normal intensity of my career as an investment banker. Having arrived home late from work the previous evening, I did not leave my apartment until mid-morning the following day.

Waiting for the bus on the corner of Columbus Avenue and West 86th Street, my regular stop, it was impossible to ignore how excitedly strangers spoke with one another. It was the first time I had experienced this in New York since moving there seven years previously. The anxiety and confusion in their loudly whispered and frantic conversations was impossible to ignore.

Several planes had crashed into the World Trade Center and nobody knew quite what to make of it. The questions flew thick and fast among this small group of commuters, cruelly punctuating what was a delightfully crisp early autumn morning. *"Was it an accident or was it deliberate?"* *"What sort of planes were involved?"* *"How badly had the buildings been damaged?"* *"Had anybody been killed?"* Furthermore, and most importantly of all, *"What did it all mean?"*

Travelling east on the bus, the bright tapestry of light-infused green that was my normal Central Park vista passed by in a blur. This was the last time my view of the city was free from the horror unfolding downtown. For, as the bus crossed out of Central Park onto Fifth Avenue, a quick look to the south, where a plume of black smoke smudged a pristine cerulean-blue sky, confirmed something terrible was indeed happening.

Arriving at work that morning, the first tower had crumbled while the second tower was clearly losing its battle to survive. What I most remember is that none of the modern communication tools worked. The internet and cell phones were down so the information I received was entirely from email as family and friends in Australia watched the day unfold live. Even the remotest cattle stations in Australia, where several of my friends lived, had a better idea of what was happening than I did in the Midtown Manhattan offices of Bear Stearns where I worked.

Sitting at my desk, the email sprang to life with an unexpected frenzy as I turned on my computer; its barrage of short, stabbing questions from around the world bringing tears to my eyes. *'Where are you?' 'Are you OK?' 'Are you safe?'* Sadly and incredulously, following those brief, heartfelt concerns for my safety, I was updated on the destruction wrought downtown, paradoxically, from the other side of the world.

Following the collapse of the second tower later that morning, we were told that work was finished for the day. We were to make our way home as best we could. Along with my colleagues I headed out, north up Park Avenue in my case before cutting across Central Park back to my apartment. It was in the pristine splendour of Central Park I was accosted by a most unforgettable, brutal image. For, in the clear, crisp cerulean-blue sky, a grotesque, ogre-like black cloud rose slowly over the midtown skyline. Its menacing and brooding feel cut me to the bone more than any other image from that day. As if hypnotised, I watched the cloud slowly metastasise, disbelieving such a shocking and disfiguring sight could ruin what had become one of my favourite views of the city.

My other disturbing memory from that time was the smell that blew uptown the following evening as the wind changed direction and came from the south. For the first time, for those of us who had not been downtown, the all-consuming cloud entered our lives. The smell of burning plastics, aviation fuel, crushed concrete, and lives lost, their particulates unwillingly and unwittingly inhaled, ensured I would always be part of that day. It had a rotting, sickly stench that pervaded every part of my apartment, and my being, no matter how hard I tried to block it out. For me, that rotting cloud bookended those horrific days much as the first black smudge on the pristine cerulean-blue sky the previous morning also did.

With the destruction of the World Trade Center, and the associated economic uncertainty swirling around like a viscous East Coast blizzard, something had to give. And the investment banking business was certainly no exception. The funny thing is my day of 'liberation' from Bear Stearns was actually something of an anticlimax. I already suspected it was coming. I had heard the rumours and seen how the interest in our small group within the firm had suddenly waned.

As I sat listening to the quiet, supportive tone of my 'liberator', all the while enticed by the crisp, clear October day outside his window, I felt I was receiving a unique opportunity to rediscover my life – a chance that would likely never come again. Whatever the cost, now was the time to follow my heart, without fear or favour, to where it would lead and what it would teach, knowing it would be a life-changing experience. Of the 830 employees 'let go' that day from Bear Stearns, I suspect there was only one who overtly thanked the firm for its appreciated and benevolent act of 'liberation'.

Leaving work that last day, boxes in hand and a wry smile on my face, my heart continued to speak its words of encouragement. It reflected on the wheel turning full circle, the importance of embracing change, and the lessons an Outback walkabout would surely teach. Despite this completely unexpected change, I believed the experience would play a fundamental role in my life though I had no idea how. Nevertheless, that was all I needed to embrace this most unexpected life circumstance.

Little was I to appreciate how my 'liberation' would prove to be the blessing in disguise I hoped it would be. Not only did it provide a welcome respite from the intensity of effort endured during the previous seven years, it was also the ideal opportunity to understand the detrimental impact such a demanding schedule had taken on my whole being: my mind and body, heart and soul.

As I increasingly started to listen to my whole being, I was startled and confused by the intellectual, physical, emotional, and spiritual paralysis I felt. My exhausted mind was a constant chatter of thoughts that would never rest, yet it was difficult to think and reflect in a manner that was self-controlled. My sapped body had almost no form, no strength, and no energy despite having been an athlete for much of my life before living in New York. And, as I lost touch with my body, so I had also lost contact with my emotions and was living with a numbness never previously encountered.

Most alarming of all, at a soul level, I felt drained having lost the sense of adventure and connection to the natural world that previously defined life for me. Life had become a never-ending grind as I sacrificed the critical aspects of my health and happiness, both ignorantly and complicitly, on the altar of a Western lifestyle infused with American self-destruction.

Much of it was my own fault. One of the lessons I failed to heed when undertaking this particular life path was the importance of balance and a healthy regard for all parts of my being. What I ultimately came to appreciate, during this time of reflection, was the single-minded dedication I initially brought to the lifestyle I chose and the opportunity it represented, which was initially a strength, had become a crutch for other parts of my life to which I paid less attention. As I came to realise, if I did not make a change and reconnect with that life balance, this misguided focus would become the Achilles' heel of everything possible in a life well lived.

Through my own ignorance and laziness, I had unwittingly failed to appreciate the risk of long-term damage to my whole being from the pressure to perform and live without regard for the inevitable consequences of such destructive behaviour. As it turned out, it was ultimately the destructive elements of this lifestyle that made me stop and listen to Nature's siren call and the wisdom it had to speak. Ultimately, and paradoxically, it was the detrimental nature of the path I had consciously but naively chosen that made me aware of the changes now required to undo its effects.

As I increasingly focused on this awareness, for the first time really taking off the rose-coloured glasses inherited on being born into Western society, I realised my self-inflicted problems primarily came from ignoring the wisdom of the natural world. I had done everything asked of me professionally and still found myself on the scrapheap. I had focused on trying to stay fit and healthy, and live well within my means, only to discover it was the greedy and selfish who were promoted and protected. I had learnt how self-entitled Western society has become with respect to looking after itself, using politics, deceit, and hypocrisy to ensure a most unequal and unfair allocation of scarce resources and opportunity.

I began to feel I did not belong, and did not want to belong, to such an increasingly sick society. I needed to return to a place where I could once again believe in what I felt, where I could achieve a state of true health and happiness. It was time to leave New York to replenish what had been taken from me, to take full responsibility for my whole being, and to understand how to live in a manner that supported and sustained my life. Now was the time to undo the damage being part of such an intrinsically self-destructive society had wrought.

My final realisation from this period of deep self-reflection was the extent to which a feeling of perpetual exhaustion now defined my every day. This realisation did not come immediately. It felt more like the slow rousing from a deep sleep where the more I woke, the more I realised how out of kilter my life had become.

Paradoxically, the prism of heartbreaking grief surrounding me every day made this awakening easier. As the bagpipes' sad lament echoed plaintively through the streets of New York, and the dead from that dreadful day were remembered and farewelled, the reality of not living my life to the full, of not embracing the adventurous life possible, accosted every waking moment. Each day, I was brutally reminded of the ephemerality of the human experience and the importance of living our life with no regrets. In particular, the obituaries for the dead became required reading as I tried to comprehend the totality of what happened that day. Most of the stories left me shocked at the loss and the unfulfilled potential. Many cut to the bone while others left me with tears in my eyes, if not actually crying.

As I quietly and consciously sat in this space of grief and shock, unemployed with my visa expiring and no career opportunity to fill the blank canvas I stared at each day, my mind wandered to those things I now missed most of all. I missed the Australian bush and its nurturing caress. I missed the tangy smell of eucalyptus trees after the rain and the sweet scent of a worked horse. I missed the open plains and the wandering path of the Southern Cross across the magnificent Southern Hemisphere night sky. I missed Nature, what it offered, and what it represented. As I listened to my heart, it became strikingly clear how important it was to faithfully follow my own compass, to always find the good in any experience no matter how painful or confusing, and to not have any regrets when my time on Earth is done.

Reflecting on what had happened that day, I put myself in the shoes of the dead and asked myself one question. *"What would I have most regretted not doing if I had been among them?"* And the answer was easy. I would have most regretted not connecting more fully with the natural world, not understanding the lessons the Australian bush had long sought to teach, and not having the courage to follow my heart in the direction it now called. Most importantly of all, I would have regretted not following the seductive call of walkabout, from the vastness of the Australian Outback, first heard as a child all those years ago.

Broken Hill is an enduring though remote town on the dry, dusty edge of civilisation: a speck in the vastness of the Australian Outback. It is also my birthplace since first seeing the light of day in May 1966: a Taurean born in the Year of the Horse. At the turn of the 20th century, Broken Hill was among the most important towns in Australia. Most maps today show it as a small dot in the middle of nowhere; a hint of civilisation in what is incorrectly defined as the daunting, empty space of the Australian Outback.

Broken Hill was, and remains, a mining town whose long exploited silver-lead-zinc orebody was discovered by one of the many curious adventurers who wondered at the colour and weight of the rocks on the 'broken hill'. The 'broken hill' is now almost gone; its 'Line of Lode' mined above and deep below the surface with only residual mullock heaps hinting at its meaningful contribution to Australia's development. Yet, despite the lack of any overt recognition, its enduring legacy stubbornly remains. It was core to Australia's growth as a nation, funding much of her early infrastructure, while many of the skills and assets it forged served as the foundation for several global mining companies today. It also provided the early impetus to the development of a social safety net that remains one of the most respected across the world today.

People born and raised in Broken Hill are known as 'A-graders'. Being Broken Hill-born guaranteed life employment in the mines. Unfortunately, the depletion of its orebody means there are few mining jobs for which to stay today. The purpose of this distinction was to encourage those locally born, unlike the general mining populace who are itinerant by nature, to make their home in this outpost of civilisation.

Neither of my parents were A-graders. Although they were 'from away', they were actually typical of the breed that made Broken Hill their home. My father was an immigrant from Scotland, a mining engineer who moved to Australia in the late 1950s as a mineral boom beckoned to adventurous souls from around the world. Dad's paternal ancestors originated in the Shetland Islands, a unique combination of Scottish and Viking blood history tells us is resplendent with the adventurous spirit of walkabout, while his mother was from the Scottish mainland.

Although my mother was Sydney-born, her ancestry also reflects the immigrant beginnings of all but the First Australians. Like my father, her parents were immigrants from the Old World who sought opportunity and freedom in a very different land. Mum's ancestry was also Scottish and Nordic: her Norwegian and Danish paternal grandparents immigrating to Australia in the 1870s while her mother came to Australia from Scotland as a child. What their collective Scottish and Nordic genes thought of Broken Hill I can only imagine!

Although Mum grew up on the shores of Sydney Harbour, her training as a teacher saw her move to Broken Hill where she met my father. There they subsequently married and produced a small, sometimes unruly, brood of three children of which I was the eldest. I do not remember much, if anything, of Broken Hill. We only lived there for two years before moving across Australia to the small, even more remote, town of Tom Price in the Pilbara region of Western Australia.

Like Broken Hill, Tom Price was also on the Australian frontier. It was the next chapter in humanity's attempt to subdue Nature, to impose its will over what was then, and still is, a tough, character-forming land. One of the largest iron ore deposits in the world had recently been discovered and, like previous mineral booms from the beginning of European Australian history over 180 years before, it beckoned to those attracted to opportunity and adventure on the frontier in this most remote of continents. And as with many other significant mineral discoveries in Australia, it too was located in one of the hottest and driest environments on Earth.

It was as a three-year-old child in Tom Price I experienced my first connection to the mystery of the Australian bush. I remember walking to the end of our street, one that petered out into the all-encompassing vastness of the bush. I remember looking into that vastness, a fantastic vista of spinifex, eucalyptus trees, and rocky ridges, enthralled with what was out there and the mysteries and adventures it clearly held. Its presence called to me with a sincerity and attraction that made its stirring voice impossible to resist. I remember feeling a strong desire to connect with it, to explore it further, to head into its remoteness, and to discover its great secrets and riches.

Fifty years later, I can still remember that exact moment and the profound sense of connection I felt. My connection to the bush, my desire to understand it, my need to listen to it, and my choice to be part of it determined the direction of my life from that moment. It defined the sports I played and the career I undertook. It governed the mentors I chose and those kindred spirits from whose lives I try to learn. Moreover, in the moment of being 'liberated' in 2001, it was that same siren call that beguilingly called me back to the land of my birth.

After several years in Tom Price, we moved east across the breadth of the continent to Central Queensland, and the mining town of Blackwater, where school now became part of everyday life. Fortunately, that was not the primary attraction of this small, nondescript town surrounded by large open-cut coal mines in the Brigalow Belt.

For it was in Blackwater, a far less remote town than Tom Price, where my parents finally became more comfortable with their eldest child wandering off for days on end exploring the bush at will. It was also in Blackwater where horses first became part of my life, a connection that burns bright to this very day. The parents of my best school friend owned a cattle property outside Blackwater, where most of the work was on horseback, and it was there I first learnt to ride.

Despite the long years that have passed, I can still see us riding Clancy, their little pony, all day and as late into the night as we possibly could. It did not seem there was ever enough time in the day to indulge our exploration and adventures atop this very patient pony. Even when not riding, I spent much of my time with horses reflecting on a life path in which they would play a significant role.

Several years later, given the itinerant nature of the mining industry lifestyle, we moved to the mining and cattle town of Clermont. It was here my connection with, and fascination for, the bush in all its forms really evolved. Many weekends were spent on camping trips with the local Scouts: our evenings enjoyed around the fire mesmerised by the intriguing majesty of the night sky.

Overhead, as the Milky Way, Southern Cross, and two pointers journeyed their way across the sky, interspersed with the slow moving light of a satellite or the brightness of a shooting star, the moon mesmerised me on its lone walkabout through the night. The Southern Hemisphere night sky, which first captivated me in those early childhood days, remains one of my favourite panoramas anywhere in the world.

Longer camping trips were also undertaken around the region with each day spent discovering the innate workings of the natural world. I learnt to track native animals through the bush, with their footprints and tail marks far more interesting than any subject at school ever was. I learnt to find my way through the bush, day or night, using the sun and stars, while trying to survive from the fat of the land with a knife and little else. As a group, we built canoes and rafts, often unsuccessfully, with a dunking on a cold winter's morning the most frequent reward for our toil. Other weekends were spent climbing and abseiling from several volcanic peaks around the town. Wolfang Peak, a 30 million-year-old volcanic plug, was my favourite. It was dangerous and sheer making for slow, challenging climbs and fast, thrilling abseiling descents.

In addition to adventures with the Scouts, the other great attraction of Clermont was working cattle at the local stockyards. Working the crush on a hot weekend afternoon with ringers and stockmen, as they branded, castrated, dipped, and yarded their cattle, was the ultimate in excitement as far as I was concerned. The bellowing of cattle as they were yarded, the pungent smell of burning hide as they were branded, and the yelps of cattle dogs as they lunged for 'bush oysters' as a young bull calf lost its manhood were the sounds, smells, and sights that made the bush such a vibrant, fascinating, and exciting place in which to live.

Working wild cattle was the most exciting part of those childhood days. They had an energy and spirit that drew me to them, that intrinsically resonated with me. Seeing them occasionally escape the yards by pulling themselves over a six-foot high log fence, or going through it with the top rail splintering like matchsticks, only induced a greater respect for them along with the men who worked them.

It was also in Clermont, at the local stockyards, I was able to follow my fascination with horses. As stockmen and drovers often left their horses in the yards, as they worked their mobs of cattle, it gave me the chance to spend time alone in their gentle equine presence. Many an early morning, on the weekend or before school, was spent with these nameless stock horses just patting them or trying out my latest hackamore idea with a piece of baling twine. As I walked amongst them, I think they were as curious in the small 10-year-old child wandering in their midst as I was fascinated with them.

I remember one horse in particular, an older brown mare with a very soulful manner, who I loved spending time with, and whose tender touch I remember to this day. Looking back, I think she may have somehow understood my life path entailed connecting with her species, and Nature, and so further nudged me in that direction with her gentleness. She was a most remarkable horse whose photo is one of the few I still have from those days.

Given my fascination with horses and attraction to the cattle industry lifestyle, I was convinced, much to my parents' disbelief, my purpose in life was to become a stockman or a drover. Whatever it was, it would involve working with horses in the bush and that was all I wanted. Being inspired by, and becoming increasingly comfortable in, the natural world were the most important lessons from those days. At that time, they were even more important than what I learnt at school!

Propitiously, or unfortunately as I thought at the time, those bucolic days ended when I was 12 years old. My father selflessly decided it was time to move our family to Sydney to ensure his children received the education we missed through continually moving and living in ever-changing remote mining towns. To our eternal gratitude, he sacrificed the full potential of his career to ensure we had the same schooling opportunity he had. While his choice was not appreciated by me at the time, with the thought of living in a city an idea to be feared, it has come to be one of his decisions as a parent I am most grateful for.

Moving to Sydney was, at times, a difficult and disorienting experience as report cards from my five years at the Shore School certainly attest! Yet, despite the challenges and many self-inflicted mistakes, the consistent grounding of Shore helped me to develop a broader life framework;

one that encouraged an increasing intellectual awareness to balance the physical, emotional, and spiritual insights gained from growing up in the bush. In hindsight, the opportunity to be part of the Shore community, to develop my personal understanding of my place in the world, one that ultimately facilitated how I undertook my walkabout, was a most fortunate experience.

The other appreciated choice my parents made, thereby ensuring our transition to the city was not as traumatic as it could so easily have been, was moving to the Northern Suburbs of Sydney. Fortunately, our house looked over the bush surrounding Middle Harbour with the freedom and space of Garigal National Park across the street the perfect location to indulge my increasing fascination with Nature's delights. Although most of my classmates preferred studying or socialising, I could not ignore my need to be in the natural world. Accordingly, I often wandered down to Gordon Creek, or to Middle Harbour itself, to just light a small fire and boil my quart-pot, simply savouring the peace and serenity Nature afforded. It was all I truly needed.

While school was engaging intellectually, the opportunity to pursue a career represented the chance to move in a more interesting direction. Not surprisingly, given a childhood spent living in remote mining and cattle towns across Australia, and working as an underground miner at Myuna Colliery one summer holiday, it was the natural resources industry that most strongly called.

Undertaking a bachelor's degree in business at the University of Technology Sydney, followed immediately by a master's degree, provided the career direction initially sought. While the focus of my study was accounting and finance, its application to the mining and energy industries was the most interesting part of that education. It was the intellectual challenges of the business world balanced with the rigours of the natural world that made life a fascinating adventure each day.

Accordingly, when my university exams were finished and the books finally closed at semester's end, I returned to the natural world and the pleasure of working with horses once again. Most holidays were spent working on several cattle stations around Clermont with friends I had made while living there. The joy at being back in the saddle, of spending long, hot days covered in dust and sweat, was the perfect panacea to the soft hands and sapped body incurred during my university days. My need to be part of the Australian bush, personally and professionally, is one from which I have never been able to escape. It is one from which I never want to escape.

It was my fascination with the natural resources industry, and increasing desire to work in corporate finance at a global level, which occasioned my move from Australia to New York. On finishing university, I felt an investment banking career provided the most practical opportunity to follow this dual fascination. The opportunity to work with mining and energy companies, starting with my first career position at Macquarie Bank in Sydney, provided the intellectual balance I intrinsically sought. It provided the strong intellectual connection to the natural world much as working with horses provided the physical, emotional, and spiritual connection. I felt there was a lot to learn by following this path though I had no idea how it would actually unfold.

Given the position of the United States as a powerhouse in the production and consumption of metals and energy, and its role as a global centre for corporate finance and capital markets, my next career step focused on working there with entry achieved through the intellectual rigour of a Master of Business Administration degree. After half a dozen applications, and almost as many rejections, I was fortunate to gain acceptance into the MBA program at the Kellogg School of Management, Northwestern University. Accordingly, in August 1993, I left Australia on my career walkabout for the United States not knowing when I would return to the nurturing embrace of the Australian bush.

From Kellogg, my fascination with natural resources and corporate finance was followed to New York and an investment banking career, first at Lehman Brothers and later Bear Stearns. Investment banking offered an exhilarating career path at this time with its exposure to mergers and acquisitions, corporate finance, and capital markets providing a fascinating learning opportunity. Whether it was the all-consuming intensity of the work, the challenging nature of the problems solved, the personality types the industry attracted, or the ruthless manner in which pecuniary baubles were distributed, there was never a dull moment.

Experienced bankers have likened it to running a marathon at a sprinter's pace and that is exactly how it felt for seven years. The work never ended as one project evolved into the next. From valuation spreadsheets and complex merger and acquisition models analysing corporate combinations, to high yield debt and equity capital raisings funding corporate growth, each day blurred into the next as I tried to keep senior bankers happy with the work product they required. From joint ventures, spin-offs, and divestitures to initial public offerings, private capital investments, and restructurings, I lived and breathed the strategic, operational, financial, and timing aspects of the transactions we pitched and executed for our clients.

While much of the work was quantitative, which I thoroughly enjoyed, writing the 'pitch books' we used to explain our ideas was also fascinating. Telling the story around a transaction, of why it made sense and how it would be executed, provided the qualitative balance I required to remain somewhat sane in the world of spreadsheets, formulas, and numbers otherwise inhabited.

I lost count of the number of times I worked until the early hours of the dawn, finally getting into a cab just as the sun first spread its golden-orange glow over the East River. With the mining and energy industries in a state of flux, as low commodity prices drove consolidation on all levels, we were on the cutting edge of that change and in some ways driving it. While I found the work intellectually challenging and physically demanding, my fascination with corporate finance and natural resources kept me perpetually enthralled until the day of my 'liberation' finally arrived.

My intellectual fascination with, and physical, emotional, and spiritual connection to, the natural world focuses on its geology in particular.

Understanding the story of the land's evolution, of the myriad of events that went into its creation, gave it a history that made it come alive. It gave Nature a persona with which I wanted to connect. Whether it was the ancient iron and basaltic ranges of the Pilbara, the volcanic peaks around Clermont, the hydrocarbon-focused sedimentary basins of North America, or the metalliferous provinces of Africa and South America, the processes by which the Earth evolved fascinated me.

Having a mining engineer for a father, who could explain geology in detail, further increased my interest in all things related to rocks. By focusing my career on the natural resources industry, I was able to maintain my interest in the Earth's geological history and the stories within the rocks. Understanding structural and stratigraphic maps, base maps and isopach maps, facies maps and geological columns became almost as important as the financial modelling, valuation, accounting, tax, and structuring skills primarily used throughout my career.

Learning how the Earth evolved, how its unique stature reflected the interaction of geological elements and processes from the beginning of time, further enhanced my belief in the creative capacity of the natural world. It was ultimately this creative capacity I most wanted to connect with on my walkabout as I sought to heal myself from the dissonance and destruction of modern-day society.

The geology of Australia, and its resultant geography, biology, and zoology, is as varied and fascinating as that of any continent on Earth. Australia has one of the longest geological histories of any continent; its creation reflecting residual pieces of ancient lands combining over several billion years in a chaotic and random walkabout of their own to forge the marvel of today.

Simply explained, the Australian continent has been a work in progress for over 4 billion years. At its core, the continent comprises three cratons: the Western Craton in Western Australia, the Gawler Craton in South Australia, and the North Australian Craton comprising much of the Northern Territory and the Kimberley. These three cratons today account for the western two-thirds of the continent. Formed separately and in different processes 1.8-3.5 billion years ago, they coalesced around 900 million years ago forging a geological kernel that subsequently underwent a number of profound changes over the next 600 million years to create the landmass of today.

Yet Australia only evolved as an island continent relatively recently as its host, the supercontinent Gondwana, was slowly rent asunder. Its long birthing process, as Africa, South America, India, Antarctica, and finally Australia separated over 150 million years, only ended when the Australian continent split from Antarctica around 50 million years ago – a lone continent on its own walkabout during which time its flora and fauna developed almost untouched until modern times.

Geologists hypothesise that, in another 100 million years, the tectonic forces driving the geological evolution of the Earth will move the continent north to where it will collide with, and become part of, Asia. It will only have existed as an island continent for around 150 million years: an immaterial fraction of the Earth's existence.

Reflecting these dynamic and ancient processes, the rocks defining the continent's character today have undergone profound transformations. Some were formed at the birth of the planet as it coalesced from the debris of exploded stars. Australia was already ancient at the evolution of life when the first organism sallied forth from its ancient sea floor home around 400 million years ago. Its rocks reveal the geological, biological, and zoological history of the Earth so ancient are their origins and so limited has some of the erosion and tectonic destruction been.

From glacier-carved rocks along the Australian coast to glacial till found deep in the desert, from the remnants of mountain ranges once as high as the Alps and Himalayas to one of the oldest rivers on Earth, from rocks showing the beginning of life to rocks from space, the Australian continent is a fascinating compendium explaining the true genesis of our world.

Moreover, the best way to experience and explore these places is on walkabout. A slow, in-the-moment journey where Nature seducingly reveals the lie of the land and its ancient story. And while the flora and fauna of the continent will beguile, mesmerise, and scare the intrepid traveller on an Australian walkabout, it is the land, most of all, that will leave the deepest and clearest impression of what is so enchanting and inspiring about the Great South Land.

Walkabout has been my life philosophy since my first memory. Whether it involved living on the intellectual, physical, emotional, or spiritual frontiers, new beginnings have always inspired me despite the personal and career cost of never living in one place for too long.

Since childhood, I have found it easy and exciting to be on the move, to see and connect with new places. There has always been something challenging and galvanising about a life based on mobility while remaining connected to the natural world. This belief is so ingrained to my being it fundamentally influenced all the significant decisions I ever made. Not surprisingly, as I discovered, this feeling is actually a core genetic part of who I am as a human being. My ancestors, on both sides, showed similar proclivities.

My paternal grandfather worked as a steamship engineer on the China route before returning to Scotland and volunteering for the First World War in 1914. My maternal great-grandfather left Norway as a young man in the 1870s and travelled to Australia by sail, meeting his Danish wife-to-be on the same ship, only once ever returning to Norway. My father was a mining engineer in some of the remotest regions of the world.

It is no surprise that walkabout comes so easily to me. Not only was I nurtured in this lifestyle growing up, my genetic make-up reflects that of several adventurous peoples from history. With Viking and Scottish ancestry defining my bloodline, my predilection for walkabout was probably a key part of my DNA well before my birth. We may think we have freedom of choice, though I cannot help but wonder if our in-the-moment decisions are more often a reflection of who we intrinsically are as a human being than who we may think we are as a person!

Walkabout, at its essence, is a uniquely Aboriginal Australian activity, expression, and philosophy. It represents the rite of passage by which

Aboriginal Australians learnt to connect with the natural environment so critical to their lives. Walkabout was the ritual by which their whole being connected to the country where they were born, lived, and died, gaining insights into its functioning and their place in that. In many ways, the call to walkabout is Nature's purest call, certainly its most revitalising. Having always been inspired and fascinated by cultures whose people were inextricably linked to the natural world, and how they lived in relative harmony within that realm wherever it may have been, it now made sense it was my turn to follow this path.

Going walkabout felt the most natural thing to do as I sought answers to the many questions now burdening my mind and soul. And what better way to do so than in the manner practised by the most ancient and successful of itinerant peoples? My immense respect for Aboriginal Australians, and their innate ability to connect with the Australian continent, played an equally important role in my decision. To appreciate and understand Nature's teaching, I felt I had to connect with its intrinsic wisdom in much the same manner as Aboriginal Australians also had.

As a child, I had an innate sense of the importance of connecting with the rhythms of the Australian bush. In many ways, it was my first love. Whether rising with the sun for early morning exercise, being respectful to the plant and animal beings around me, or connecting with the energy of its many different places, the natural world felt more energising than when I spent my days surrounded by people. Whether it was the myriad calls of birdlife in the early morning, the cool sweetness of a creek in the hot afternoon sun, or the gentling of the country as the warmth of day passed into the cool of dusk, the natural world was far more interesting than school lessons, completing my homework, or being 'entertained' by the television.

Nature gave me everything I truly needed. All it required, in return, was making that connection to its endless generosity through respect for its wisdom and a desire to follow its teaching: the easiest things to do. Apart from my family, who gave me the support and encouragement to follow this call, Nature has always been my guide, my inspiration, and

my sustenance. And, as I became older, I learnt how easy it was to connect with its ways, and how important it remains to our life on Earth.

Nature, to me, is omnipotent. It is the ultimate creator of which humanity is simply another of its evolutionary branches as the many cycles of
the 4.5 billion year history of the Earth clearly illustrate. I have always
found the wisdom of nature-based peoples far more insightful than Western religions, with the idea of our dominion over birds, fish, and animals
the most ignorant and repugnant idea ever conceived. Especially when
much of humanity today is increasingly dealing with the self-inflicted
consequences of this mostly limiting and damaging belief!

What is increasingly interesting is the often practical, ancient natural
wisdoms Western society rejects include prescient insights science is now
finding to be of significant benefit to us. Which is why many Westerners
are increasingly turning to nature-based philosophies for help and direction as we discover the root cause of our dis-ease is a lack of connection
with the natural world. For when we understand Nature's wisdom, when
that comes to define the core insights of how to live in harmony with the
environment and ourselves, nothing else is required. Which is why my
connection to the Australian Outback ultimately resonated so strongly
and made my journey the profound awakening it turned out to be.

Of all the nature-based peoples whose teaching and philosophy I
respect, it is perhaps not surprising my Nordic ancestors' beliefs strongly
resonate. Therefore, like other Nordic wonderers and wanderers from
time immemorial, I too sought the blessing of a patron. The patron who
most inspired was a deity my Nordic ancestors would also have once
looked to for help and protection during their travels: the Nordic all-
father, Odin, my walkabout talisman. As a fellow wanderer, and one who
sought a similar connection to the natural world, Odin's travels in search
of wisdom most resonated as I planned my journey.

Seeking wisdom from the natural world made complete sense to
me. Far more so than the path deemed appropriate by Western religion.
Odin's experience of learning from Yggdrasil, the Tree of Life, of gaining

his knowledge from the teaching of the natural world, deeply resonated. I could understand why he spent a lifetime seeking wisdom in this way. With his eight-legged charger Sleipnir, the perfect partner for a long, meandering walkabout, there was no other deity whose patronage I would rather entreat. Seeking to connect intimately with the wisdom of the natural world, it was with Odin's blessing and life philosophy I undertook my walkabout trusting in Nature to teach me the knowledge it readily makes available to all humanity.

Accordingly, with the Pile at Ground Zero still smouldering and the economy laid low, my bags were packed and I left the United States for Australia not knowing if or when I would ever return. At that moment, I felt alive, reinvigorated. I felt a great enthusiasm for what my life was about to entail – a fascinating journey across the length and breadth of the Australian continent reconnecting with the land of my birth. This was the time to follow the mesmerising call first heard as a child from the wilds of the Western Australian Pilbara. A call whose refrain through my university years saw me travel back to the bush to work horses and cattle during the holidays. A call that had remained a gentle exhortation since first arriving in the United States, and all through my time in New York, with weekends of polocrosse and short holidays to the deserts of Australia my only connection.

However, from the moment of my 'liberation', it was no longer just a call. It was now my reality. Nature's siren call, as loud and clear as it had ever been, told me the moment I had been waiting for had finally arrived. Now was the time to leave the life that was slowly destroying me. Now was the time to throw caution to the wind, to follow my heart, and learn the wisdom Nature had long sought to teach. Now was the time to follow Nature's siren call to walkabout across the vastness of the Australian Outback to rediscover the life of health, happiness, and adventure I more willingly and urgently sought.

2

Rolling the Swag

'The hoofs of the horses! – Oh! witching and sweet
Is the music earth steals from the iron-shod feet!
No whisper of lover, no trilling of bird
Can stir me as hoofs of the horses have stirred.
They spurn disappointment and trample despair,
And drown with their drum-beats the challenge of Care;
With scarlet and silk for their banners above,
They are swifter than Fortune and sweeter than Love.'

Will Ogilvie – The Hoofs of the Horses

Whether starting the day as a ringer in a stock camp, a drover in a remote part of Australia, or a traveller somewhere in the far-flung reaches of the Outback, the first act of the day is to roll your swag. A swag is not only your bed. It is your castle and wardrobe. It is often your only respite from the harsh toughness of the Australian bush. When looking for a seat to sit around the fire, your swag is that seat. When choosing a place to rest on the hard, rocky ground, mesmerised by the moon and stars above as the fire slowly burns into the night, your swag is that support. When it is raining with no shelter available, your swag will provide the little protection enjoyed. When it is winter, when the chill of a cold morning forms as ice on top of a horse's water bucket, your swag keeps you warm and dry. The older it becomes, the more it reflects its owner's very persona. In many ways, it tells the world its owner's story. Reflecting its sanctity and importance, the unwritten rule of the bush is to never interfere with another man's swag. Moreover, when it is time for walkabout, when it is time to travel the rugged vastness of the Australian Outback, it is one of the most important possessions you will actually take.

Returning to Australia, my initial act of walkabout was to roll my swag. To protect against the weather likely to be experienced on such a journey, I first thoroughly waterproofed its six by nine foot canvas wrap. On the middle third of the wrap, I lay an open sleeping bag over which I placed several blankets with two pillows at the top completing the ensemble. Kneeling at the top of the swag, I pulled the left-hand third of the wrap over the bedding and the right-hand third over the top. With seven push studs equally spaced down the left-hand side of my swag, I then clipped the open edge to the swag to hold it all together. To finish, I tightly rolled the canvas-enveloped bed from the top down, around which I wrapped two leather straps, old stirrup leathers, about a hand's width from each end, buckling each one. That was it, easy and simple. My swag was rolled.

While the physical act of rolling my swag for the first time brought a wry smile to my face, the philosophical act was even more important. For it ensured the past was now truly in the past. This act represented the moment I took the first step into the future and started my work under Nature's respected tutelage. It was in this moment my former life started to fade, along with the disappointments from my recent past. Not only did this act signify the start of my walkabout, it initiated a daily ritual for the duration of my journey. A ritual that came to represent the slow maturing of the wisdom I sought thereby making its daily repetition the most important of my journey.

With the swag rolled, I turned my attention to the rest of the preparation required. I spent several days buying a Toyota 4Runner 4WD, recovering gear from storage where it had been sitting for the previous nine years, and organising the other pieces of equipment required. I greased my saddle and bridle, cleaning off the light dusting of mildew that had covered everything in its soft grey and yellow blanket. With two spare tyres, a 20-litre jerrycan for petrol, a small gas-fired stove, a cooking grate for the open fire, a shovel and bucket, a personal emergency beacon I always carried, a duffel bag of clothes, my quart-pot, and my camera, I had everything I could possibly need.

That is what makes walkabout so easy and liberating. It does not require many possessions. For it is the act of travelling lightly that singly creates the freedom and space necessary to learn from its different experiences. The essence of walkabout being that minimum possessions facilitate maximum connection with the natural world; a connection that is not otherwise possible when surrounded by the accoutrement of our daily lives.

It was fascinating how easy it was to leave the past where it belonged, especially my possessions. On leaving New York, I placed them in half a dozen boxes where they remained in storage until finally retrieved three years later on resuming my career. I felt no attachment to anything in those boxes except my books, photos, and music. Whatever else I needed, or acquired, was happily left for others. It was such a pleasure leaving everything behind, not caring if it was there, or not, on my return.

This experience, of cleansing my life of non-critical items, helped me to understand that real freedom comes from having less possessions, not more, despite what much of society tells us today. It was this lack of possessions, of having saved and stayed away from debt, which made this journey both possible and actionable.

Then again, I never thought it made sense to die with a house full of possessions having forgone an adventurous life. So maybe I was just reacting to the situation in which I now found myself. Either way, my newly discovered freedom came from having less, not more, which was one of the most important realisations of my journey. It is a lesson I will never forget.

My walkabout plan was simple – to travel throughout the Australian continent visiting its spectacular geography and learning as much as possible under Nature's expert tutelage. Apart from that desire, and deep-seated need, there was no set path, no mapped out course. The spontaneity of meeting different travellers, of hearing their stories of places to visit, and trusting the journey would unfold as it needed to was the totality of my plan. There was no attachment to a defined path or a defined timetable. It was about learning as I went, of being surprised and awed every day by the plethora of different experiences. It was about keeping an open and quiet mind, and heart, to help the pieces of the puzzle coalesce in a way that enhanced my connection with the natural world best of all.

Much of the benefit from my walkabout came from ignoring the linear, intellectual mindset that had previously defined my life. Of putting it into a box with everything else and leaving it behind, not knowing if or when it would ever make sense to open that box again. To learn the wisdom I sought, I realised it was necessary to leave the expectations and limitations of the past behind and open my whole being to a new way of life. It was something anybody could do, which alone made the journey the profound experience it turned out to be.

To enjoy my walkabout as completely and intimately as possible, I chose to travel alone except when joined by a couple of old friends along the way. The idea of being alone in the bush, camping under the stars in the remote Outback's vastness, responsible for all aspects of my own wellbeing, was the most critical part of my decision to undertake this journey. There was no fear of the unknown; just a healthy respect for the risks involved and an awareness of the importance of always having a backup plan should anything go wrong.

This was the only way to remove myself from society, and its increasingly unhealthy behaviours, for Nature would teach me at its own pace. To go with others would only limit my ability to move at the right pace and gain the greatest insight from the experience. My family and friends accepted my decision without reservation, or any real surprise. Mum, in particular, understood this was something I needed to do and only asked that I be careful, stay in touch, and be home for Christmas. There are not too many understanding mothers like that. And with one last, slightly teary hug from her on the morning of my departure, I was ready to finally embrace the uncertainty that was now my life!

The morning I left Sydney rose with a special glow, its warmth mirroring the stomach-churning excitement that had slowly built from the day of my 'liberation' several months before. As the rotations of the Earth had moved towards this day, with the same certainty of purpose now driving my own direction, I knew this was the right path. I did not know exactly where the path would lead, but it was the right path and that I could trust. The freedom I felt in all parts of my being quickly eroded any fear as to the consequences of leaving the professional world behind for some time.

Laughing at the randomness with which 'success' and 'failure' are doled out in the capitalist system, I made a note to always remember that real success comes from living the life that calls. Others, with a self-absorbed approach, may end up with a bigger slice of the pie, but they would likely pay the price in terms of their health and happiness. Sitting in the driver's seat, the key in the ignition, I relished the fullness of that moment. I felt relieved, light, and excited simultaneously: a most stirring sensation. I now appreciated how the last three months had synchronised perfectly to bring me to this unique moment to finally follow the path that had long called.

Turning the key, the engine's full-throated roar heralded my journey's start. There could be, there would be, no turning back.

Heading north, the harshness and ugliness of the concrete and bitumen jungle of Sydney was soon nothing more than a shrinking image in the rear-view mirror. As the city slowly disappeared from view, the bush increasingly whispered its welcome return as the leaves playfully rustled, the grasses joyfully waved, and the sun happily danced across the sparkling waters of numerous creeks and rivers crossed. The excited shimmering of the sandstone ranges and plateaus in the distance reflected the intense delight I felt at being back within my spiritual home.

Letting my senses take control, I listened to the relaxed hum of the engine as it effortlessly propelled the vehicle forward. I felt the vibration of the tyres on the road as the first few kilometres passed: the first few of the 50,000 kilometres ultimately travelled over the course of the next two years. I felt the sun on my arms and the wind on my face. And through the windscreen, the vista that is the visual magnificence of Terra Australis slowly unfolded, only occasionally hinting at the incredible splendour it would reveal on such a journey.

While I travelled alone for most of my journey, I was never lonely. For travelling with me were the experiences and philosophies of men whom I had come to regard as mentors – the early Australian explorers and adventurers whose journeys played a critical role in the crafting of my own life philosophy. This was my chance to walk in the physical and philosophical tracks of human beings whose accomplishments had inspired me to live my life as they had. This was my chance to intimately connect with their thoughts and deeds, to better understand their philosophy for a life well lived, and to understand the critical role of Nature's teaching to that.

It was the lives and achievements of my 12 mentors, my own philosophers and guides from the desert, which came to define the core threads of the journey's tapestry yet to unfold. It was the opportunity to follow their unique life paths, in their respective tracks, which made this journey the life-changing experience I hoped it would be.

My life mentors hail from the early pages of European Australian history. While they lived quite different lives, the one common thread was their connection to what inspires me about life – that we achieve success and happiness where we live our life as an adventure in harmony with the natural world.

Equally inspiring was their sense the world was their oyster, and the opportunity this represented to construct their life in their own unique image despite the significant limitations often imposed by society. That they were able to throw off the shackles that bind many people to a safe, predictable path, instead of forging their own way unhindered by society's risk mitigating fakeness, highlights how much freedom we could have if only we saw life as the adventure they did. It is to the deeds of explorers and adventurers we must look to understand our intrinsic capabilities when much of modern-day life seems focused on subverting those instincts instead.

Who has not been called to a great adventure or been fascinated by the explorers of the past? Who has not dreamed of undertaking their own journey into unknown country to connect with the life force that creates the experiences we intrinsically seek? Who, at some point, has not desired to leave everything behind and trust their ability to live an adventure in pursuit of a worthy goal? Who has not wished to undertake a great exertion that challenges and expands us as individuals, testing our limits and capabilities, while learning the fundamental lessons of life? Who has not wished to leave the emotional and cultural shackles of the past behind and become a freethinking human being without the baggage inherited on being born in a particular time and place? Who as an adult has not looked back into the days of childhood and seen how divergent our life path became from what we sought when our thoughts were empowering and true?

For these reasons, now was the time to undertake such a journey. Now was the time to follow in the tracks of those whose lives had inspired me since childhood. Now was the time to undertake my own walkabout to determine exactly what I needed to learn at this stage of my life.

My 12 mentors all had a connection with the Australian Outback. Growing up in the bush, I was fascinated to read the journals and biographies of these explorers, drovers, and adventurers on their journeys of discovery. I cannot remember how many times I followed their tracks on a map of the Australian continent, on the random walk of their expeditions, looking for places they had camped or passed through. At that age, I wanted to have been born at a similar time to be part of their expeditions so deeply did their exploration of Australia call to me. It was only as I undertook my own walkabout many years later was I finally able to connect with their inspiring legacies.

Reading their detailed journals, often in the locations they were written, helped me to connect fully with the spirit and meaning of their lives. Their respective philosophies came to represent the key threads of the walkabout fabric I clothed myself in during this journey. Most importantly, their life philosophies mirrored their words giving them an honesty and integrity difficult to find today when many, if not most, of our political, business, and religious leaders talk and walk two distinct and often hypocritical paths.

While these adventurers have long since died, their legacies remain an inspiring example of what is truly possible when the comforts of society are forsaken for walkabout. As would be expected, many played a critical role in opening up and developing the Australian frontier: a foreign and difficult land to most Australians at that time.

The expeditions of John McDouall Stuart, Ernest Giles, Burke and Wills, Captain Charles Sturt, Sir Augustus Gregory, and John Eyre, as they explored the harsh, unknown Australian interior, remain as exciting as when they were first undertaken in the mid-1800s.

The pioneering cattle drives of Patsy Durack and Nat 'Bluey' Buchanan, as they opened up the barely explored interior of the continent in the mid-1800s, inspire today as much as they did at their initial undertaking.

The intellectual approaches taken to understanding and respecting the Australian environment, as advanced by Essington Lewis and Sir Hubert Wilkins in the early to mid-1900s, are even more important today than when they were first articulated.

The inspiring and heartfelt words of the Australian First World War correspondent, Captain Charles Edward Woodrow Bean (known as C.E.W. Bean), highlighting the importance of the Australian bush to the Anzac story, remain a source of inspiration for those who seek an adventurous life path.

The resonating poems of Will H. Ogilvie, with their eloquent insights into the majesty of the Australian bush, written in the 1890s while he worked as a stockman, drover, and horse-breaker, helped me to appreciate and understand the richness and unique benefits of Nature's teaching in a way nobody else could.

From the first Will Ogilvie poem I ever read, I have repeatedly returned to his stirring works to reconnect with the Australian bush. Not only was he an accomplished poet, he was also a great horseman spending 10 years working in cattle camps and breaking in horses during his time in Australia in the 1890s. His beguiling poetry succinctly captures the essence of the Australian bush, and the importance of Nature's wisdom to our lives, in a way few other poets do. Even his memorial, near Selkirk, Scotland, reflects his life on the Australian frontier. For there, surrounded by the misty-green rolling hills of Scotland, is a bronze image of an open book showing the dry, dusty Australian Outback he made his home.

Few poets can take you to the core of Nature's wisdom through their works as Will Ogilvie. That a Scottish-born poet could capture my heart, in a way few Australian-born poets ever did, says much for the integrity and honesty of his work. His poetry became the most enduring voice of the bush during my travels so meaningful was its verse and so honest was its message. Especially his poems and verses highlighting the virtues of an equestrian lifestyle!

Horses have been a part of my life since I can remember. Their beauty, power, and elegance have inspired a fascination and deep respect from my earliest days. To feel the power and agility of a horse as it races to turn a mob of cattle charging through the timber, to watch the symmetry and elegance of a well-muscled horse playing polocrosse or working in the dressage arena, or to hear the gentle whinny of a mare seeking its foal are some of life's simple but most endearing pleasures.

On starting my career, with the financial security it afforded, I spent almost every weekend working with horses. Whether it was trail riding, working in the dressage arena, or playing polocrosse, all enjoyed with my trusted equine companion, Banjo, I could not get into the saddle often enough. There was no better panacea for any ailment than a long, slow ride through the ranges north of Sydney or a hard, fast game of polocrosse.

Reflecting my predilection for an equestrian lifestyle, most Saturday nights were spent camped alone in the bush, with my meals cooked over a small fire, embraced by the starlit night sky and wrapped in a heady swathe of dust, horse sweat, and smoke. Working with horses all weekend, embraced by the natural world, was an experience I could not, would not, give up. Balancing the intellectual challenges of my career with the physical exertion, emotional resonance, and spiritual power of the natural world made life worth living. The nightlife of Sydney held no appeal compared to spending time enveloped by the magnificence of the natural world and its myriad charms and adventures.

During my time in New York, my strongest connection to the natural world was also through horses. Whenever the opportunity arose to work a horse, or just go for a ride, it was taken. Riding through the leafy splendour of Central Park on a cool spring morning, with joggers taking the place of kangaroos and emus, maple and elm trees taking the place of acacia and eucalyptus trees, and Central Park apartment blocks taking the place of sandstone ranges, was an opportunity not to be missed. Nor were the polocrosse carnivals played in various eastern and southern states when a free weekend infrequently arose.

However, it was not the same. The deep connection I previously felt to Nature was not there given how sanitised the environment had become. My desire to return to working with horses not only reflected a need to return to the bush. It reflected a need to return to a life outdoors:

a strenuous life. A life based on the resonance of man with the energy of the natural world. A resonance whose benefits I had lost reflecting the long-ignored calls of my body for a healthier life.

Following this important realisation, in the waning days of my time in New York, my journey commenced on a small property north of Sydney in the Hunter Valley; a place I felt I could reconnect with the energy of the natural world aided by the soothing guidance and support of one of its most majestic beings – the horse.

Starting down this path, I relished each day as if returning from a long and relaxing holiday. Slowly reconnecting with the energising circadian rhythms of the natural world through my connection with the horse, my own internal rhythms increasingly resonated with the natural vibrations of life. Each day, Nature's gentle teaching inspired a profound realisation – the integrity we bring to four basic behaviours, or elements, determines the quality of our life. As I discovered, or more importantly rediscovered, the more I engaged in these activities, the more balanced, happy, and energised I became. It was easy, simple, and motivating to undertake this work every day with minimum effort and commitment. It made me wonder why I had ever given them up in the first place.

Regular meditation gave my mind the time and space required to access cleansing and energising thoughts, an appreciated change from the exhaustion previously endured. Regular exercise ensured I felt alive, refreshed, and motivated no matter the task whether riding horses, cleaning stables, or fixing fences. A healthy diet gave my body the nutrition it required to reconnect with Nature's life force, while nights of the deepest sleep allowed me to slowly consign the feeling of exhaustion to the past.

As I came to realise, the only 'meds' I truly needed for the life of health, happiness, and adventure I sought were meditation, exercise, diet, and sleep. That was it. It was daily doses of these four simple, natural elements that initiated, facilitated, and enhanced my connection to Nature's life force. In essence, these simple 'meds' represented the elixir of life I was now seeking!

On returning to my life with horses, most days started at dawn just as the sun first spread its golden-orange glow across the eastern horizon. From my bedroom door, I could watch my equine companions in the lingering shadows of dawn. Sometimes I did not even have to look for I woke to the melody of their contented chewing and sighing directly outside my window. At other times, I had to strain my eyes to see them down in the creek or hidden within a clump of trees.

However, when I called them, when I gave that first clang of the feed tin or water bucket, they would appear and work their way towards the horse yard. Often, one broke into an excited canter up the hill sending the others into a similar frenzy; the thunder of hooves and flying manes and tails all adding to the spectacle of the occasion. At other times, they showed little interest and only a small bucket of feed or a handful of hay would stir them from their lethargy.

Of course, on the coldest of mornings, I often found them on the other side of a small creek, which meant taking off my boots and wading over barefoot. Just as I crossed, they often burst into a gallop back through the water leaving me mud splattered and laughing. Much of the day was spent with a similar smile on my face given their perpetual antics and the playful approach they brought to most aspects of their lives.

Feeding and watering these horses early in the day gave them time to digest their food before our work commenced later that morning. It was fascinating to watch their behaviour as their food was prepared, in particular the power plays my four-legged friends indulged in and the pecking order created. I came to realise the social dynamics among this small mob of horses was actually no different to that at any Wall Street firm. It was all about getting to the feed bins first, of ensuring nobody pinched your food, and letting fly with a small kick or bite if anybody came too close. I often laughed at how the behaviour of this small mob of sometimes-unruly horses was no different to that of many senior Wall Street bankers despite the latter's pretence at class and civility.

Thinking about my experiences with both groups, there was one difference I came to appreciate with my equine companions most of all.

They could always be trusted to behave in a fair manner. Whether it was the swish of their tail, the set of their ears, or the roll of their eyes, their thoughts always matched their actions. After my experiences in New York, it was especially gratifying being around someone whose behaviour did not constantly change with an unexpected and often self-entitled randomness. Even if I could not understand their language, I knew I could trust them: bad habits and all.

One of the more engaging aspects to being around horses all day was learning the differences in their personalities. Each horse had its own distinct temperament when it came to interacting with human beings and one another. They were all unique beings in their own way and could be very funny at times whether splashing in the spray from the hose, galloping around like rodeo buck jumpers, or just letting their curiosity play out with anything that caught their attention.

In the small mob of six horses I worked during this time, one stood out in particular – a young chestnut mare of about 15 hands. Her name was Can-Can and she was the horse I most connected with during my stay. I loved her tenderness and her soft, silky touch as she rubbed her muzzle on my chest and arms. Most of all, I just appreciated being in her space – a quiet, feminine space that was a welcome change from the destructive masculine I had been surrounded by during much of my career. The same destructive masculine that precipitated the World Trade Center's obliteration and the unnecessary, even more obscene, invasions and humanitarian crises following that fateful day. After a short while, it made complete sense why a mare had chosen me, and how important it was I intrinsically connect with her gentle, soothing, and compassionate ways.

Can-Can and I worked together every day and spent many enjoyable weekends playing polocrosse throughout the Hunter Valley north of Sydney. I am not sure why her name was Can-Can for she did not have the long legs of a French dancer conformation-wise and thankfully did not throw her hindlegs around being quite relaxed temperament-wise.

Given her curious and compassionate nature, I loved working with her. She had a very relaxed seat at all gaits that made for a smooth and comfortable ride. As I worked on her fitness and form during my stay, she developed a lean, muscled look. With the hot Australian sun igniting her chestnut coat, she came to resemble a bronzed version of the exquisite equine statues seen in museums and art galleries around the world today.

'There is nothing like the outside of a horse for the inside of a man' is a sentiment that has echoed across multiple cultures and multiple continents for the last 6,000 years. To ride well is to connect with a life force of Nature, maybe *the* life force of Nature. Moving in time with the rhythms of a horse, staying balanced at all gaits, being in control yet riding on a gentle rein, I slowly relearnt how to live in harmony with the natural world around me.

Most appreciatively of all, as I gently worked my horses so they gently worked me in equally subtle and important ways. Whether at the walk, the trot, the canter, or the gallop, bareback or in the saddle, the sound of hooves striking the ground became a soothing melody that resonated through my whole being. A melody that helped me slowly make peace with the disappointments from my recent past and inspire hope for what the future now held.

To feel their gentle yet powerful movement beneath me, whether under the saddle or bareback, to move in harmony with their motion, became the goal of every day so beguiling and relaxing did it feel. Communicating with my body, learning the language of Equus with all the subtleties and nuances that required, took me far from the intellectual comfort zone I had previously inhabited. I started to feel I was connecting with Nature in a way I had never known possible. Simply riding around the paddock, while practicing polocrosse or working on my dressage skills, connecting with the natural world through my body, heart, and soul, gave me far greater pleasure than what society had offered in quite some time.

When not working my equine companions in the paddock, I took them into the ranges where they were free of the conformity imposed by the predictable path of the dressage arena. On those days, I could feel their palpable joy and excitement at being back in a role they had lived for countless generations: one whose genetics, I suspect, still call to them today. Cantering through the open bush, with the sun over my shoulder and the wind on my face, was an absolute luxury money could not buy. Feeling the power beneath me, as a horse stretched into a hard, fast gallop, surrounded by the majesty of the natural world, was an indulgence of which I never grew tired.

It was these indulgences from the natural world that, if undertaken more often I suspect, would help us place our lives in a more meaningful perspective than we currently do. Feeling that power, trusting that power, was to slowly reconnect with the energy and youthfulness of the natural world remembered as a child. During times like this, it was easy to understand why, and how, horses have played such an important role in humanity's evolution from a physical, emotional, and spiritual perspective over the millennia. Despite being unemployed with no opportunity to resume my career, I felt as light and happy as I had in a long time. I would not have chosen anything else over those moments of pure, simple, nature-based joy.

After our workout, whether in the paddock or in the ranges, our walk home was always a slow, cooling walk on a loose rein letting the horse be a horse. There I unsaddled, hosed them down scraping off the water, sweat, and mud, and lightly rugged them. After a tussle of their mane and a pat on their neck and wither, which we both equally enjoyed, they wandered out to re-join the mob. After working my first horse, I then caught and saddled the next to undertake the same process all over again. With between four to six horses to work each day, I spent much of my time in the saddle. It was certainly a far more pleasurable and healthy experience than what I remembered from working at a desk.

While working these horses provided a natural euphoria for me, there was also a more practical reason. The polocrosse season was about to begin in Australia and it was time to start playing. *"Polocrosse, what is that?"* people often ask out of curiosity given the word sounds vaguely familiar.

Polocrosse, a uniquely demanding and exhilarating horse sport, developed in Australia in the late 1930s, is essentially a combination of polo and lacrosse. It is a game where, at the highest level, the skill and nuance of a dressage rider fuses with the rough and tumble of cavalry combat. To see it played at that level is to see everything achievable between humanity and the horse. The art, the skill, and the magnificence!

Polocrosse, or 'Polox' as most signs say, with an arrow pointing down a narrow dirt track, is probably the most fun anyone can have on a horse… in any sport. It requires teamwork, tactics, and daring mixed with calm, cool intellect at the gallop.

It represents a chance to ride as the Mongols from the Eurasian Steppes once rode or as the Native Americans once rode. It represents a connection to a time long past when the skill of riding could mean the difference between life and death. Yet the sport offers more than the opportunity to enjoy a weekend of hard, fast riding – it represents an opportunity to spend time with like-minded souls doing something we love. Probably the most important attribute of all.

The polocrosse carnivals I played were a full three-day experience, especially when significant travel was required, as I often did not get home until late Sunday night. While Friday was always busy getting to the carnival grounds, and setting up camp, the real work began early Saturday morning as we fed and watered our horses before eating breakfast and then preparing for play.

Before feeding Can-Can, I slowly walked her around the grounds to help remove any feelings of tightness or soreness from travelling the previous day. On a cold, misty morning, with the sun's rays barely able to pierce the fog covering the grounds, she and I could walk alone and have no idea that all around was a bustle of activity. It was simply my horse and I, enveloped by the quiet of a winter's morning. If it was a very cold winter's morning, with ice thick on the top of Can-Can's water bucket, it made leaving the warmth of my swag even more difficult!

After walking and feeding our horses, the early morning was spent around the most appreciated warmth of the communal club fire preparing breakfast. While my teammates enjoyed a breakfast of bacon, eggs, and other treats, I preferred the lightness of a bowl of porridge and a cup of tea boiled in my quart-pot. What I remember most from those times was the joy and contentment I felt on waking to a day of excitement and laughter. It was an uplifting experience to start the day in this relaxed manner compared to the perpetual rush and exhaustion remembered from my career days.

After breakfast, our efforts primarily focused on getting our horses ready to play. First, I groomed Can-Can, platting her tail and cleaning her hooves before wrapping her forelegs and hindlegs for protection, and finally pulling on her bellboots. Next, I saddled her, after which I gently placed the bit into her mouth as I slipped the bridle over her head. With Can-Can ready, I changed into my team shirt, moleskins, and boots. Taking my helmet and racquet, I walked Can-Can over to the warm-up area where we gently worked for half an hour, slowly at first, getting our collective heart rates up and blood flowing so we took the field fit and ready to play.

A polocrosse team is comprised of two sections of three players. Each section plays alternate chukkas thereby allowing the horses, and probably most riders, sufficient rest to play the four to six chukkas required each day. Each weekend, we typically played four games – two on Saturday and two on Sunday, of which the last would be the final if our team remained unbeaten over the weekend. Getting to the final was the intention of every game on Saturday. For, even if we were beaten in our first game, there was always a chance of getting through to the final if our team scored enough goals or the team that beat us was also beaten.

The shrill call from the umpire's whistle started the game. On hearing the whistle, the six horses and riders from each team rode towards centre field, from opposite ends of the field, shaking hands or touching racquets as we passed one another. As a polocrosse field is the size of a rugby or football field, there was often much good-natured banter among our-selves as we rode towards the opposing team, and especially on meeting them! Following the last handshake, all players converged around the umpire to hear their views on how the game would be refereed and the rules they would pay attention to.

"Second sections off" were the umpire's final words before the game commenced in earnest. As the second section left the field, moving to the sidelines or to the back of the field, those remaining gave our horses one last canter and moved into our respective positions in the lineout.

The whistle's shrill scream announced the start of play as the umpire threw the ball into the lineout. Instantly, the scene came alive as six riders stretched to catch the ball; racquets clashing and bending, horses jostling and pushing, players stretching and yelling until the ball is caught in a racquet. In that instant, the rider with the ball has spun her horse out of the lineout and started to gallop down the field. In that same instant, the lineout dissolved as the opposing team pursued their quarry down the field in a fantastic moving spectacle of colour and movement; the red, white, yellow, green, and blue of our team shirts exquisitely contrasting against the chestnut, bay, black, and grey of our horses in the brown dust that slowly rose into the azure-blue sky.

Despite a frantic, weaving pursuit, the player with the ball cannot be stopped. In one quick motion, she bounced the ball into the goal scor-ing area, then caught and threw it between the posts. Immediately, the umpire's whistle sounded as their racquet waved: a goal was scored. Back we returned to the lineout for another chance at the ball, another chance at a goal, another chance at glory on this field where no quarter is given and none is expected.

On finishing the chukka, our horses were typically a lather of sweat with nostrils flaring and flanks heaving much like their riders. At the first opportunity, we dismounted, loosened our girths, and slowly walked our horses to help them catch their breath while our team's second section played its chukka – our words of advice blown away on the wind or bur-ied in the dust that washed over all. Although polocrosse is only a game, it did not look that way at times. It appeared a battle of old with racquets replacing swords and maces as charging horses and racquet-on-racquet clashes defined the personal nature of the contest.

Before long, as the second section finished its chukka, we tightened our girths and quickly mounted before returning to the field. After a quick handshake with the opposing team, or a touch of racquets, we returned to the lineout where the shrill scream of the umpire's whistle signalled another six minutes of play had commenced.

Snagging the ball out of the air with a twist of my racquet, jumping into a gallop to find open space with a dozen thundering hooves behind me, and charging towards the goal was a thrill unlike any other. The surge of power beneath me as Can-Can stretched into a hard gallop, and the dazzling speed the ground passed beneath her, was a delight of which I never tired. Working in harmony with her, playing as one, left me completely fulfilled. It was this feeling of unison with her, of moving and playing together as a single being, that reinforced how important my time with her was. It was this feeling of connection, of oneness with the natural world, that increasingly reminded me how critical it was to connect with Nature's wisdom and the insights from its teaching.

By the close of play Saturday, the empty paddock of Friday had become a spectacle of horse and rider surrounded by trucks, cars, and trailers of all types and colours spread around the grounds. People of all ages, from children in strollers pushed around by proud parents to grandparents watching their children and grandchildren play, lined the fields enjoying the camaraderie and sportsmanship under the azure-blue Australian sky. There were often more horses than riders as spare horses were brought to train for the game or to be used by the umpires.

Swirling around this ever-present hive of activity, the smell of eucalyptus smoke filled the air from club fires that smouldered away during the day, only to be subsequently brought back to life for the ritual cooking of dinner on Saturday night. Sitting around the fire on a cold, starlit night, talking and joking with my friends as we cooked, ate, and rested, surrounded by the tender, contented whinnies of our equine teammates, was the closest I will come to Nirvana for some time.

At those times, covered in dust and sweat from a long day of playing, I realised our happiness around the fire came not from possessions or wealth. It came from simply having our health and the opportunity that provided to experience the thrill of the game with like-minded souls. Nothing else was wanted, or needed, for Nature had provided it all. Looking into the starlit bounty of the night sky, with the flames from the fire throwing a warming glow over all, there was no other place I would rather have been. Quite simply, working horses during the day and spending the night wrapped in the smoke from the fire or the warmth of my swag made me far happier than any possession possibly could.

My last act on Saturday night, before crawling into my swag's appreciated warmth, was ensuring Can-Can was settled for the evening. As she meandered to the front of her yard, looking for the reward she expected and deserved, I gave her several biscuits of hay. As she stood there, chewing away with an occasional contented sigh, I loved nothing more than to give her a big hug, pushing my arms far down her neck into the warmth under the heavy rug she wore. Feeling her warmth against the chill of a winter's night, inhaling her sweaty scent with that of the freshly cut hay, listening to the crackling of the fire and the laughter of my teammates, made me feel very at peace. I was content with the Universe and my place in it. I did not have to understand how it all worked – it just did not matter.

My former life was so far away it could have been another lifetime ago. The past no longer existed so full was the present. With a tussle of her forelock and a pat on her neck, I left Can-Can to enjoy her hay while I crawled into my swag for an appreciated and relaxing slumber until the laughter around the fire the following morning brought me back to life.

As Saturday was a full day of playing, so was Sunday, especially where we reached the final. And whether our last game was the final or a play-off game, it was undertaken with as much enthusiasm and energy as the first. Sunday always ended with the A-grade final, the ultimate show of horsemanship and polocrosse that never ceased to inspire and beguile so athletic were the horses and nuanced were their riders. Seeing what was truly possible between a well-educated horse and a skilled rider inspired my return to cold winter mornings of working with Can-Can in the hope I could one day achieve a similar level of finesse and harmony. Seeing the nature of the bond possible between horse and rider continually reinforced how strong our connection with the natural world can really be.

On reaching home, often late on Sunday night, one last act defined the end of a weekend away – Can-Can's whinnying and the excited reaction of her friends as they cantered up and down the fence as we drove in. Yet, while this act marked the end of one weekend, it also marked the beginning of the next and the work required to play an even better game. Working with horses certainly teaches you there is always something to improve that only ever comes with effort and focus. Which, coincidently, is also the reality for a life well lived!

After three months of working horses and playing polocrosse, this part of my journey came to a close. It was time to roll my swag and begin exploring the vastness of the Australian continent in earnest. For the first time in many years, I felt balanced and energised, fit and relaxed, rested and whole. Working in this manner, before starting the next stage of my journey, was the perfect way to transition my whole body feeling from one of exhaustion at the moment of 'liberation' to one of health at the moment of returning to the road less travelled. In many respects, my return to a life of hard, physical work was a transforming experience with the old skin now left behind and the new fresh to the world.

Yet, despite the siren call of the Australian Outback and the opportunity to follow the tracks of my life mentors, it was difficult to leave. The end of close friendships is never easy. Can-Can was the friendship most difficult to end. We went for one last ride before I left. We rode across the country up into the ranges, just her and I, with the sounds and smells of the bush invigorating every sense: the chill of the early morning air enhancing our feeling of being completely alive. I felt her relaxed power as she cantered up the hill, her breathing barely audible, her strides barely noticeable. I felt connected to her spirit. She and I were one. It was ultimately Can-Can's tender soul that helped me to reconnect with the fundamental elements of Nature's teaching so critical to a life well lived.

For that, I will always remain incredibly grateful. For that, I will never forget.

Thank you, Can-Can, for sharing your beauty and wisdom with me.

3

Waltzing Matilda

'I have woven a verse from the glory
Australia sheds on her plains;
I have stolen her heart for a story
And crossed it with rowel and reins;
I have gathered a song from the starlight
On camps where her cattle-men lie
With shining spurred feet to the firelight
And swarthy bare brows to the sky.'

Will Ogilvie – From Hearts of Gold

There are three songs guaranteed to bring a tear to the eye and a lump to the throat of even the most nonchalant and carefree expatriate Australian: *Advance Australia Fair*, our national anthem; *I Still Call Australia Home*, Peter Allen's call to those far from their native land; and *Waltzing Matilda*, 'Banjo' Paterson's ode to a uniquely Australian character, and characteristic. To 'waltz matilda' is a very iconic form of travel. It means to carry your swag, to be on the road, to travel the Wallaby Track. In the early days of Australia's development, it was often the only realistic mode of travel for those whose destination was the Outback. During the Great Depression, over a third of the Australian workforce spent time on the track, 'waltzing their matildas', as they sought employment across the length and breadth of the country. *Waltzing Matilda*, Australia's best-known song, was one of the first songs heard from space. It was somehow fitting this song from Earth's last frontier should be the first Australian song heard from the final frontier. Accordingly, on commencing my own walkabout, and 'waltzing matilda' on my own Australian journey, it was fitting the first stop be Combo Waterhole: the billabong the swagman threw himself into all those years ago.

Driving north from the Hunter Valley, leaving Can-Can and her equine companions to enjoy their well-earned break from polocrosse, I tracked north into Queensland to the city of Rockhampton, quietly nestled beneath the Berserker Range. From there I headed west, following the narrow strip of bitumen to the horizon, and Longreach, where the vast expanse of the Australian Outback impinged on my consciousness for the first time.

The increasing lack of trees as the scrubby landscape slowly petered out into the grassy plains of Western Queensland was the first hint of its presence. The emptiness of the bare paddocks was only matched by the never-ending vastness of the azure-blue sky. Apart from a fence and the road, Nature's realm filled the windscreen. The enormity and emptiness of the landscape, the shimmering mirages on the horizon, and the lack of any structure to pen me in brought a contented, wry smile to my face.

There was nothing to confine my view of the world. There was nothing to constrain the journey now embarked upon. It was on reaching this physical and philosophical place I realised the past was now truly being left behind. This was the moment my connection to New York and my former life, which had slowly weakened in the previous months of working horses and playing polocrosse, was now broken and my walkabout fully began. Following my 'liberation', I had finally returned home.

The feeling of pure exhilaration that welled up from deep within my soul, the same feeling from childhood when each day was a new adventure, made me appreciate how important this journey was to my life path. It made me question the beliefs I inherited on being born into Western society and their relevance to a life well lived. All the questions that had rattled around my mind at 'liberation' and in the subsequent months, which I had initially been unable or unwilling to consider, now pushed to the surface demanding my attention. Moreover, they were very loud and very succinct!

Why do we dedicate the best years of our life to work only to find exhaustion is the reward in our retirement years? Why do we knowingly pursue a lifestyle that destroys our whole being when a few simple changes would completely empower us? Why do we allow society to define happiness as based on consumption when that is the source of most of our ailments? Why do we refuse to understand that ignoring Nature's teaching regarding our whole being ultimately facilitates our own demise?

Travelling Australia's vastness alone, with Nature's bounty providing far greater happiness than any possession, I reflected long and hard on each of these critical questions. Intriguingly, the questions kept coming as if Nature first required I accept responsibility for the self-inflicted predicament I now found myself before teaching me the wisdom I sought.

Combo Waterhole, the best-known billabong in Australia, lies northwest of Longreach between Winton and Kynuna on the Diamantina River. Like many other places in Australia, its exact location was marked with a rusty piece of battered corrugated iron wired to a fence with a tired, worn arrow showing its direction as being somewhere in the distance along a winding dirt track. The other sign, the bush sign, highlighting its general location to more educated eyes, was the narrow line of eucalyptus trees snaking their way through the yellow-brown grasslands.

Driving towards the waterhole, the words of *Waltzing Matilda* came alive as the scene unfolded before me. It seemed the dust from the squatter's thoroughbred and troopers' horses' hooves was still gently drifting across the land as a light breeze played upon the track. There was even a hint of smoke from the swagman's fire further down the creek, along with the tangy smell of burning eucalyptus hanging in the air, from recent bushfires. On arriving at the billabong, I felt the same sense of anticipation and trepidation felt by the song's unique characters all those years ago.

Although I arrived in the middle of winter, I was welcomed by a glorious sunny day that warmed my body and fired my soul. To reach the billabong, I followed a track over an old stone-pitched overshot weir to the famous waterhole itself. Walking along the track, its cleared path provided an intimate introduction to the region's wildlife. From the long-toed prints of kangaroos and emus to the smaller etchings of possums and birds, the dust was alive with the tell-tale signs of bush life. The few kangaroos seen lounging in the shade slowly hopped off to the next patch of shade, if I got too close, or stood their ground daring me to come closer. In those moments, a few steps back always seemed to disarm them of their attitude.

Walking through the quiet sanctuary of the bush on that clear, sunny winter's day, a sparkling glint through the tangle of wiry trees and brown flowing grass first hinted at the billabong where the swagman camped. As the grasslands opened up, the billabong slowly revealed its true extent: a small, muddy waterhole surrounded by trees and scrub indicating this was a dry time of the year. Resting under one of the many coolabah trees lining its banks, my thoughts turned to the swagman and the unfortunate confluence of events that brought about his tragic demise.

Waltzing Matilda is not merely a jingle. It is an intriguing commentary on the political and social undercurrents of that time in Australian history. The song, written in 1895 while 'Banjo' Paterson was visiting Dagworth Station, the property driven through to get to the waterhole today, reflects a period of significant unrest and political activism in Australia.

Shortly before Paterson's visit, during the 1894 Shearers' Strike, shearers burnt the Dagworth shearing shed to the ground with 140 sheep unfortunately still inside. Following the shed's destruction, Dagworth's owner, along with three mounted troopers, rode to arrest the arsonists. On the banks of Combo Waterhole, they found the body of Samuel Hoffmeister, one of the shearers' leaders, who had shot himself after torching the shed the previous night during a covering gun battle. On another of Paterson's visits to Dagworth, he was shown the carcass of a sheep killed by a swagman for food, but left to look like a dingo was responsible.

These specific events, set against the social and political tensions of the times, were the catalyst for the song. Put to the music of an old Scottish tune, *The Bonnie Woods of Craigielee*, with the help of Christina MacPherson, a visiting school friend of Paterson's fiancée, it had its first public singing later that year at the North Gregory Hotel in Winton. From there, as they say, the rest is history.

From its humble beginnings on a Western Queensland billabong, *Waltzing Matilda* has become one of the most recognised songs across the Western world. It has followed Australians, like a talisman, around the world through good times and bad, feast and famine, war and peace. To hear it played by the Massed Pipes and Drums during an Anzac Day march in Australia, with the bagpipes in full cry supported by the drums' resonating percussion, by a symphony orchestra with a gentler, nuanced tone, or by Slim Dusty around a campfire is to hear it in its full-throated, emotionally charged glory. Given its resonance in so many ways, *Waltzing Matilda* remains a key thread in the fabric of Australian society today.

Yet, despite the ease with which the song rolls off the tongue, despite its whimsical lyrics, it remains a tragic story of conflict between the 'haves' and the 'have-nots', between the landholders and itinerant workers whose respective beliefs still form the cornerstone of the policy platforms of Australia's two primary political parties. Resting on the dry, dusty banks of Combo Waterhole, under the sparse shade of a stunted coolabah tree, I reflected on the circumstances the swagman found himself and why he believed suicide was his only way out.

Today, tragically, a class of Australian citizens remains in that same unenviable position despite how much most things have changed for the better since the song was first written. Aboriginal Australians, the original itinerant Australians, remain subject to many of the same economic and social forces that brought on the tragedy at the billabong all those years ago. Today, the health and prosperity measures for the First Australians remain at unacceptably and distressingly low levels reflecting the toughness of life for a marginalised people and their constant battle to survive.

Despite Australia's advances in so many ways, despite how well its citizens have fared over the last hundred years, the reality of the song's themes remain a sad reminder of the tragic situation for Australia's underclass today. Furthermore, this shameful reality was a theme I experienced many times during my journey as my path took me far from the privileged position most Australians enjoy today.

Seeing firsthand how much of Aboriginal society had been blown to the wind, how their lifestyle and culture had almost been destroyed, made me aware that a great wrong has been done. A wrong that today's Australians have much to right before we have even remotely repaid our significant debt to the original Australians.

Despite the swagman's tragedy at the billabong, and the echo of its implications for today, the majesty of the encompassing bush made Combo Waterhole a delightful location to enjoy a rest from the road. Similar to much of Australia, there was a splendour to find at all times in what Nature had created despite the dry conditions prevailing.

Sitting on the edge of the billabong, in the cool shade of an undisturbed winter's afternoon, my feeling of connection with the bush continued to strengthen. Appreciating the gentleness of its authentic embrace, I got a good fire going and pulled out my swag for the first time on the road: its dirty-green colour matching that of the vegetation along the creek. Resting on its rolled, supportive form, listening to the talkative bubbling of my quart-pot as I boiled my first cup of tea, while savouring the appetising aroma of saltbush-raised lamb and roasted vegetables cooked on the coals, I felt my reconnection to the natural world had finally begun.

Delighting in the tangy smell of burning eucalyptus leaves as the smoke from my fire wafted into the branches overhead, while listening to the distinctive calls of corellas and finches as they cavorted in the trees, made me appreciate how much I came alive in Nature's realm. Watching the sunlight splash over the Mitchell grass and saltbush plains, as it changed from the bright, harsh yellow of the afternoon to the more gentling hues of dusk, I felt seduced by Nature's soft touch across the landscape. The feeling of joy that simply came from being part of the natural world reminded me how important it had been to undertake this walkabout and reconnect with the Australian bush.

As the evening cool slowly descended, and the dusk's golden rays began their slow turn to purple and orange, it was soon time to leave this historically and culturally unique place. Yet the natural charms of Combo Waterhole made it difficult to leave, which meant it was close to dark before I returned to the road. This was not very smart as the level of carnage seen alongside the bitumen during the previous days' driving suggested travelling at night was only to be undertaken in the most necessary of circumstances.

With the drought tightening its grip across the land, much of Western Queensland increasingly found itself in a dry state as water levels dropped and paddocks turned to bare ground. These circumstances drove the native animals out of their usual feeding areas to wherever they could find fresh grass, most often along the side of the road. Unfortunately, the effect was similar to the meeting of technology and steel with flesh and bone that caused the devastating carnage of the First World War. Accordingly, it was with a sharp lookout and a distinct lack of speed I followed the bitumen northwest into the vastness of the Outback, and Mount Isa.

Mount Isa is a remote town in a tough environment. It is another of the resilient mining towns that sprout from the rugged Australian landscape much like spinifex, the equally resilient desert plant that surrounds the town today. Mount Isa's birth reflects the discovery of its underlying lead-zinc-silver orebody in 1923 which facilitated the development of one of the most productive mines in the world. In its heyday, its motherlode generated a cascade of wealth that served the nation much as the Broken Hill orebody did the previous century. Even with the distractions of its modern conveniences, however, the harshness of the surrounding country reminded me this was Nature's realm and, accordingly, worthy of my respect at all times. There may be no second chance if I did not.

From Mount Isa, the road headed west through the old droving town of Camooweal and onto the Barkly Tableland, one of Australia's primary beef producing regions. More importantly, this was where I crossed into the Northern Territory, as named on a map, or 'The Territory' as called by its citizens. The vastness of the plains was liberating. There were few trees and, apart from an occasional windmill or gate, there was nothing to remind me of humanity except the ever-present strip of bitumen leading to the horizon and the fence running parallel to the road. It was a world of two halves: the azure-blue sky and the dirty brown grasslands stretching to, and meeting at, the horizon, with only the shimmering of a mirage ahead to distract me.

Then the mirage changed and the horizon showed signs of movement. At first, it appeared cattle were crossing the road. Then, as the mirage evolved into reality, the cattle become cars and trucks. I had finally reached the Stuart Highway, the narrow strip of bitumen running longitudinally through Australia's geographic heart, which remembers the achievements of its pre-eminent explorer: John McDouall Stuart. The Stuart Highway is reached at Three Ways; its name defining in laconic Australian style a driver's only option at one of the remotest highway junctions in the world.

On reaching this junction, I turned north towards the Top End and the delightful geological, biological, and zoological diversity that makes it one of the most mesmerising of Nature's havens across Australia. Yet this road north was more than just a road. It represented the opportunity to follow in the tracks of a mentor whose adventures had inspired the curiosity of a child for the Australian frontier many years previously. A mentor whose crossing of the uncharted Australian continent ranks among the most inspiring of all the journeys of exploration undertaken across the New World.

John McDouall Stuart is one of the most successful and accomplished of the early Australian explorers. He was the first person to cross the continent from south to north, through the harsh deserts and dry plains of Central Australia, and successfully return. In his six expeditions into and across Central Australia, from 1858-62, not one man died under his command. He did not try to conquer the bush like many of his contemporaries. Instead, he sought to understand its natural rhythms and cycles, organising his expeditions to travel light and fast within those cycles. He was also unlike most explorers of that time in terms of his relationship with the Australian continent, with his diary a reminder of his appreciation for Nature's splendour at a time when most other explorers found the continent a bleak and frightening place.

The other remarkable aspect to Stuart's legacy was his exploration was undertaken entirely on horseback. With horses requiring water regularly, his journeys across the driest regions of Australia also rank as one of the finest feats of horsemanship ever achieved. Not surprisingly, reflecting the enormity of his achievement, many landmarks passed on a journey through Central Australia today were discovered and named by him, including Central Mount Stuart (which he originally named Central Mount Sturt): a fitting monument in the heart of the continent. The Royal Geographical Society awarded Stuart a gold watch and subsequently the Patron's Medal for his conspicuous success in the field. It was an honour only accorded to one other person: David Livingstone, the African explorer.

Stuart's expeditions into Central Australia taught me some of my most important life lessons. He taught me that most paths are not a straight line but often a convoluted track requiring its unique lessons be learnt, choices made, and difficulties surmounted. His experience taught me that being stopped in our tracks and retreating to try another day is often a better preparation for life than having an easy run to the top.

His journeys taught me that life as an adventure would not be easy, that it would have its thankless days when nothing went right and when fate dealt some heavy-handed blows. He reminded me that success in any venture requires we remain self-reliant and able to resolve any issue at any time. Most importantly, his ultimate success showed that endurance and commitment can overcome most, if not all, the difficulties and challenges fate puts in our path.

On being 'liberated', it was Stuart's example that most resonated as I dealt with an unexpected and challenging situation. For where we live our life with a fraction of his tenacity and resilience, life's unexpected obstacles can never defeat us and may actually point us in the right direction. Which is why I increasingly saw my 'liberation' as the gift it truly was!

The Top End of Australia, with its breathtaking diversity of geological, biological, and zoological DNA, is a veritable paradise in today's world. It is quite simply one of Australia's most spectacular and awe-inspiring regions. From serene waterholes, craggy sandstone escarpments, and the majestic waterfalls of Litchfield and Kakadu National Parks, to the inspiring majesty and tranquillity of Edith Falls and Katherine Gorge, its geography inspired on every level. Nature's DNA, left to its own devices for around 2 billion years since the first sediments were deposited from which the North Australian Craton subsequently evolved, has created a geological base and biological ecosystem whose spectacular symbiosis left me in perpetual awe.

From small, delicate waterlilies providing the lush green carpet where many birds and insects lived their lives, to tough eucalyptus trees capable of surviving the countless fires that swept through the country in the Dry, it was a biological extravaganza. From lethal, much feared saltwater crocodiles, survivors from the distant age of the dinosaurs, to small, architecturally brilliant termites building cathedrals from raw earth, it was a zoological wonderland. It made me wonder what humanity can possibly hope to achieve by manipulating DNA that Nature has not already tried and discarded as being inferior to its plethora of life forms today!

The seasons in the Top End, or the top half of Australia for that matter, like many of its plants and animals, have their own unique character: not for them the mild and regular resonance typically found in the southern states. Up here, it was either the Wet or the Dry though Aboriginal people recognise up to six stages of a yearly cycle. The Wet lasts roughly from November to April while the Dry lasts roughly from May to October. The Wet is a time of intense rainfall, monsoon conditions, and flooding creeks and rivers when up to two metres of rain will be recorded.

The Dry, on the other hand, is a time when the land reverts to one that is parched and dusty eagerly awaiting the humidity, lightning, and afternoon storms indicating the life-giving rains of the Wet have returned. The Dry is characterised by bushfires whether experienced through the burning scrub at the edge of the road, the acrid smell of smoke perpetually in the air, or the black smudges randomly defiling the horizon. The Dry is the time to see this country, when the raging waters of the Wet sweeping through its creeks, rivers, and over its waterfalls have returned to the gurgling trickle that does not put the life of man and beast at perpetual risk!

The prolific natural wonderland of the Top End was best experienced in its national parks. Litchfield National Park, just outside Darwin, was an enchanting location to visit with its tumbling waterfalls and pristine waterholes just the place to relax and enjoy Nature's gentle pampering. While it did not have the size and grandeur of Kakadu National Park to the east, its waterfalls and billabongs were an appreciated relief from the toils of the road. Three waterfalls stood out in particular – Sandy Creek Falls, Florence Falls, and Wangi Falls. Each had a trickle of water gently flowing over and down their face, tumbling into their respective waterholes, which made for a most appreciated swim.

There is much to be said for the simple pleasure of swimming across a tree-lined billabong, after checking for crocodiles of course, feeling the coolness of the water against your skin while the sun's rays warm your body. I felt completely cleansed and embalmed by these most soothing of places. The water was crystal clear and tantalisingly fresh; far more a nectar of the gods than wine could ever be. In fact, the waters here were some of the freshest and sweetest tasting I experienced. After several days enjoying the pleasures of different billabongs, with the nights spent wrapped in my swag under the moon and stars, I felt completely refreshed by the myriad of charms in this part of Nature's domain.

While Litchfield National Park gentled the aches and pains of travelling, Kakadu National Park to the east, named for the extinct Aboriginal language previously spoken in Arnhem Land, invigorated and cleansed my whole being. Its billabongs and waterfalls, in particular, were inspiring and insightful tributes into Nature's ability to create spectacular works of art for the appreciation of all humanity.

From the chiselled grandeur of the Arnhem Land escarpment, over which Jim Jim Creek cascades, to the breathtaking panorama from Gunlom Falls across a broad swathe of valley and range, Nature's masterpieces appeared carved by a genius sculptor. From the serenity and peace of Sandy Billabong, as the rays of the early morning sun streaked the rising mist purple, orange, and gold, to the calm and wonder of the Yellow Water wetlands in the glow of the setting sun, Nature's masterpieces appeared painted by a genius artist.

Kakadu offered everything required to ease the busy mind, replenish the tired body, inspire the ambivalent heart, and calm the restless soul. I felt Nature realised how difficult humanity would likely make its time on Earth and, accordingly, created the perfect sanctuary in which we could find the necessary respite from that chaos. For maybe, in such a place, we would finally appreciate the benefits of consistently living in harmony with the natural world instead of constantly seeing ourselves as separate from it.

Jim Jim Falls was one of the most spectacular locations in Kakadu, made more so by the slow, jolting drive down the rough bush track required to access its majesty. Its seducing touch slowed my walk into the gorge as its reflection off the creek provided the first glimpse of its chiselled grandeur. The vegetation along the creek banks, applying a salve of green, gentled the rocky foreground. The gorge walls towered above me for much of the slow walk in; the fractured sedimentary layers creating the distinct impression a somewhat laconic builder was responsible for their initial construction. There were even a couple of spare blocks resting on the cusp of the falls suggesting an Australian builder had yet to finish the job! At the bottom of the falls, in the dark plunge pool surrounded by a gleaming white sandy beach, the water was cold. The sun did not spend too much time warming these waters though I did not complain when the chance came to indulge in an invigorating swim.

Similar to other places in Northern Australia, particularly during the cooler winter months when the sun did not glare with its full intensity, it was the contrast of colours during the day that most captivated me. From the azure-blue sky to the contrasting brown, green, yellow, white, and grey of the surrounding country, Nature's palette inspired awe at the slew of colour across its canvas.

While Jim Jim Falls captivated me with its rugged battlements, inspiring waterfall, and wild gorge, so Gunlom Falls beguiled me with its breathtaking serenity and sensuous pampering. Swimming in the shallow, blue-green waters of its waterhole or resting in the small rocky pool on the cusp of its falls while looking across the waterless ranges in the distance, I felt caressed by Nature in a most tender way.

The waterhole at the bottom of Gunlom Falls was the most idyllic in Kakadu. Its succouring feel balanced my whole being, especially as the quiet returned at dusk with the departure of tourists for the day and its population of nocturnal native animals slowly came to life. Swimming in its clear, shallow waters, surrounded by the gentle rustle of leaves and the calls of its birdlife, was pure rapture as the sun's rays surmounted the top of the gorge and spread their warm tranquillity over all. At the top of the gorge, in the sun-drenched pool overlooking the broad sweep of valley and range, the natural resonance of the land beguiled and inspired me on every level. And if that was not sufficient to rejuvenate and humble, there were other places offering equal scenes of rapture and tranquillity though unfortunately most of these were unsafe to swim!

Sandy Billabong was one such place: a serene, scenic stretch of water bound by a forest of paperbark trees and covered in a swathe of green, broad-leafed waterlilies topped with snow-white flowers. It was especially captivating at sunset when the sky and land seemed to ignite; the water's reflection mirroring the blazing sky as Nature's paintbrush of light moved across its Australian canvas mesmerising me in a way humanity's artworks never could. It appeared a ball of fire had ignited the clouds in a fantastic fury, as it raced across the sky, with the reflection off the water a faithful representation of the scene unfolding above. In the dark of night, the sky became a cornucopia of pulsating stars with their light applying a gentle silver salve over the land and water. And in the early morning, as the mist gently rose off the water and the sun's rays coated the paperbark trees and waterlilies in a subtle orange-pink tinge, there was no other place I would rather have been.

Awakening to such an ancient landscape, I quickly came to appreciate how strong and enduring Aboriginal people's attachment could be to this country. In fact, I felt twinges of a similar connection to the land after only being in Kakadu for several weeks. It was another valuable lesson in how strong a life force it would become if my ancestors had lived there for at least 50,000 years like the Aboriginal people of today. This was especially the case at Ubirr where a wander among its caves, filled with ancient rock art from the earliest days of Aboriginal habitation of the continent, perpetually reinforced the bounty of the land and the respect its Aboriginal custodians had for it.

Seeing images of barramundi, catfish, goannas, turtles, wallabies, and a plethora of other fauna, painted in white, yellow, and red ochre across the cave walls in either an x-ray style or a more solid form, amazed and awed with their attention to detail and natural beauty. The rock art here, and throughout the Top End and Northern Australia, further enhanced my respect for Aboriginal people as they clearly respected, and took the time to understand, the land, its flora, and fauna in both an artistic and practical manner.

Sitting atop the sandstone outcrop of Ubirr, originally part of the vast Arnhem Land escarpment until carved off by an ancient shallow sea into its isolated position today, the panorama over the Nadab floodplain was breathtaking. Watching the sunset pastels reflected off the stilled waters, dappling the lush green carpet spreading to the horizon, I experienced a landscape Aboriginal Australians would have lived in for tens of thousands of years. There are not too many places left in Australia today to experience a view like that!

It was experiencing the land in this way each day that reinforced my increasing connection to the Australian continent and its importance to my life. Each evening during my journey, I contentedly watched the sunset with nothing but a clear mind and an open heart. It was impossible to do so in any other way as the combination of colour and movement created one inspiring vista after another. As the sky slowly darkened, in the twilight before the stars and moon fully lighted the night sky, I then organised my camp and prepared dinner.

To understand Nature, to connect with its teaching, I ate only a simple evening meal: mostly canned tuna, rice, and vegetables along with a little meat, supplemented with fresh fruit and salad when available. This was essentially my diet for most of my journey with the food washed down with a quart-pot of boiling tea or an appreciated cup of red wine as a special treat.

When it was possible, and especially in the cold of winter, I lit a small fire for cooking and warmth. Then, resting on my swag, with nothing but the dull red pulse of the fire's coals and the silvery pulse of the night sky for company, reflect on what I had seen and learnt that day. I spent most evenings just enjoying my fire, the flames a hypnotising and welcoming presence that kept me company during the night. I felt very relaxed in this most primal of meditations as I underwent my own awakening and transformation.

These experiences connected me to the thoughts and feelings of my Scottish and Nordic ancestors from times long past. They connected me

to at least 65,000 years of Aboriginal habitation of the Australian continent and their intimate connection to the land. And they connected me
to 700,000 years of human history when fire had been a practical and
spiritual survival tool. And while the mesmerising presence of my small
fire was one to be enjoyed whenever possible, especially as it burnt down
to its pulsating coals late in the evening, it was the allure of the night sky
and its pulsating lights that held me in its thrall most of all.

At night, especially when there was no moon, the stars provided a
light show that always inspired, awed, and humbled. My favourite con-
stellation was the Southern Cross; its familiar shape and position in the
night sky a friend from childhood. A friend who had always warmly
welcomed me home on plane rides back from the Northern Hemisphere.
Most nights, the moon and stars were the crowning glory to the bounty
of wisdom Nature generously imparted that day. At these times, bathed
in the magnificence of the night sky, I felt completely part of the natural
world even more than the human world. The bush was my home and I
was fully content with my new reality.

Farewelling the delights of Kakadu and Litchfield National Parks, my path
headed south to Katherine and its magnificent gorge. Katherine Gorge, part
of Nitmiluk National Park, was the perfect place to wash off the dust and
smoke from my time on the track. Its grandeur from the air, seen on a heli-
copter ride along its length, was even more impressive once I understood it
was actually 13 gorges carved through an ancient sandstone plateau.

While Katherine Gorge was truly impressive, it was another gorge
a short distance to the northwest that enraptured me completely. Edith
Falls, known as Leliyn to Aboriginal people, was simply one of the most
exquisite gorges I visited on my travels. It had a peace and serenity experienced in few other places across the Australian continent. Its sheer size,
the simple elegance of its inclined and fractured walls, the freshness of its
clear waters, and the shade from its pandanus palms and eucalyptus trees
lining the waterhole made it the perfect place to roll out my swag and
stay for some time.

Edith Falls was clearly a very different place during the Wet as the grass, sticks, and branches high in the trees overhead starkly reminded me. In the Dry, however, it was a peaceful and relaxing place. Slipping into its embracing waters after a long day of walking or driving was a pleasure unmatched by simple human rewards. As I lazily swam out into the middle of the gorge, the azure-blue sky contrasting exquisitely with the surrounding ochre-red gorge walls, I could not imagine a more enjoyable place to be. Moreover, as the natural diversity of Edith Falls inspired me with its bounty, so the cultural diversity inspired me with its humanity.

Similar to other places where people are able to set aside the concerns of everyday living, Edith Falls was the ideal location to get to know a large number of people in a short space of time. In the evening, as we prepared dinner, the number of different accents wafting on the breeze seemingly mirrored the diversity of the surrounding flora and fauna. From the musical tones of blonde-headed Scandinavians to louder, harder German voices, from broad, laughing Australian accents to the ordered, respectful tones of the Japanese, all races were peacefully represented in the mini United Nations camped together during those days.

Travelling alone had a number of distinct advantages not the least of which was the flexibility and opportunity to speak with anyone. From older couples who were especially generous in providing meals to that *"nice young man in the swag"* to European travellers who were exploring the bush just like me, it was a pleasure to walk over to a group with a bottle of wine or just a *"G'day"* and connect. There was a feeling of being part of an international family. We were all in this together and helped one another with directions, advice, or simply sharing our food. It was at Edith Falls, in exactly this manner, I enjoyed one of the most memorable nights of my journey – an impromptu dinner party with citizens from around the world, all relishing the pleasures that simply came from being in the company of like-minded souls.

The catalyst was meeting up with a Swiss family whose path I had crossed at Sandy Billabong several weeks before. They had already camped at Edith Falls a short while and made friends with a couple who were professional classical guitar players. As we sat down to dinner that evening, an older Australian couple came over and introduced themselves. That made it a party of ten, children included.

Under the star-lit opulence of the cool night sky, the white bark of the surrounding eucalyptus trees shining with a silvery glow, our group was bathed in the mesmerising and pulsating light of the moon and stars. As our fire burned low into the evening, throwing its warming glow over all, we talked, joked, and laughed our way late into the night through several tantalising bottles of wine. And when the soft, harmonious sound of gently strummed guitars floated over the bush, much like the meandering smoke from our fire, it made each of us reflect on how incredibly lucky we were.

At times like this, surrounded by the true essence of life, I felt no grief from the loss of my former life. I felt no regret at what could have been. At that moment, I felt only joy at being able to follow my own life path with all the unexpected benefits that entailed. As I crawled into my swag later that evening, cocooned in its warmth and the moon's silvery embrace, my gratitude for 'liberation' was complete.

From Edith Falls, the road headed south to Alice Springs following the route pioneered by John McDouall Stuart 142 years previously. To have one of the longest highways in the world record his achievement is the ultimate tribute to Stuart's tenacity, resolve, and pragmatic strength of purpose. When driving through this country, I came to appreciate the magnitude of his accomplishment more clearly. The unflinching nature of the sparse, waterless terrain, the intensity of the all-consuming heat, the danger from Aboriginal people defending their country, and the profound isolation of his journey only hardened his determination to find his way through – and my respect for him.

While the country Stuart traversed at great hardship often appears empty, every now and then the modern-day traveller comes across a most unexpected oasis: a watery jewel through which Nature reminds us of its inherent propensity to provide sustenance in many ways. Mataranka

Pool and Bitter Springs were two such places: turquoise-blue jewels set in a ring of pandanus palms and lush foliage that kept the dust and heat of Stuart's world at bay. The chance to wash off the track's dust and sweat via a long, slow swim through their crystal clear, mineralised pools was a most sensuous experience. It was another of those small and vital pleasures that make a journey through the desert worthy of the effort required, and a reminder of the unique and enchanting pleasures only found within its realm.

Following the narrow strip of bitumen leading to the horizon, as it had since first leaving Sydney six months previously, the ancient oxidised sands of the desert slowly gave way to rocky country and the wonderfully sculptured Devils Marbles. Known as Karlu Karlu to Aboriginal people, their general name for the area, there were eroded and carved boulders of all shapes and sizes. From a 1.7 billion-year-old solid granite intrusion initially exposed through erosion, the Devils Marbles have been carved over hundreds of millions of years into the plethora of rounded and splintered boulders seen today. Some barely maintained their connection to the host rock so pronounced had the weathering process been. If I had inadvertently leaned against one of them, I may have been crushed in their path as they rolled off their pedestal.

Walking among the Devils Marbles, their timeless simplicity and beauty called to me in a way I had not felt before. I felt connected to the continent and its unique geological heritage in a way not previously experienced. Many people new to Central Australia also feel this way as I came to learn. The glow of the setting sun reinforced the magnificence of this place: the granite tors igniting a fiery red in exquisite contrast to the cobalt-blue sky arching over them. It was another ideal location to quietly sit and watch the evening light transform the landscape as the dusk slowly turned to night.

This was especially so on the trunks of the stunted eucalyptus trees, randomly scattered among the granite boulders, across whose white bark the rays of the setting sun radiated a changing mosaic of the desert's primary colours: red and orange, purple and white, and finally, silver and gold.

That night, however, I had an experience that caused me to interpret the name of this place quite literally. As the regular campground was full, the only place left to roll out my swag was in the parking bay at the foot of the Devils Marbles themselves. After another nourishing meal of canned tuna, vegetables, and a cup of tea from my quart-pot, boiled on the gas-fired stove I travelled with, it was soon time to crawl into the appreciated warmth of my swag under Nature's starlit canopy with nothing but a light wind and the rustle of the nocturnal native animals to keep me awake.

Or so I initially thought. Unexpectedly, it turned out to be the most uncomfortable night of my travels!

As I tried to sleep, the top of my swag was continually blown off no matter how often I clipped it down. Yet the wind was not that strong. Throughout the night, I felt I was being watched. I felt something or someone was out there. Whether it was a person or an animal I have no idea, but I got up and walked around the boulders in the moonlight several times trying to determine what it was. All to no avail. When I crawled back into my swag, the wind picked up and tugged at its edges until the cover was blown off again. I felt a very mischievous spirit was playing games with me.

Clearly, I was not wanted and it was not going to leave me in peace until I moved on. Despite my tiredness, after a long day behind the wheel, I did not sleep a wink all night!

After a seeming eternity, the uneasy dark of night slowly dissipated as the first rays of dawn lit the eastern sky. Even then, the feeling of unease that hung over me all night remained. Why that was, I will never know. Despite the splendour of the dawn sky and the warm glow slowly spreading its way west across the landscape, I did not feel the normal joy on being part of Nature's waking. There was little to stay for as had been made very clear. Accordingly, I rolled my swag, boiled a cup of tea, and, with a parting look, left the Devils Marbles and their unfriendly spirits as a disappearing vista in the rear-view mirror. During my entire journey, it was the only time I experienced such a profound feeling of not belonging in a particular place!

Yet, several days later, I had good reason to remember that feeling. For, on arriving in Alice Springs, the capital of Central Australia, I experienced firsthand how unfairly Aboriginal people are still treated in their own land. The uncomfortable and confused feeling of not belonging experienced at the Devils Marbles, in a land I otherwise felt profoundly connected to, came to define the same feeling I subsequently learnt reflects the unfortunate reality for many Indigenous Australians today.

I realised my unease at the Devils Marbles helped me to understand that Nature would not fully share its wisdom with me until I recognised the destruction wrought on the First Australians was by the same culture that was slowly destroying me. It was not until I recognised the full scope of this destruction, and accepted my complicit role in its ongoing influence through my lack of attention, would Nature share its most valuable and important teaching with me. Which, at this point in my journey, made complete sense to me!

4

Nature's Cathedral

'They curse her desert places!
How can they understand
Who know not what her face is
And never held her hand?–
Who may have heard the meeting
Of boughs the wind has stirred,
Yet missed the whispered greeting
Our listening hearts have heard.'

Will Ogilvie – The Bush, My Lover

Geology defines the character of the Australian Outback. It was the
deserts, ranges, and gorges that most enticed me with their collective
grandeur, and where I found my greatest connection with the country.
In the ranges, in particular, the history of their creation told a fantastic
story. In some places, the rocks had been twisted and buckled, their original form faulted and fractured, folded and uplifted. In other places, the

sedimentary layers remained just as initially deposited hundreds of millions if not billions of years previously. These rocks provided the means to discover the unique history of the Australian continent. It was gleaned from the small pile of glacial till in a baking desert. It was divined from ripple rock where the waves of ancient oceans once washed over the land. It was garnered from the meteorite and comet craters on an otherwise empty desert plain. Everywhere I travelled, my appreciation for geology, and my love for the land, grew as I discerned a new twist on the old story of the Australian continent's evolution. Of the many inspiring places visited, however, there was one I came to appreciate most of all. It was a gorge carved in the West MacDonnell Ranges; a natural cathedral in the continent's desert heart whose magnificence inspired from first sight.

Alice Springs is billed as one of the more remote towns in Australia according to the map. On arriving, I soon discovered it was not that remote with the bitumen heading in most directions, a small airport, and a host of modern conveniences that converted this ancient breach in the MacDonnell Ranges into a relative oasis. My appreciation for the pioneering days that facilitated the region's development was certainly enhanced given the historical sites to visit in and around the town. Similar to the travellers of old, both Aboriginal and European who previously relied on its life-giving resources during their journeys, it was an important location to recharge my provisions and refill the water and fuel cans before heading out into the vastness of Central Australia.

Yet, Alice Springs was more than simply a supply depot for those who travel deep into the heart of Australia. It was, in fact, a vivid reminder that Europeans were not the first people to find the Central Australian deserts an inspiring and spiritual place. It was a stark reminder there were a people who long before Europe was even settled, let alone civilised, had made this land their home and had come to love it like no other.

Alice Springs, to me, defines Australia's fractured and difficult relationship with its indigenous people. It was impossible to spend any time here and not become painfully aware of the tragic plight of the First

Australian within his or her own land. Watching young and old Aboriginal people as they struggled to find a new resonance with the Australia of today filled me with intense remorse and shame. It was cruel and unfair this proud, noble, and ancient people, brutally forced to the fringes of society not through their own doing but through over two hundred years of active and wilful neglect, still paid the price for European ignorance.

Watching European Australians, many incapable of surviving without their modern conveniences in a land the First Australians were once the masters of, look down their noses at the prostrated figures lying around the town filled me with a deep sadness for the disrespect we show Indigenous Australians today.

While I would have preferred to focus on the natural wonders of my walkabout, it was impossible to ignore the plight and disenfranchisement of Aboriginal people and their country. How could anybody who travels into the Outback not see the tragedy unfolding before their eyes, let alone want to do something about it? How could people with a European heritage, in which fairness and the less debased versions of Christian morality supposedly underlie their approach to life, continually ignore the destructive impact of their culture on this most ancient of peoples?

The more I saw the active neglect of the First Australians, and the land itself, while the European part of society increasingly took and never put back, the more I felt a deep sense of shame for the country and its choices. Our reconciliation with Aboriginal Australia clearly has a long way to go before the wrongs of the past are righted if my experience in Alice Springs was any guide.

The magnificent West MacDonnell Ranges, known as Tjoritja to Aboriginal people, tower over Alice Springs with a rugged grandeur that promotes their dominance of this land. On every level of my being, these captivating ranges called to me with their exquisite beauty. Their presence was omnipotent. They were all-powerful and all-knowing. Their look of wisdom and strength instantly inspired my respect. With the original sediments deposited around 800 million years ago, when much of inland

Australia was covered by a shallow sea, the ranges evolved around 350 million years ago in a burst of tectonic activity during the Alice Springs Orogeny.

The ranges today reflect the tremendous heat and pressure required in building this most alluring of places. I could feel it in the hot smoothness of the rock. I could see it in the white splash of quartz across the ochre-red quartzite. Their physical grandeur drew me to them, encouraging me to discover everything I could about them, knowing it would be a life-changing experience. So inspiring was their majesty, so revealing was their presence, they became my lodestar every time my walkabout brought me back to Central Australia.

Named by John McDouall Stuart on their discovery in 1860, the MacDonnell Ranges rise from the ground much as a wave rises from the ocean with a similar, regular form. Yet they are suspended, held in a geological trance, where they will remain until brought low by erosion like any other structure that dares rise above the safety of Earth's flat parapet. Across the desert, similar ranges also rise from the flat ground with an almost regular monotony reflecting how often the continent has been impacted over its 4 billion year history by geological events of which each left its own unique tectonic scar. Many of the ranges seen today were created from similar events as pieces of ancient crust collided with, and became attached to, the existing continent.

As these pieces of ancient crust crashed into the evolving landmass, the weakest parts of the crust buckled, folded, or sheared up creating mountain ranges across the continent, sometimes on a scale equal to the Alps and Himalayas of today's world. In the MacDonnell Ranges, the crust folded up inducing the tilt of the sedimentary layers seen today: the fracturing and faulting of the ranges further highlighting the toughness of enduring those times. It may also be what defines the toughness of the land today.

While the ranges defined the landscape, their unique features seduced me to the wonder of this land. For, as I came to learn, it was in these places Nature displayed its most precious natural jewels. It was in the gorges of the West MacDonnell Ranges I experienced stately brilliance as only created by Nature's hand. The gorges were as different as they were unique given the 350 million years Nature had to carve these earthly masterpieces. From the aptly named Standley Chasm, a rocky path chiselled into the ranges, to Redbank and Serpentine Gorges, both snaking through the ancient uplifted strata, each gorge was a physical, emotional, and spiritual delight.

Exploring these gorges, climbing through their rocky ramparts, and swimming in their pristine waters was the perfect opportunity to connect with Nature as much more than just an observer. Especially at sunrise, as the first rays of light struck the gorge walls igniting them a fiery red, when I could immerse myself physically and philosophically into Nature's world. It could have been the dawn of time so unspoiled was the environment and so often was I the only person there. And while each gorge visited engendered a feeling of awe and respect for Nature's work, there was one gorge in particular whose resonance and grandeur I remember above all others.

Ormiston Gorge, known as Kwartatuma to Aboriginal people, remains my most treasured and revered part of Australia. I can still remember the feeling of trepidation and awe that gripped my stomach when it first came into view. It drew me to it with an unexpected intimacy I never expected though I had never previously seen it. Driving across the sandy bed of the creek that carved this gorge from the ranges, as they were slowly uplifted, its magnificence was tantalisingly revealed. In those first moments, I felt an overwhelming sense of belonging. It was the only time I experienced such a strong initial connection to a single place during my two years of walkabout.

Walking into the gorge, inspired and fascinated by everything I saw, its natural eminence enraptured me. The gorge walls stretched to the horizon and into the cobalt-blue sky; their fractured and faulted form only broken by a number of quartz veins hinting at the difficult birth this place had endured. Everywhere I looked, the rays of the setting sun set the gorge walls ablaze. Walking deeper into the gorge, I felt I was returning to a place I had never left yet it was a place I had never been. I felt enchanted by its splendour. I could not imagine a more inspiring and perfect place. That was until I reached its eastern end for its view to the horizon was one of the most inspiring vistas I have ever seen.

In that moment, I felt Nature had granted me a great privilege. I felt I had been granted entry to its most magnificent cathedral. It seemed that Nature had set to work, with nothing but a hammer and chisel, and carved a natural amphitheatre much like the sanctuary in the most inspiring of humanity's cathedrals today.

At the base of the gorge walls, the natural faulting and fracturing of the rock had created the perfect seating arrangement with the blocks towards the front lower than those at the back. The gorge walls were transformed into perpendicular pillars as light from the setting sun slowly moved shadows across them. The roof of this cathedral was the cobalt-blue sky of day or the sparkling black of night: its floor a soft, sandy creek bed with several small eucalyptus trees forming a rostrum from which Nature would inspire with its wisdom and humbly explain the importance of its teaching to our lives.

Standing alone in the cool dusk air, enveloped by the majesty of the surrounding gorge, I felt deeply connected to the natural world in all its forms. As if to highlight the significance of that moment, the glowing heights of Mount Giles in the distance reflected their gentle light into the gorge illuminating the amphitheatre as the slowly encroaching dusk spread its shadow over all. In that moment, I knew my ashes would be scattered here once my time on Earth is done.

While the eastern end of Ormiston Gorge awed and inspired with its geological majesty, the western end of the gorge was just as special but more alive. It was here the main waterhole, a magnificent Aboriginal sacred site, was found. Sitting under the canopy of an ancient eucalyptus tree, a sentinel from a time when Aboriginal people were masters of this land, I was enthralled to watch Nature's realm transform as the evening cool slowly descended. And it was not just in the evening natural masterpieces worthy of their own gallery were to be seen. For the morning revealed vistas of equal splendour as the glassy waterhole reflected the cobalt-blue sky, the ochre-red gorge walls, and the startling quartz splashes in perfect symmetry.

The waterhole was also home to most of the gorge's wildlife. From agile wallabies bounding over the rocks to the odd dingo quietly sauntering across the sand, from raucous galahs to spinifex pigeons careening through the bush, the area's wildlife was prolific and fascinating. Early morning and late evening were the best times to enjoy their antics as most animals only emerged once humanity's overt intrusion into their world was finished for the day.

Yet, despite the magnificence of the gorge, the array of its wildlife, and the diversity of its flora, I was continually surprised at how many people never stopped to appreciate the plethora of natural delights surrounding them. Most people walked into the gorge, and through the gorge, at the same pace, with their heads down as though nothing about their surroundings was even worth noting.

Astonishingly, this was not just a few visitors passing through. It was tour group after tour group. It made me sadly realise how removed much of society has become from Nature, and how the natural world has become a location to travel to rather than a place to stop and be part of. Many visitors barely walked to the waterhole before turning back, not even glimpsing the magnificent vistas further into the gorge, as the physical exertion was too great though only sand and small rocks barred their way.

Many who visited Ormiston Gorge appeared to view it more as an item to cross off a list instead of truly appreciating the gifts it had to offer in so many ways. It made me fear for the future, for, if an intriguing, inspiring place like Ormiston Gorge no longer captivates many of those who visit, what chance does Nature have for our attention and protection when competing against the destructive and debased forms of so-called 'entertainment', information, and religion in our lives today?

Nevertheless, while much of humanity did not appear to appreciate the majesty of this sacred place, it was a very different story for its native inhabitants. One came to hold me entirely in its thrall: the galah. *Eolophus Roseicapilla,* a member of the cockatoo family, single-handedly defines the wonder of much of Australia's native birdlife. Its bright pink and grey colouring, topped with small dark eyes and a pink-white crest, was exactly what I expected of a bird with a devil-may-care attitude. Watching these birds hurtling through the bush, a wildly screeching pink flash, always left me smiling.

It was hard to say who relished their show more: the galahs or those fortunate to be watching them. For, in the quiet of dusk, as they slowly, nonchalantly flew above the landscape with just a few flaps of their wings, I felt they were content with their life, singly appreciating the importance of freedom and space to that happiness. As I sat watching these birds, in different places at different times, it always struck me how much I could learn from their ways. Their curiosity for all things, their happiness in the natural world, and their joy at simply being alive defined many of the lessons I learnt on my journey. While Nature taught me these important lessons frequently, it was my pink and grey-feathered friends who defined them most succinctly of all.

I spent several days exploring the myriad of natural charms within Ormiston Gorge and the rocky ramparts of its surrounding Pound. Walking deep into the gorge each day, I simply watched and savoured the changing landscape as the sun moved across the sky. The gorge walls, in particular, were most intriguing. They started as a light ochre-red in the early morning, slowly darkening to a deep ochre-red by the afternoon. As the day slowly evolved to dusk, the colours continued to change. First, from deep ochre-red to purple, and then to white. Intriguingly, as the colours changed, so the gorge walls seemingly came alive as the shadows rose and fell.

From two-dimensional walls to three-dimensional pillars, the gorge seemed alive. It appeared to be breathing with the rise and fall of its lungs reflected in the changing hues across its walls. It had a character and personality I grew to love. Leaving several days later, as my journey resumed, I felt sad not knowing when I would enjoy its multiple pleasures once again. However, it was a place I would return to – of that I was certain.

From Ormiston Gorge the road headed west, past the delights of Glen Helen Gorge and the sleeping woman of Mount Sonder, into the geographic and spiritual heart of Australia. Shortly into this part of the journey, I left the bitumen that had carried me this far. I was now on the dirt, with the narrow strip of dust and rocks stretching to the horizon a jarring, life-shaking experience reflecting corrugation after corrugation until I was not sure my 4WD would hold together for much longer.

There was something cathartic, for me, about spending a lot of time driving the dirt roads of the Australian Outback. I suspect it may be because this was the closest I would ever come to experiencing what the explorers and pioneers endured: the heat constantly draining the moisture from their body, the smoke and dirt ground into their clothes and skin, and the continual taste of dust whipped up by the wind. The other aspect to driving these tracks I appreciated was slowing down. It was the perfect opportunity to absorb the lie of the land and the nuances of the country passed through. It allowed me to connect with the land in a way travelling the bitumen never quite did.

One of the unexpected features of Central Australia were the meteorite and comet craters scattered across the landscape with an alarming regularity. Gosse Bluff, known as Tnorala to Aboriginal people, was one such place. Created around 140 million years ago as a meteorite struck at a speed of up to 30 kilometres per second, blasting a 22-kilometre-wide crater compared to its two-kilometre diameter today, it remains a powerful reminder of the power of the Universe.

Standing within the crater, discovered and named by the explorer Ernest Giles in 1872, even a rudimentary knowledge of geology tells its visitors everything required to understand the cataclysmic nature of its birth. The walls thrust up at different angles, the rock fragments scattered across the spinifex-clad floor, and the crater's random location on an otherwise featureless plain highlighted its apocalyptic story. Gosse Bluff was another location in which I fully appreciated how vulnerable the Earth remains and our relative insignificance in the scheme of the Universe.

As the last mass extinction on Earth came about through a similar event, on the Yucatan Peninsula in Mexico 65 million years ago, Gosse Bluff was another place where I also appreciated that humanity is just another branch on Nature's tree of life. A branch capable of destruction in the geological blink of an eye as other species have been since the dawn of time. As Nature has always survived, and ultimately prospered, from such events, this realisation gave me further 'grist for the mill' as I increasingly understood its profound role in my life.

Heading away from Gosse Bluff, the corrugations like small waves on a desert ocean bore me to another of Nature's masterpieces, and one of the inland's most precious jewels. Palm Valley, known as Pmolankinya to Aboriginal people, is a place of the most unexpected biological wonder in Central Australia's vastness. It is a throwback to a time when the Australian continent was a very different place to that of today. Palm Valley is located in the Finke Gorge National Park, named for the Finke River that flows through its heart. Fascinatingly, the Finke River is one of the oldest rivers on Earth, one that has slowly carved its way through the desert and ranges for over 300 million years. Like many other significant features of Central Australia, it too was discovered and named by John McDouall Stuart.

Palm Valley was a difficult place to access. I definitely needed a 4WD to traverse the track in. On arriving in the brightness of the afternoon sun, with a full moon rising above the ancient ramparts protecting their precious treasure, the valley was a remarkable sight. Ancient palms and cycads, whose forbears were once part of a forest that covered regions of Central Australia in earlier, wetter times, were scattered along a small creek seeking its precious liquid riches under the sand. Several palms in the small oasis of Palm Valley are only found here with the recent discovery of isolated relatives hundreds of kilometres to the north suggesting a most interesting evolutionary history.

Not having seen these plants anywhere on my journey previously was another intriguing reminder of the fascinating evolution of the Australian continent literally from the dawn of time. Not only of its rocks, but also of its biological creations as Palm Valley showed.

Palm Valley had a quite surreal feel to it. After days of travelling through the heat and dirt, with nothing more than the dusty road and low spread of the horizon on which to focus, my senses were invigorated by the coolness and respite offered from the heat and glare of the desert. It was a pleasant change to rest under one of its many palm trees with the contrast of their luminescent-green leaves against the cobalt-blue of a late afternoon sky similar to that found on a remote desert island.

Interestingly, for all intents and purposes, Palm Valley was a remote desert island. It was an ancient biological island today surrounded by a sea of corrugations and spinifex, an oasis in the middle of a tough and challenging desert. The deep ochre-red of the sandstone walls magnified the intensity of the green and cobalt-blue hues with a darker reflective tone to that expected from the white sand of a beach. To complete the majesty of the vista, the pearl-white full moon slowly rose above the valley walls and their precious biological cargo – Nature gently reminding me, once again, of its inspiring creative powers in the otherwise seemingly empty vastness of the desert.

That night, with the campsite a plethora of accents and cultures, one of the rangers undertook his regular lecture series about the region. As he spoke about the destruction of native flora and fauna due to introduced species, it was interesting to watch how people responded. Most people were shocked at how much destruction had occurred in just the previous 20 years. The most telling comments came from European tourists as they sadly reflected on how little Australians had learnt from the mistakes of the Old World, and how destructive those collective behaviours unfortunately still were.

Most European tourists, most tourists overall in fact, had come to Australia for its purity and sanctity given how much of the natural world has been destroyed elsewhere: tarred and concreted over by humanity's ugly yet efficient process of sedimentation. All the more reason to protect the special places that remain, not only for ourselves but also for future generations so they may fully appreciate the bounty of the natural world. As I crawled into my swag that night, with the sounds of different accents wafting on the chilly night air like the smoke from my fire, it was with a feeling of hope that humanity, one day, will learn to live in harmony with Nature. We have so much to gain if only we make that choice as I was increasingly coming to learn.

From Palm Valley the track continued west, out into the desert, to another of Nature's inspiring geological creations. Kings Canyon is a spectacular canyon butting back into the George Gill Range; the view from its rim out into the vastness of the desert another of the mesmerising images taken away from Central Australia. On a clear day, it is possible to see all the way to Uluru with Australia's most recognised landmark a small purple-blue smudge on the horizon to the southwest.

The enormity of Kings Canyon was the characteristic that most left me in awe, especially when looking into its chasm, as the vastness and flatness of the surrounding country magnified its depth and breadth. As in other gorges throughout Central Australia, the sun's positon relative to the land played a leading role in how I experienced the majesty of this place.

I arrived quite late in the day for the walk along the canyon rim took longer than expected as I sought to understand the different rock types defining the country. A fascinating aspect was how varied the underlying rocks were, further hinting at the long evolution of this part of the continent from the ancient sea floor it had once been. From sandstone domes reflecting 400 million-year-old sand dunes on an ancient beach, to ripple rock, a rippled sedimentary rock reminiscent of a beach at low tide, everything pointed to the land as once being covered by water as today it was covered by sand. Even more interesting was how the same rock types had been carved into quite different sculptures depending on where they lay in the deposition sequence and the weathering processes subsequently applied to them.

While the flora at Kings Canyon was also unique, including 400-year-old cycad trees that only survive in this ancient part of a long forgotten world, the primary magnificence of Kings Canyon lay in its curved sandstone walls, carved then polished by the elements into one of the desert's most impressive sculptures. For when the western sky blazed in the rays of the setting sun, the canyon walls ignited with such a ferocity it seemed the very ground would burst into flames. As in Palm Valley, and throughout much of Central Australia, the contrast of the ochre-red canyon walls with the cobalt-blue Outback sky held me raptured until the dusk darkened into night. It was only then I left, confident I would miss nothing.

Only then did I return to my camp and an appreciated meal, watched over by the brightness of the moon and stars casting their silvery glow across the desert, to reflect on the illuminating wonder of Nature's work. It was an important ritual that closed each day much as rolling my swag in the morning started each day.

There is something physically and philosophically compelling about travelling through the soulful vastness of the desert that has spoken of awakening and learning since the earliest days of humanity. Whether in Africa, the Middle East, or the Americas, the deserts have called to people across the ages as places to seek the answers to the questions burdening their minds and souls, and to discover their place in the world. In this regard, the Australian deserts are no exception.

Late at night, wrapped in my swag, with the light of the moon and stars bathing the landscape in their silvery hues, the sands of the desert provided the perfect backdrop to let my mind wander unbound as it focused on the important questions of life, and their ultimate answers. The quietness of the desert, only interrupted by the blaze of my fire or the rustle of leaves as a breeze wafted through my camp, provided the ideal location to reflect on life. It provided the freedom and space to let my mind and soul relax, and empty of the societal detritus that had previously filled them. It ensured I could trust in the integrity of the questions it was now most important to answer.

It was during these desert evenings the answers I was increasingly seeking, to the questions that kept bubbling up like the steam from my quart-pot, slowly began to reveal themselves. It was during these nights, alone by my fire with the delights of the natural world as my only companions, Nature began to slowly imbue me with the richness of its wisdom. It was during these nights, most importantly of all, I started to feel my whole being slowly come back into balance as my mind and body, heart and soul integrated the increasing insights that came from time alone in Nature's realm.

After months on the road, seeking to connect with Nature's wisdom, I felt it had finally accepted the integrity of my request and was now willing to share the teaching I respectfully and appreciatively sought. Following my 'liberation', I was finally on the cusp of learning the most important lessons of my life.

Despite the mesmerising splendour of these desert jewels, my journey required I return to the sea of corrugations that bore me roughly from one to yet another of equal brilliance. This was a fascinating and captivating feature to Central Australia. Its jewels were of such refinement it was impossible to believe they existed until actually experienced. They could have been another desert mirage so unexpected was their presence until the delights of their sanctuary were seen and enjoyed.

Another interesting feature to the Central Australian landscape was how it slowly changed and how subtle those changes were. Since leaving Alice Springs, the ground had been very rocky with most of the vegetation, except around the waterholes and creeks, stunted and sparse. It had a toughness to it, a prickly feel that warned potential intruders to stay away.

Yet, as I drove away from Kings Canyon towards Uluru, the character of the country slowly changed. Instead of the never-ending vibrations of grinding tyres and working suspension on rocky ground, the timbre became more a slow purr as the rocky landscape gave way to one of sand. Instead of stunted mulga and prickly spinifex offering little in the way of succour, wispy desert oaks with their welcome provision of shade increasingly became the dominant vegetation.

Uluru first appeared as the purple-blue smudge seen from Kings Canyon, only this time much bigger. As I drove closer, I felt it was pulling me towards it so great was my desire to experience one of the most iconic of Australia's spiritual places. It appeared to grow before my eyes as the narrow strip of bitumen was followed across the sand: the desert oaks, mulga bushes, and desert grasses forming a guard of honour along its path reinforcing the significance of this place. As I approached Uluru, its grandeur increasing before me, I felt stirred by its stark elegance as its character slowly unveiled. It was at moments like this I intimately understood why Aboriginal Australians felt these places were such powerful and important elements in their lives.

It was especially on seeing Uluru in the evening light, my first night there, which reinforced this understanding most of all. For, as the dusk slowly lowered its pastel curtain of pink, orange, and purple radiance across the eastern sky, the sun's rays set Uluru ablaze; the full pearl-white moon sitting atop its summit the crowning glory to the majesty and serenity it inspired. Each viewing moment was more stunning, more extraordinary, than the last as its character evolved in an enrapturing dance. I watched its slow transformation transfixed by its beauty and inspired by how this living masterpiece was created from the most basic elements of earth and fire, wind and water. It was another reminder of how these basic elements are responsible for Nature's most inspiring creations.

Watching that mesmerising sunset over Uluru reinforced my understanding of how fundamental these basic elements are to the creation of the natural world. It was another reminder of how the most basic of elements are equally important to humanity's evolution – only in our case those elements are meditation, exercise, diet, and sleep. As I had come to learn, these basic elements are the only 'meds' we intrinsically need. For where we instead rely on artificially created poisons and fakeness to build our whole being separate from the natural world, so we ultimately destroy ourselves. However, where we instead build a life of connection to the natural world through these basic elements, we too can resonate with the same elegance and majesty as seen in that sunset at Uluru.

Furthermore, that is Nature's gift and its promise to all.

Watching Uluru from a distance was one way to appreciate its magnificence. Another was to walk around its base seeing it in all its intimacy. This was also the way to appreciate its unique geological history.

Uluru was created around 350 million years ago, during the same Alice Springs Orogeny that uplifted the MacDonnell Ranges, from sandy sediments washed into a shallow basin from the erosion of the Petermann Ranges; a mighty mountain range to the west now laid low as all mountain ranges ultimately are. The sediments originally forming Uluru, subsequently impacted by a number of geological forces, were ultimately uplifted through 90 degrees. Today, those now vertical layers of sandstone give Uluru its uniquely ribbed character. Either up close or from afar, these ribs provide the constantly changing shadows and features that make it such an intriguing place at any time of the day.

From smooth, almost expressionless features to the rough, wrinkled surfaces that barely hint at its ancient age, Uluru beckons us to understand the unique confluence of geological events and time that went into creating one of the world's most recognisable landmarks. They equally conspire with the surrounding desert and sky to remind us of Nature's power to create places and vistas that captivate and inspire the human soul.

Walking around Uluru was also the best way to appreciate its ancient human history for Aboriginal people have lived there for at least 30,000 years. One of the best ways to understand their connection to the land was through the rock art found tucked away in the caves that irregularly line the base of Uluru. Not surprisingly in the desert, many of the paintings showed locations to find water and the different foods available. They even highlighted important creation stories regarding Uluru that, though very different to its geological history, were equally interesting as I came to see its physical characteristics with a different, more nuanced perspective.

As at Ubirr in Kakadu National Park, the primary painting materials used were white, yellow, brown, and red ochre. Interestingly, one of its sources was an ochre pit to the east of Ormiston Gorge. Here, on the banks of a small, dry creek, the vertical layers of clay once mined by Aboriginal people for their ceremonies and paintings, and for trading with other clans throughout Central Australia and beyond, can still be found. Another hint of how Aboriginal people deeply connected with the very essence of the land itself.

Reflecting the dynamic history of the Australian continent, and the myriad of geological events it experienced, Uluru was not the only inspiring creation found in the sands of the Central Australian deserts.

To the west of Uluru lies Kata Tjuta, another majestic, beguiling, and inspiring monolith though quite different in many ways. The less winnowed nature of the sediments eroded from the Petermann Ranges, as they were deposited further upstream, and the slightly different geological forces applied, meant Kata Tjuta had a different look and feel to that of Uluru. The conglomerate layers comprising Kata Tjuta were less uplifted than the sandstone layers of Uluru, though more fractured. It was the vertical fractures in this rock, subsequently eroded over hundreds of millions of years, which form the captivating domes and valleys of today. Uluru and Kata Tjuta remind us of how minor differences in geological processes can result in quite different natural creations over time.

Walking quietly through the Valley of the Winds, with barely another soul around, I felt I was in another of Nature's cathedrals. The smoothness of the walls had the same cool, powerful feel as Ormiston Gorge with the surrounding space just as inspiring. The domes of Kata Tjuta, scattered through the desert as if places of worship from a long lost civilisation, were fascinating to explore with each having its own unique character to be deciphered once examined up close. From larger, elongated domes to smaller, rounded domes and one lightly covered with spinifex, there was no end to the geological diversity of this extraordinary, ancient place.

While Kata Tjuta was particularly unique, it was similar to other desert places in one respect. Just when I thought I had seen it at its most magnificent, Nature's changing mood showed me a different though equally stunning vista, especially into the evening. In the rays of the setting sun, as the intensity of the ochre-red monolith waxed then waned in the light show unfolding over its domes, Kata Tjuta glowed with a beauty unique to anything I had seen in the desert before. The backdrop for this display was the eastern sky, subtly layered pink, purple, and orange in the same horizontal style as the sedimentary layers comprising Kata Tjuta itself. Against the empty vastness of the flat desert horizon, Kata Tjuta's slow unveiling was as much a pleasure to behold as the beguiling sunset enjoyed at Uluru several days before.

Enhancing this scene, rising directly over Kata Tjuta, the full moon spread its silvery glow across the landscape. It was the type of flawless scene humanity has longingly sought to capture on canvas. It was the subtlest combination of colour and shape only master painters have been able to achieve. It was another powerful reminder that, for all our intellectual, technological, and cultural achievements as human beings, Nature will always be the first place to seek the treasures most valuable to us.

Visiting Kata Tjuta was also important for another reason, however. For it was here, in the sands of the Great Sandy Desert, I crossed the tracks of another mentor: Ernest Giles.

Ernest Giles discovered Kata Tjuta on his 1872-73 expedition into Central Australia; the first of five expeditions he undertook through the Red Centre of which two crossed the continent to and from the West Coast. Giles was Australia's last real explorer with his bravery and tenacity in twice traversing the driest regions of Australia unequalled by any other explorer. Not only did he traverse the harshest regions initially with horses, before subsequently also using camels, and a minimum of equipment, he did so with an exultation of spirit for the splendour of the natural world that shines through in his journals. He was the most poetic of the Australian explorers, finding pleasure and wonderment in places most other Australians at that time regarded with absolute dread.

Giles was also very respectful of the Indigenous Australians he encountered, often retreating to ensure no violence ensued. Even when confronted by aggression from local Aboriginal people, he only fired to scare them off recognising he was the one trespassing on their land. Much of the desert Giles crossed, for which he received the Patron's Medal from the Royal Geographical Society, remains off limits to all but the hardiest adventurer even today. To cross it twice successfully, with horses, remains one of the most impressive achievements from the history of Australian exploration.

From Kata Tjuta the track headed southwest, passing through the Petermann Ranges before neatly bisecting the Gibson and Great Victoria Deserts: places all named by Giles. This track, the most direct path through Western Australia to Perth, represented another 1,000 kilometres of sand and rocks, dust and corrugations until the small mining town of Laverton was finally reached. Initially, the sands of the desert framed every view with small clumps of desert oaks the only relief from the spinifex-clad land to the horizon.

On reaching the Petermann Ranges, the view changed completely and what a stunning sight it was. Broad ramparts of ochre-red quartzite rose majestically from the spinifex-covered ground; the remnants of the Petermann Orogeny around 550 million years ago when the mountains were cleaved from the ground as Gondwana continued to coalesce. They were an ancient memorial to the power of the Earth and its unique geological impact on the Australian continent.

Today, though only a shadow of their former majesty, the ranges remain untamed despite the unimaginable passage of time. They were a place where Aboriginal people maintained their lifestyle in the old ways and where the traditions of the past still held strong. As this was

Aboriginal land, the ranges were not accessible to me. I could only observe their grandness from the road and leave it to my imagination as to what geological treasures existed within their rugged domain.

From the Petermann Ranges to the end of the track at Laverton, where I turned back to Central Australia, the vistas passed were generally ones of sand and clay dunes interspersed with the remnants of ancient ranges. The lack of geological activity at the surface meant the flora really defined this country. From thick mulga scrub to spinifex, the vegetation systematically changed depending on whether I was passing through a well-watered region or one that was very dry. Where it had recently rained, I passed a sea of wildflowers and waving spinifex. Where it had not, the land was instead dotted with dead trees and brown-grey patches of dead and dying spinifex. Out in the desert, I was certainly reminded of how the vicissitudes of the season ultimately played the key role in the vistas experienced!

Reflecting the desert's changing offerings, and the length of time required to travel this track, I found several bucolic campsites to roll out my swag for the evening and enjoy the majesty of the starlit night sky quite literally in the middle of nowhere. From broad swathes of sand over which eucalyptus trees spread their welcome shade to rocky ranges where only stunted mulga trees survived, each camp was a unique location few others had enjoyed. These were the perfect places to appreciate and connect with the vastness of the desert and the night sky completely alone.

And while these sands were called a desert, they were in fact a quite unexpected intellectual, physical, emotional, and spiritual oasis: one that enabled my whole being to gratefully reconnect with the resonance of the natural world. It was the integrity and peace of Nature's desert realm that ultimately prepared me to receive the wisdom Nature will share when we show our respect for its ways and creations.

The final destination of my journey through Central Australia was Chambers Pillar, known as Itirkawara to Aboriginal people. Discovered and named by John McDouall Stuart on his 1860 push to the north, it was the last remnant of an ancient sandstone plateau that today stands alone on the western edge of the Simpson Desert.

I arrived late in the evening with the full moon spreading its silvery glow across the landscape. Rising above the sandy flatness of the plain, the same plain Stuart had crossed 142 years previously, was a towering and glowing beacon. The glow from the full moon that night turned Chambers Pillar into a plug of pure silver rising from the desert floor. What made that moment even more precious was its proximity to Stuart. Nothing had changed about the country for it was exactly as he had first seen it all those years ago.

Resting on my swag that evening, I half expected Stuart to loom up out of the darkness. For maybe he was not as far away as I thought. Maybe his spirit had returned from the cold of his grave in London's Kensal Green Cemetery to the scene of his greatest triumph. It was the closest I ever felt to him during my entire walkabout despite the number of times I actually crossed his tracks.

The following morning, after a quick quart-pot of tea boiled on my gas-fired stove, I hesitatingly returned to the track. Driving away from Chambers Pillar, back through the rocks and sand of the desert to the bitumen, it was with a sense of sadness I left. Central Australia is an incredibly pristine and inspiring part of the Australian continent. Everywhere I travelled, there was a spectacular vista over a ridge or around a corner I felt compelled to pull off to the side of the road and simply appreciate.

Experiencing these captivating scenes reinforced how important Nature was to my whole being. For it was only in Nature's domain was I able to meditate on what was truly important in life and, more importantly, on what was now required to develop the strength and health necessary for its accomplishment. Everything I could possibly require to choose a more fulfilling and meaningful life path would be found in the natural world. Moreover, the more I appreciated this critical realisation, the more it reaffirmed the deep connection I first felt to the bush all those years ago.

5

Down The Track

'There are stars of gold on the Wallaby Track,
And silver the moonbeams glisten;
The great Bush sings to us, out and back,
And we lie in her arms and listen;
Our dull hearts quicken their rhythmic beat
For a wild swan's southward flying,
And gather old memories sadly sweet
From a wind-swept pine-bough's sighing.'

Will Ogilvie – The Wallaby Track

The expression 'down the track' is one of the more frequently used Australian idioms. It conjures up feelings of remoteness, of going to places where few others venture, of the dry, dusty environment that is so often the heart of Australia. Whether it refers to a time, a place, or a direction, it is as part of the everyday Australian vernacular as "*G'day*". It is also a throwback to the days of an earlier Australia when to 'hump the bluey', to 'waltz matilda', or go down 'the Wallaby Track' were an accepted part of the itinerant workforce lifestyle and lexicon. It is a throwback to a time very different to the Australia of today. Yet there are still parts of Australia where it remains possible to go 'down the track' physically and philosophically. Many of these tracks are through remote and vast expanses where the Australia of today resembles the Australia of those long gone days in many ways. Similar to those times, it is in those places the allure and quiet of the bush can still be found. Not only is it where Nature's propensity to set out its teaching clearly and precisely can be easily discerned; it is where the freedom and space encourages an understanding of this teaching in a way few other places do.

Driving south from Chambers Pillar, following the faithful path of John McDouall Stuart, the bitumen somehow detracted from the quality of my walkabout. Maybe it was when travelling faster I tended to notice less. Maybe the lack of dust and corrugations made me less aware of the nuances of the country passed through. Maybe the ease of the journey removed me from what the original pioneers and explorers would have experienced. Most likely, it was a combination of all these things.

Accordingly, when the opportunity arose to return to the dirt of a remote bush track, at the equally remote town of Marla on the Stuart Highway, the decision was an easy one to make. The Oodnadatta Track, a 620-kilometre journey through the semi-desert country of South Australia, named for the small town through which it passes, is one such track. Like other tracks through Central Australia, its early history reflects the feats of John McDouall Stuart. Given the historical nature of the route, it was the best way to understand the country he explored and the magnitude of his extraordinary achievement.

Driving the Oodnadatta Track in the winter of 2002, it was very dry. And despite being the middle of winter, it was actually quite warm. It was a joy to be back on the dirt, seeing and feeling the nature of the country as I passed through it. Mind you, there was only one direction to look and that was to the front. The dust cloud trailing my vehicle filled the rear-view mirror with a brown haze making it impossible to see behind. I always knew if someone was coming in my direction as an equally long and wide dust cloud announced their arrival long before the first glinting flash of their vehicle.

Returning to the dirt, the vastness and harsh majesty of the landscape was the dominant geographic trait. It was not difficult to see this country as the ancient sea floor it had once been when a shallow sea covered much of the Central Australia of today. Apart from the odd hill or gully, and its associated stunted vegetation, there was almost nothing to see in the never-ending vista of sand and rock stretching to the horizon. It appeared Nature had decided to leave this part of its canvas fallow for the time being at least.

Yet, every now and then, as if to keep me aware of Nature's propensity for life, a kangaroo, lizard, or bird made its presence felt as a flash of colour or movement in the otherwise motionless landscape. The vastness of Central Australia, especially when travelling alone, made me feel small and insignificant. Driving all day and seeing only a few vehicles, the odd fence, or even less frequent windmill made me very aware of how difficult it must be to live here given humanity's predilection to settle even the marginally economic areas.

One of the more interesting features of the Oodnadatta Track is the gibber country through which it passes. A gibber is a small, flat stone just like any other small, flat stone. There is nothing especially unique about this stone until surrounded by a sea of them stretching to all points of the compass. In the heat of the day, with the dark mat of stones shimmering to the horizon in all directions, I could have been driving through a slagheap from Nature's ancient magmatic furnaces. However, at dusk, as the desert became awash in a sea of purple and orange hues, the gibber country became a welcoming place. It was almost as if, during the day, Nature wanted to test my resilience by constant trial after which, at dusk, having proved myself, it succoured me with its cool air and the wonder of the night sky. This was no different to similar experiences in other parts of Australia, but somehow in the desert it was always far more appreciated.

My first camp along this track was on the only permanent source of water available: the Algebuckina Waterhole on the Neales River. Despite seeing barely a hint of humanity's existence along the track, here at the waterhole it was a quite different story. For a long, wrought-iron, rusting truss railway bridge spanned the waterhole in the otherwise almost featureless terrain.

What a spectacular sight it made at dusk as the sun set directly behind its starkly defined girders: their form and shadow the only hint of a straight line in the desert's curves. The bridge, built in 1889 as part of the old Ghan Railway, when the track was first pushed north to Oodnadatta as part of a plan to reach Alice Springs and ultimately Darwin, was a sign of great progress at that time. Today, it is instead a relic of those times: a reminder of Nature's ability to reduce humanity's grand plans to the very dust from which we come.

Relaxing at the edge of the waterhole that evening, Nature again seduced me with its magnificent visual prowess. No matter where in Australia I camped, I remember the sunset as the most spectacular time of the day. And no more so than when experienced in the desert's vastness as the dusk colours cascaded across the sky setting the horizon ablaze. Each sunset was an event eagerly anticipated and often so mesmerising it always left me humbled.

That sunset on the Oodnadatta Track was another of the spectacular light shows Nature unfolded across the vast, empty landscape. As the colours in the evening sky danced across the horizon, so the waterhole mirrored that ballet. Contributing to its opulence was the light dusting of clouds that ignited when first touched by the sun's setting rays. As the light show blazed in the western sky, so it unfolded on the land as the salty edge of the ancient waterhole glowed in unison. It appeared the Earth was igniting in a slow conflagration as the waterhole reflected the ever-changing orange and purple hues of the clouds and sky above.

As the colours and shadows moved in a natural dance, so the bridge stood still: its rigid shape in stark contrast to the long curves and moving ripples of the ancient desert landscape. As the sun slowly sank to the west, the light of a full moon and stars replacing the waning glow of dusk, the waterhole was transformed into a silvery, rippled sheet with the bridge a hulking shadow slowly lost to the night. As the flames of my fire reflected off the waterhole that evening, the sparks intermingling with the reflected stars above, the land embraced me in a way that made me never want to leave.

Reflecting the scarceness of water throughout the desert, my camp that night was in a location Aboriginal people would have relied upon for thousands of years previously. I was merely another traveller in the long line of humanity to appreciate its bounty. Much of the track today follows an old Aboriginal trading route with the track's direction defined by Nature itself. Mound springs, which provided the sustenance used by the track's initial Aboriginal users, dot its path with an impressive regularity. Without these springs, there would have been no reason to follow this particular track through the desert.

Mound springs are exactly what their name suggests. A warm spring bubbling up from a small mound created from the slow deposition of minerals over time. These springs are outlets for the underlying Great Artesian Basin, one of the largest aquifers in the world. Originally filled from ancient rains that fell along the western side of the Great Dividing Range to the east, the geological spine that runs almost the full length of Australia's east coast, it today underlies one fifth of the continent. For the most part, there is nothing very special about these springs unless you are dying of thirst. That is until experiencing their captivating charms in the dawn of a cold winter's day as the snaking streamers of steam cast rainbows across the desert sands.

Following the track southeast, I was introduced to its more recent European history that was just as significant and just as interesting. I passed Anna Creek Station, the largest cattle station in the world, covering 24,000 square kilometres. A single cattle station as large as a small European or Asian country. Yet, reflecting the marginal nature of the desert country, it only carries around 16,000 head of cattle in a good season.

In addition to the odd sign to other cattle stations and the occasional windmill, I also came across relics from a time when prospects for developing these wide-open spaces seemed endless in the exciting period of Australia's version of nation building. Derelict train stations, former watering points, and bridges from The Ghan railway dotted the landscape with their distinct angular shapes very visible in the desert's flatness and gentle curves. And reflecting the randomness of their location, most passed by in a blur of dust and the endless horizon.

Along the old Overland Telegraph Line, the only connection Australia once had to the outside world, remnants of ruined telegraph stations that once played a vital role in that connection lay baking in the sand, today mere shadows of their former glory. Walking through these historical ruins, the continuing deterioration of this important part of Australia's history made me sad. Yet it also appeared the most natural process in the harsh extremes given the elusive nature of life in the desert. It was here I learnt to appreciate how quickly Nature can displace even the most concerted efforts of human interlopers.

Following a relaxing overnight camp just off the track, I continued along its path the following morning; a somewhat blinding experience as the sun slowly crested the eastern horizon. After a short time, the vastness of the country slowly gave way to the vastness of Lake Eyre South and its saltpans. Lake Eyre South, and Lake Eyre to the north, discovered by John Eyre in 1840, are one of the largest water catchments in Australia. Almost one sixth of the continent drains into these lakes when floodwaters reach this far. The lake was a blinding expanse of white, slowly increasing in size until it spread to the horizon. While it was a giant saltpan for my visit, it can become an awe-inspiring oasis once the life-giving rains west of the Great Dividing Range spill down the inland creeks and rivers to reach its salt-lined shores.

As most rivers west of the Great Dividing Range flow inland, several early Australian explorers undertook expeditions to discover the extent of a fabled inland sea believed to exist at that time. Unfortunately, for those early explorers, this was not the geographic reality of the continent. It was a mirage. They were around 100 million years too late.

The fabled inland sea did exist but in ancient times when warmer climates ruled the Earth and the water now held in the polar ice sheets instead resulted in higher sea levels. Yet, every now and then, the country shows what it is still capable of when tropical lows send huge volumes of water down the creeks and rivers feeding these lakes. They become an inland sea of the most majestic proportions. However, to see the blindingly white saltpans exquisitely contrasted against the cobalt-blue sky, it was a place of such radiance I was content to appreciate it just as it was.

Following the track east past the blinding glare of Lake Eyre South, I soon came to another of humanity's attempts to control the workings of the environment: the Dingo Fence. Originally built to keep dingoes out of areas considered suitable for the breeding of sheep, it has probably created as many problems as it has solved. As a pair of dingoes can kill many sheep in a night, the fence was required to protect the introduced flocks. Today, it is maintained constantly, all 5,600 kilometres of it, and those dingoes that do get through are pursued with bullet, bait, and trap. The downside of the fence, and the watering points introduced for stock, is Nature's fine desert balance has been distorted such that many animals dingoes once kept under control, such as kangaroos, now have no predator so other means of keeping their numbers under control have been required.

Shortly after passing through the Dingo Fence, I finally reached the town of Marree: another small town in the middle of nowhere. Another attempt by the early pioneers to impose some form of civilisation on the empty vastness of the rolling gibber plains. On reaching Marree, the Oodnadatta Track was now behind me: a receding vision in the rear-view mirror along with the dust cloud that had followed my vehicle since turning onto the dirt several days previously. While Marree represented the end of one desert track, however, it also represented the beginning of another I had always wanted to follow – one of the toughest droving routes ever pioneered.

The Birdsville Track is the best known of Australia's many droving tracks. It is also infamous for the number of men and cattle that died along its route as drovers pushed their herds down its length from some of the remotest cattle stations in the world.

The track, named for the small town that sits at its northern end, stands out as one of the remotest tracks anywhere in the world. The vastness and emptiness of the country I passed through was palpable. It did not matter where I looked. It was the same to the horizon at all points of the compass. It appeared Nature's palette consisted of only two colours when painting this part of its canvas: cobalt-blue for the sky and dirty brown for the land, with each applied in equal measure.

The scenery remained quite similar along the entire track, all 520 kilometres, with the most significant difference being between the gibber plains of the Sturt Stony Desert and the sand dunes of the Strzelecki, Tirari, and Simpson Deserts. The flora and fauna here seemed more of an afterthought given the empty vastness of the surrounding country as I passed through it.

Yet, it is the ability of the country to transform itself, into plains of waving Mitchell grass and saltbush, which represents one of the most interesting observations from the journals of the early explorers and pioneers. Given the vagaries of the seasons, one explorer would find a wasteland of epic proportions while another explorer several years later would describe the land as a veritable paradise. Today, like those times of old, it is the promise of those good seasons that supports the life of the region today.

Leaving Marree, I passed through the Dingo Fence once again. Heading north, one kilometre quickly dissolved into the next as the shimmering mirages on the horizon enticed me to believe a magnificent waterhole lay tantalisingly ahead. Just the thing I was seeking to wash the dirt and smoke from my body and clothes. Yet the waterhole never appeared for it was just like the mirages of old that led many an early explorer or pioneer to an early grave. Given the starkness of the views to the horizon, this was a place where I particularly appreciated the tender touch of Nature's evening mood while remaining respectful for its apparent daily disdain for all living things.

I always found travelling through regions like this to be very cathartic. I found they provided the freedom and space to calm my mind, relax my body, expand my heart, and inspire my soul. There was nothing to react to. There was nothing to focus on. My whole being slowly found its resonance with the natural world for there was nothing dissonant to generate the stress or frustration that is so often part of today's society. My experiences across the desert encouraged me to believe in Nature's majestic power to create and sustain our environment, and ourselves, far more so than when living in a city where humanity is fundamentally removed from the inherent wisdom of its actual creator.

The Birdsville Track's primary purpose was the droving of cattle. To ensure the watering points required for the movement of men, horses, and cattle, bores were drilled along its length to tap the Great Artesian Basin: the same source of water bubbling from the mound springs on the Oodnadatta Track to the west. Along the Birdsville Track today, a number of these bores can still be found from which steaming water pours making them the perfect place for an overnight camp. The early morning was the time I most savoured these places. For, as the sun's rays struck the landscape a brilliant gold, the steam caught the same light, casting a multitude of rainbows across the hard gibber stones and sand, gentling the rocky ground in a way never experienced at any other time of the day.

It was around these bores I also came to appreciate the life of the desert. Numerous dragonflies and small birds darted in and out of the reeds and grasses, while the paw prints of kangaroos and dingoes, fresh in the mud from the night before, made their ghostly presence known. Yet, with the steely glint off the gibber plains stretching to the horizon, it was easy to understand why the early explorers felt they had reached their own version of Hell after months of crossing these plains.

Heading north, the character of the country slowly began to soften as the dunes of the Simpson Desert first appeared. While this softened the country to my eyes, it was an illusion as highlighted by the random memorials to those who had perished out here. Yet, as I continued my journey through this most elusive of Nature's domains, the country once again began to change in a most wonderful manner.

The Diamantina River, one of three inland rivers whose episodic flow remains the lifeblood of this land, controls the landscape in either the wet or the dry times. In the dry times, its floodplain is a barrier against the sands of the desert while its life-giving waters provide moisture for the mosaic of vegetation along its banks. Yet, when this river comes down in flood from rains to the north and east, its reach from horizon to horizon, with only the tops of sand dunes protruding from the yellow-brown waters, reminds humanity once again of Nature's power to transform the country in an instant through a breathtaking flourishing of life.

For, when the rivers come down in the Channel Country, spreading their precious liquid volumes along its network of braided channels and out onto its plains, the waters become a magnet for life of every possible variety; the desert's bloom transforming the dry, empty land into a veritable biological and zoological utopia. Even though I arrived at a dry time of the year, it was a pleasure to see eucalyptus trees and lignum bushes thickly lining the river and extending into the sand dunes. It certainly gentled the land in a way I had not experienced when further out in the desert.

Reaching the Diamantina River represented the achievement of my travelling goal for, in a land where distances were long and landmarks few, this was how I measured the extent of my journey. From the Diamantina River, it was only a short drive into Birdsville and the most appreciated pleasure of a warm shower to wash the smoky, dusty reminders of the track back to the land from which they came.

However, this was not the primary reason for my journey to Birdsville. It was in fact poignantly related to the first siren call from the bush heard as a child. I wanted to visit and experience the place where several of the mentors from my youth had been a part. I wanted to pay my respects to their memory in the most appropriate way possible. It was, therefore, with a deep sense of gratitude to those men of the past, and the history they left behind, I camped on the bank of the river that became part of my life when first enthralled by its tales of explorers, stockmen, and drovers many years before.

I built a roaring fire that evening: the smoke from the burning coolabah branches rippling into the dusk sky with the same laziness as the water's playful ripples at the river's edge. I dipped my quart-pot into the Diamantina River, filling it to the brim.

And in memory of those who inspired a bush child many years previously, I boiled my quart-pot and drank its hot, slightly salty brew with a sense of respect for those who had also once camped in that same place. Resting on the bank of the river later that night wrapped in my swag, with the glow of the fire reflecting off the stillness of the water, it was with a sense of gratitude for both the softness of the ground and the fascinating history of the Channel Country I finally drifted off to sleep.

The 480-kilometre Strzelecki Track runs in the same direction as the Birdsville Track, except 300 kilometres to the east primarily through the Strzelecki Desert. It was also developed for droving cattle though its genesis was far more nefarious.

The first person to drove cattle down this track was Harry Redford; a man whose story was subsequently immortalized through the actions of Captain Starlight in Rolf Boldrewood's quintessential Australian bushranging novel: *Robbery Under Arms*. The track's beginning in 1870 reflected a bold gamble – it would enable Redford to sell 1,000 head of cattle, duffed from Bowen Downs station in Southwest Queensland, into a southern market with minimal risk the stolen cattle would be recognised by their brand. Being an outstanding bushman and cattleman, the odds were somewhat in his favour for such a journey. Well, as much as they could be droving 1,000 head of cattle through mostly uncharted and unexplored desert.

To his eternal credit, Redford succeeded in his daring cattle drive through tough, dry country that had defeated better prepared expeditions in the decades prior to his epic journey. Though he was ultimately brought to trial for his exploits, a jury of his peers was so impressed by his audacious success they found him not guilty. The judge's exclamation, *"Thank God, gentlemen, the verdict is yours and not mine!"*, suggests he was less than impressed by Redford's pioneering efforts!

From Birdsville I headed east to the Cordillo Downs Track, then south to Innamincka and the northern end of the Strzelecki Track. Similar to other tracks through the desert, this also passed several homestead ruins with each serving as another reminder of what a difficult region this was to run a pastoral business. It was fascinating to wander through these old ruins with their thick brick walls, majestic fireplaces, and assorted equipment rusting on the ground outside. Often there was a small, fenced-in cemetery with many of the graves for children who had died during the heat of summer or from one of the many illnesses we have almost forgotten about today. It was sobering to read the epitaphs on those gravestones and reflect on how difficult it must have been for those pioneers who took on the desert. It certainly increased my respect for the enormity of their challenges, the toughness of their chosen lifestyle, and the intensity of their commitment.

Heading south, my map showed another crossing of Cooper Creek ahead. Driving towards it, I first thought I was seeing another mirage. The same pulsating mirage of trees, water, and shade I swore I had seen countless times on the track that always melted away just as it came within reach. Just when I thought this one too would vanish, the bush surprised me. For there, in all its natural sumptuousness, was the Cooper Creek of my childhood fascination. It was an oasis and quite the antithesis of its namesake on the Birdsville Track downstream, which was really just a dry gully. It was a most appreciated sparkling jewel gently rippling under the midday sun.

The creek was alive with the sounds of a menagerie of birds in an ornithological orchestra. Screeching cockatoos, squawking corellas, and swooping, screaming galahs all strove to be heard in the somewhat dissonant cacophony swathing the land. It was a sanctuary to kangaroos, wallabies, possums, echidnas, and their most feared enemy after man: the dingo. It was a cornucopia of insects from friendly bush flies to dragon-flies and cicadas; their hum a reverberating reminder of their perpetual delight at living in such a sanctuary. It was a reptilian paradise with goan-nas, snakes, and lizards sunning themselves in the more secluded areas. The banks, lined with coolabah trees that lurched at every angle to the water, were a tangle of lignum and grasses. It was the perfect location to indulge in a well-deserved break from the track.

Yet, while Cooper Creek represented a high point of my journey through the desert, it marked a low point in the history of the explora-tion of the Australian continent. For it was within this bountiful realm the leaders of one of the best-equipped expeditions were both to die.

The saga of Burke and Wills is today taught to every Australian at school almost as a testimony to what can happen when the laws of the bush are ignored. In one sense, it is a shame that for all the exciting tales of Australian exploration, for all the inspiring stories of how early European explorers learnt to work within the country's unique character, it is this particular expedition which is most remembered. Unfairly, the achieve-ments of more successful explorers never seem to garner the same degree of interest as Burke and Wills.

Yet, while they died tragically in their attempt to become the first Europeans to cross the continent longitudinally, an understanding of what they achieved and their dedication to their task has always inspired much respect in my eyes. For, in fairness to them, much of the tragedy of their failure was due to the actions of other senior expedition members who failed to deliver as required and expected.

The expedition of Robert O'Hara Burke and John Wills, with 17 other men, left Melbourne in 1860 hoping to beat John McDouall Stu-art to become the first Europeans to cross the Australian continent from south to north. From the expedition's depot camp on Cooper Creek, Camp 65, Burke and Wills, along with two other expedition members, John King and Charles Gray, successfully navigated their way 3,000 kilometres across uncharted country during the hot, humid summer months to the Gulf of Carpentaria and back to Cooper Creek.

In one of history's brutal twists of fate, their support party left their depot camp on the morning of the day they successfully returned leaving nothing more than a few boxes of supplies. These supplies were buried at the base of a coolabah tree where the immortal words 'DIG 3FT NW' were carved. It is this tree, the Dig Tree, which is the most famous of all the blazed trees in the history of Australian exploration.

Sitting under the same tree 141 years later, I tried to imagine how Burke and Wills must have felt when they arrived back at their depot camp, having successfully achieved their goal, only to heartbreakingly discover their support party had left only eight hours before their return. And having left very little in the way of supplies at a time when their journey through the remotest parts of the continent, during the most difficult time of the year, had truly exhausted them. Worst of all, on the very day of their triumphant return. Who of us can even imagine the sense of betrayal and abandonment they must have endured?

With the meagre supplies recovered, and after a short rest, the small party of three men attempted to reach the closest outpost of civilisation, which they were unable to do. There was no way out. Burke and Wills both died on the banks of Cooper Creek. Only John King, the last of the four men who successfully reached the Gulf of Carpentaria, survived, for Charles Gray died on the return journey several days before they reached their depot camp. In another brutal twist of fate, it was the day they spent burying Gray in the hard, rocky ground with their bare hands that caused them to arrive a day later and excruciatingly miss their chance for both survival and the recognition their successful endeavours deserved.

Unfortunately, like many other stories of illustrious success and tragic failure, the outcome could have been so different. If the exploration party had only arrived eight hours earlier, or the support party had instead departed the following day, we would now commemorate the Burke and Wills expedition as much a success as we do those of the Canadian transcontinental explorer, Sir Alexander Mackenzie, and the

African explorer, David Livingstone. Fate, it seems, has a way of allowing us to snatch victory from the jaws of defeat as much as it sets us up for tragic, ignominious failures.

In this case, an eight-hour difference over a four month, 3,000-kilometre journey cost two men their lives and left as their legacy a reputation for failure when their deeds deserve a lot more. Burke and Wills were tough and resolute to their cause. There can be no denying that. Both men showed unflinching commitment to the task even though it resulted in their deaths. Despite what posterity may think of their failure, their crossing of an unmapped continent at the most difficult time of the year, and their successful return to Cooper Creek, for which Burke posthumously received the Founder's Medal from the Royal Geographical Society, continues to deserve significant respect. Well, at least I think so.

While Cooper Creek is today primarily remembered for the tragedy of the Burke and Wills' expedition, I primarily remember it for the many exquisite natural jewels strung along its shaded waterway.

Scrubby Camp waterhole, on the access track to Coongie Lakes about 30 kilometres off the main track, was my favourite. The majestic, gnarled coolabah trees lining the waterhole, alive with raucous galahs and corellas, provided a well-earned respite from the rigours of the desert. When I first arrived at the waterhole, the sun was setting. The air was alive with the sounds of an avian orchestra and an insect concerto as the orange and purple radiance to the west slowly spread its fiery brilliance over the waterhole. The cool touch of the breeze, the quiet rustling of leaves, the tangy smell of eucalyptus, and the softness of the ground made it another perfect camp.

To swim in its cool waters and to lie on its soft, sandy bank, with the vibration of life all around, was an experience that left me in awe of the simple pleasures within Nature's domain. Cooking dinner that night, as the evening cool slowly descended in unison with the sky's slow darkening, it was hard to believe there was any better place in the world. Resting on my swag later that night, with the wide, pulsating starlit night sky as my only companion, was another of those times I felt an intimate connection with the resonance of the country and the many natural delights it provided across its realm.

The next morning, I followed the Strzelecki Track back into the gibber plains and sand dunes that were now so familiar. After a short time, it was impossible to believe the oasis at Cooper Creek had been anything other than a mirage, though a very enjoyable mirage. In following this track south, it soon became clear why Harry Redford had chosen this path. It followed the meandering course of a creek that, while it was often dry, meant a little more vegetation and the possibility of water along its path: a lifeline for the movement of men, horses, and cattle through the desert. And in the blur of ochre-red and cobalt-blue that defines driving through the desert, it was only on reaching the bitumen at Lyndhurst, and finally Marree, I knew the Strzelecki Track was now behind me.

However, there is another way out of the desert via the Strzelecki Track. To follow that required backtracking to the Cameron Corner turnoff and heading southeast into Sturt National Park, passing through the Dingo Fence for the last time. The interesting aspect here was the track no longer ran parallel to the dunes: it crossed over them instead as the dunes run north to south. So away I went, like a surfer bobbing on a wave, driving up and down one sand dune after another, all the while watching for the tell-tale orange flag that occasionally appeared near the top of a dune showing a vehicle was coming in the opposite direction. Heading east, my destination was another historical waterhole from the early days of Australian exploration and the chance to cross the tracks of another mentor: Captain Charles Sturt.

Depot Glen is as important in the annals of Australian exploration as Cooper Creek. It was here, on the Preservation Creek waterhole, Charles Sturt and his men lived for seven months in 1845 on their expedition to discover the inland sea. Finding the country in the grip of a terrible drought, the small party camped at Depot Glen in a vain attempt to wait for better conditions. From this camp, they attempted to reach the centre of Australia and the inland sea believed to exist.

However, it was not to be for there was no inland sea. On each attempt, the soul-destroying gibber and brutal desert sands turned them back: the privations they endured on these campaigns into the desert among the most severe of any Australian exploration party. For his expedition penetrating into the heart of the continent, at the most brutal time of the year, Sturt received the Founder's Medal from the Royal Geographical Society.

Sturt's resilience, and that of his surveyor John McDouall Stuart, came to define the level required to meet the challenges of the desert. To keep his men fit, Sturt had them build a cairn of stones on a small range to the north of Depot Glen, Mount Poole, named for the expedition's second-in-command who died shortly after the rains relieved their enforced stay. While I have always respected Sturt's toughness, it was the impact of his expedition that was ultimately the most telling. For not only did it represent the end of the belief in an inland sea, it also represented the beginning of the end to the old European ways of exploring Australia with many subsequent expeditions based on fast moving groups of men who learnt to live with respect for the country as they found it.

Heading east from Depot Glen, past Poole's grave, to the bitumen and then south to Broken Hill, the surrounding country remained dry and sparse. Often there was nothing to focus on except the horizon which remained the same for the hundreds of kilometres driven. Although the desert slowly receded in the rear-view mirror, it remained a significant presence in my thoughts. For, unlike Sturt, and most other explorers of Central Australia, I had come to love its ways and the opportunity it offered to free my mind unlike the more closely settled areas.

The sublime, nuanced nature of this country captivated me, especially in the cold of winter when its beauty was not shrivelled by the summer heat. Whether it was the sand dunes stretching to the horizon or the endless gibber plains, the rocks shimmering like an ancient slagheap, the desert beguiled and inspired as few other places did. The toughness of the country, the cleansing feel of its heat, the soulful vastness of its empty spaces, and the gentleness of its sandy touch increasingly held me in their thrall. Travelling through the desert reawakened my feeling of connection to the natural world as it cleansed my whole being. It was a welcomed reconnection to life for it was a desert in name only.

Broken Hill, the town of my birth, rose slowly from the sand and saltbush plains as a silvery shimmer on the horizon much like another mirage. On getting closer, I realised it was not going to disappear as most other mirages had done. Broken Hill is a survivor – a tough town in a tough environment. In its heyday, it was one of the toughest places in Australia. Its raison d'etre came from the primary source of its wealth: the largest, richest silver-lead-zinc orebody ever discovered. And if Broken Hill's mining pedigree is not realised at first, it quickly becomes apparent to even the most casual observer. From the headframes and mullock heaps surrounding the town to pieces of mining equipment located in numerous playgrounds and parks, everything spoke to the motherlode literally discovered and then painstakingly won from Nature's grasp.

Broken Hill gets its name from an entry in Charles Sturt's diary from his 1844-46 expedition to discover the inland sea. On passing through the region, heading northwest, a 'broken hill' caught his attention in what he subsequently named the Barrier Ranges. For many years after, explorers and pioneers wandered over, and wondered at, the 'broken hill' and its dark, heavy rocks.

Yet it lay undisturbed until 1883 when Charles Rasp, a German immigrant working as a boundary rider on Mount Gipps Station, and the station's manager, George McCulloch, formed the Syndicate of Seven to determine its riches. As fate would have it, the first shaft was sunk in a sterile part of the orebody. Fortunately, sufficient funds remained for a second roll of the dice with the second shaft literally striking the motherlode.

The discovery of Broken Hill, and the wealth generated from its spectacular mineral hoard, played a significant role in opening up this part of Australia just as the discovery of Mount Isa did for Queensland. Not only did Broken Hill's development have a regional impact, it also had a national impact so great was the wealth it generated: the taxes and dividends it paid funding the development of the nation in a manner that saw Australia on her way to the position of wealth and privilege she enjoys today.

Yet, Broken Hill was also important to me for another reason, and not just that it was the town of my birth. It was where I connected with the spirit of Australia's greatest mining magnate and another of my mentors: Essington Lewis.

Essington Lewis was a tough, self-made man in the tough business of mining. He was a child of the bush, growing up in the ranges of South Australia, skilled at bushcraft and horsemanship, before achieving his success as a mining engineer. The challenges of his upbringing prepared him well for he built Australia's largest mining company through a drive and tenacity rarely seen, even in today's world. Lewis intuitively understood how to extract value from Australia's diverse resource base, building the foundation of today's largest mining company: BHP. Not only was he also responsible for building Australia's steel industry, he played a leading role in the creation of its heavy manufacturing base.

Presciently, following his dealings with Japan in the 1930s, he became convinced that country was girding its loins for war. Backing his realisation with conviction, he single-handedly put Australia's economy on a war footing thereby ensuring the country was somewhat prepared when the Japanese finally took aim at Australia. With Australia at war, Lewis contributed mightily to the final victory through his industrial and logistics prowess as both director-general of munitions and later aircraft production. Despite being encouraged to accept a knighthood recommendation, he refused, ultimately receiving the Companion of Honour at the request of the Australian Government instead. Having driven the development of Australia's largest company and undertaken a most critical role in Australia's contribution to the Allied victory in the Second

World War, he remains one of the most inspiring citizens Australia has ever produced. And may ever produce!

While the mineral wealth of Broken Hill is considered most valuable by society, this child from the bush found its natural wealth a more valuable treasure – especially the majestic eucalyptus trees lining several of the larger creeks outside the town. I spent my last night in Broken Hill, before heading west on the next stage of my journey back into the desert, camped beside one of these trees with my swag unrolled under an open sky.

As the bark and leaves of the tree gently glowed in the rays of the setting sun, and the cool of evening descended on my camp, a pair of galahs briefly joined me on a nearby branch. It was another vision of Nature in perfection; another gift of the incredible bounty surrounding us if only we would stop, listen, watch, and learn. At times like this, I felt part of the land. I felt an intrinsic resonance with the natural world and respectfully connected with its wisdom, with its life force.

Resting on my swag later that night, as the fire slowly transformed from its initial blazing form into a pile of gently pulsating coals that mirrored the pulsating stars above, I thought back to what I had learnt on my walkabout so far. It was this – that Nature will always provide the whole being nourishment we seek if only we heed its teaching and live with respect for its wisdom. Nature had invigorated my mind, cleansed my body, balanced my heart, and inspired my soul. It had provided the environment most conducive to rebuilding the core of who I wanted to be as a human being. Most importantly of all, it had simply shown me the intrinsic path to health, happiness, and adventure it generously makes available to all humanity.

Hearing Nature's siren call, Pilbara, WA, 1969

Lachlan and Anna, Clermont, QLD, 1978

A soulful childhood friend, Clermont, QLD, 1978

Lachlan and Banjo, Polocrosse carnival, NSW, 1993

Lachlan and Can-Can, Polocrosse carnival, NSW, 2002

Termite mound and 4WD, Kakadu, NT, 2002

Yellow Waters at dusk, Kakadu, NT, 2002

Northern Australia majesty, Edith Falls, NT, 2002

Granite sculpture at dusk, Devils Marbles, NT, 2002

Waterhole reflections, Ormiston Gorge, NT, 2002

Last rays of dusk, Ormiston Gorge, NT, 2002

Nature's perfection at dusk, Uluru, NT, 2002

A glowing beacon at dawn, Chambers Pillar, NT, 2002

Nature's symmetry at noon, Kata Tjuta, NT, 2002

Nature's symmetry at dusk, Kata Tjuta, NT, 2002

Algebuckina Bridge at dusk, Oodnadatta Track, SA, 2002

Swag camp in the desert, Oodnadatta Track, SA, 2002

Gibber plains, Birdsville Track, SA, 2002

Sand dunes, Birdsville Track, SA, 2002

Cooper Creek at dawn, Strzelecki Track, SA, 2002

Swag camp on Stephens Creek, Broken Hill, NSW, 2002

Creek bed and bluff, Trephina Gorge, NT, 2002

Dawn light on Hale River, Glen Annie Gorge, NT, 2002

Alone in the ranges, Glen Annie Gorge, NT, 2002

The simplicity of walkabout, Plenty Highway, QLD, 2002

Mustering cattle, Logan Creek, QLD, 1988

Yarded wild cattle, Saraji, QLD, 2002

Looking south along Second Ridge and Monash Gully, Anzac Cove, 1995

Looking west over Braund's Hill down Shrapnel Valley, Anzac Cove, 1995

With unexploded Turkish shell behind Quinn's Post, Anzac Cove, 1995

Lone Pine Cemetery at dusk, Anzac Cove, 1995

6

Elixir of Life

'Let the wealthy hoard their gold,
Let the famous guard their wreath;
All I ask to keep and hold
Is my path across the heath;
None my freeway to withstand,
None my faith and me to part,
Just the winds to hold my hand
And the hills to keep my heart!'

Will Ogilvie – Riches

From the beginning of time, humanity has sought the fountain of youth – a single, magical elixir for the various ailments of life from which we all suffer. Many in our society continue to look outside themselves for this wonderful, elusive potion. Many of our myths and fears hint it is something found external to our being. A pill or potion that absolves humanity from doing the actual work required to achieve the state of health and happiness sought. Today, whether it is the sporting world and the taking of performance enhancing drugs, everyday people seeking surgery for ailments that arise through their own neglect, or society's increasing obsession with youthfulness at the expense of health, seeking the elixir of life remains a core part of who we are as human beings. Heading back into Central Australia, little did I realise the most important lesson of my journey was about to reveal itself. For Nature has already set out the wisdom we require to be happy and healthy with the remedies for the problems experienced by our whole being simple and free. It is by looking to the natural world and its wisdom, and actually ignoring humanity's pills and myths, we can discover the elixir of life we seek.

The road west from Broken Hill, over the Barrier Ranges and through the saltbush plains of Western New South Wales, passes through the most ancient of lands. Reflecting the age of the Australian continent and the extent to which its history correlates with the Earth's evolution, extensions of the Barrier Ranges are today found in China and North America suggesting a fascinating, ancient connection between these respective lands.

The Barrier Ranges, created through a plethora of geological events over a billion years or more, from sediments first deposited around 1.8 billion years ago, are part of the Broken Hill Block. This block represents an initial piece of continental crust, which, with the Western Craton, the Gawler Craton, and the North Australian Craton, coalesced over the next 900 million years to forge the western two-thirds of the continent known as the Australian Craton. Over the next 600 hundred million years, today's eastern third of the Australian continent was slowly melded onto this original landmass as tectonic plate movements plastered more crust to the continent's eastern edge layer by layer.

The geology of the Barrier Ranges shows that dynamic history today for the land to the north and west is comprised of much older rocks while the land to the east is primarily comprised of rocks from only the last 500 million years or so.

Driving west from the Barrier Ranges to Port Augusta, my destination was another region of ancient Australian mountain building: the magnificent Flinders Ranges. My first view of their splendour was of a purple-blue smudge rising from the ochre-red sands of the desert. Even from afar, their rugged grandeur overlooking the otherwise flat horizon peaked my curiosity knowing I would find places of rough-hewn beauty as only created within Nature's domain.

The Flinders Ranges, known as Ikara to Aboriginal people, were created from the bonding of new continental crust onto the eastern edge of the Australian Craton, when it was part of Gondwana, around 500 million years ago during the Delamerian Orogeny. As Australia slowly evolved as an island continent, finally through its break from Antarctica starting around 400 million years later, so the Flinders Ranges were rent asunder – their extension in the Transantarctic Mountains of Antarctica highlighting Australia's ancient connection to the Great White Continent.

Since their uplift from the ocean floor into an ancient mountain range, the craggy peaks have slowly been eroded to the worn stumps seen today. Worn down as other once grand ranges on this most ancient of continents were by the destructive powers of wind and water, hot and cold. Yet the geological history of the ranges can still be discerned in the rocks today. Small marine fossils, originally entombed in the sediments deposited on the edge of the ancient Australian Craton, remain suspended in the ranges high above the desert floor. The faulting and fracturing of the different sedimentary layers comprising the ranges highlight the pressures and strains of their unique geological journey. Fortunately, despite the rugged terrain, Nature's subtle touch had tempered the tough character of the land in a most beguiling way, as it is often want to do.

Of all the delightful gorges, shallow eucalyptus tree-lined creeks, and magnificently carved vistas in the Flinders Ranges, it was the geological curiosity of Wilpena Pound that most resonated. As one of the few spectacular and symmetrical features seen in Australia, it first appeared to have been created by a meteorite much like Gosse Bluff. It certainly had a similar rounded shape rising from a somewhat flat plain. Subsequently, a closer inspection revealed the rocks had a far softer look for there was none of the randomly fractured and upthrust look to this land as seen in the crater at Gosse Bluff. Through a miraculous geological transformation, a mountain amphitheatre had been constructed within the ranges shaped like a pair of cupped hands. The majestic eucalyptus trees lining the dry, rocky creek leading into the Pound, silhouetted against the dazzling azure-blue of a winter sky, reinforced the allure and majesty of this ancient place. The tangy smell of eucalyptus permeated every thought, especially in the heat of the midday sun, ensuring I would never forget such a mesmerising vista.

Walking across the Pound, the footing was quite soft. The area used to be wheat fields and grazing pasture when the rains were more accommodating. Fortunately, with the scrub and trees slowly growing back, the Pound is gradually reclaiming its original wildness and intrinsic harmony. It was another reminder of Nature's innate ability to revert to its original state from the ruination incurred at the hands of humanity no matter how severe that damage often is.

To the north of Wilpena Pound lies Arkaroola, a more remote and clearly less visited part of the Flinders Ranges. As I headed north, the country became dryer, more rugged, and increasingly appreciated. As the vegetation changed, from broad-boughed eucalyptus trees, sweeping casuarinas, and tall pines to stunted, weedier versions, so the character of the bush also changed. The land became harder and less forgiving than the southern end of the ranges, especially during the day, constantly reminding me what a hot, dry continent Australia intrinsically is.

Yet, in the cool of the early night, after watching the sunset perform another of its dazzling ballets across the ancient ranges of the Outback, I would not have chosen another place to experience the inspiring bounty of the natural world. The coolness of the evening always engendered a feeling of belonging in the bush, of being part of it. During the day, especially as the sun's draining rays beat down, my feeling of belonging was constantly tested and I often felt exhausted. However, at night, as the refreshing touch of the dusk's cool curtain of relief returned, with the splendour of the night sky stretching to the horizon at all points of the compass, I felt completely at one with Nature.

This was also the time to listen to what it would teach. This was the time to immerse myself in its bounty, to let its wisdom slowly and willingly permeate my whole being. In the Flinders Ranges, in the middle of winter, this was also the time to fully savour the wonder of the Southern Hemisphere night sky, my increasing familiarity with its gently pulsating stars, and the moon's stately position over all whether waxing or waning.

While the Flinders Ranges are today hot and dry, especially in summer, the geology tantalisingly hinted at a very different past. For among the mix of stunted eucalyptus, pine, and acacia trees, spinifex, and dust were reminders of a time around 750 million years ago when much of Australia, and indeed much of the Earth, was covered with ice. Fascinatingly, deep in the ranges today, several places show boulders of all sizes and shapes, like plums in a pudding, scattered through the sedimentary layers; pieces of ancient mountain ranges converted to rocky waste by the ice that laid siege to them.

Tillite Gorge was one such place: its rocky walls created from glacial waste that accumulated at the edge of the Australian Craton as the ice met the ancient Ediacara Sea. It was not difficult to see this place as the ancient glacial debris drop zone it had once been. Rounded boulders of granite and quartzite, stripped off mountains far to the north and west, lay randomly scattered and entombed in the fractured, sharp sandstones and shales suggesting a quite heterogeneous geological history.

As if to highlight the enormity of the continental impact of these ancient ice sheets, their detritus are found back through Central Australia and up into the Kimberley. Seeing glacial evidence across the hottest, driest parts of Australia was another of those fascinating insights into the ancient age and unique journey of this most intriguing of continents.

Surrounded by the majestic, scalloped ramparts of the ranges, and the azure-blue sky to the horizon, I felt completely embraced by the natural world's vigour and vitality. It had an energy that encouraged me to connect with its power and live as part of its community of rocks, plants, and animals. Within these ranges, as in other similar places around Australia, I came to further understand how the history of the land around me was actually an insight into the reality of our own existence. For, as human beings, we can build ourselves, and our society, into the same magnificent natural creations that surround us every day simply from utilising the most basic of Nature's elements. Alternatively, we can continue to sadly devolve into the increasingly unhealthy, self-destructive state seen in our society today through our lack of attention to Nature's teaching.

Everything needed to experience the happy and healthy life sought, the wisdom of meditation, physical exertion, emotional balance, nutritional support, sleep, and spiritual fulfilment, is found in the natural world. Along with healthy examples of what we can become as exhibited in the vistas experienced at Uluru, Ormiston Gorge, and now deep in the heart of the Flinders Ranges. Nature has so much to teach us if only we would open our mind and body, heart and soul to this reality more than we currently do.

While I would have enjoyed spending more time in the Flinders Ranges, exploring its remote gorges, walking its trails, and immersing myself in the harmonious rapture of its sunrises and sunsets, my journey north called more loudly. Accordingly, in the larger-than-life tracks of that indomitable explorer, John McDouall Stuart, I followed the narrow strip of bitumen that bears his name back to the MacDonnell Ranges in Central Australia.

It took several days to drive back to Alice Springs: another few nights enjoyed in different, random ports of waterless beauty with nothing more than the friendship of galahs and the starlit allure of the night sky for company. Another few days with nothing more than the endless plains of mulga, spinifex, and sand to reflect upon the wisdom Nature continued to teach. Increasingly, I was better able to appreciate Nature's insights for a life well lived as it now spoke a language that resonated with my whole being. A language that made me acutely aware of how much Nature can teach those who seek its wisdom, and how much we could learn if only we would listen.

The East MacDonnell Ranges are just as spectacular as their western extension though more remote. Whether physically in terms of their grandeur or philosophically in terms of the freedom and space they provided to reflect on the teaching of the natural world, their remoteness rendered them the perfect place to stay for several days. During my travels here, two places particularly resonated as I increasingly connected with the delights of this ancient land: Trephina Gorge and Glen Annie Gorge.

Trephina Gorge, the first dry gorge I experienced, was another stunning testimony to Nature's innate ability to create geological masterpieces that reinforced the insights I gained from its teaching: insights that motivated me to continue following this path. The fractured and tilted gorge walls, a deep ochre-red in the afternoon light, called me to their shade and relief from the day's heat. The broad, towering eucalyptus trees lining the creek leading into the gorge appeared as sentinels guarding the sanctity of a sacred place. The walk through the sand, with its glare dazzling in the afternoon sun, slowed my pace to a meandering crawl ensuring I appreciated the inherent splendour of the gorge. Nature, it seemed, realising the cost of speed in our lives, understood it first had to slow me down before I could fully appreciate the majesty of its intrinsic beauty and the creative capacity behind that beauty.

It was in Trephina Gorge I experienced one of the most memorable nights of my journey. That night, under a radiant moon, I was woken from the pleasure of a deep sleep by a rustle in the grass close by. Looking out from the warmth of my swag, my eyes adjusting to the brightness of the moon's light, I saw a couple of kangaroos slowly move through my camp. They hopped a few steps before stopping to chew the small shoots of grass that grew along the creek bank. Then another step or two before doing the same again. One of the kangaroos was so close that I could almost touch it, but not quite and not that I wanted to. All around were the rustling sounds of the native wildlife busily going about their lives at night as I did mine during the day.

After a short while, I crawled out of my swag and walked down into the sandy creek overlooked by a large bluff: its hulking outline silhouetted by the starlit night sky. Standing alone in the chilly night air, bathed in the light from the moon and stars, I felt connected to Nature in a way I had never felt before. I felt I had been accepted into its realm, into the clan most important to me as a human being. In that moment, my feelings give way to a primal emotion. It came with the slow rise of complete enchantment through my body from the Earth. It came with a realisation my walkabout had intended to bring me to this exact place, at this exact time, to experience this exact feeling.

In that moment, I realised how strongly I connected with the natural world: how it not only enraptured my soul, it equally enveloped my being. I understood how important it was to reconnect with its wisdom, how much it needs our protection, and how much we as humanity are slowly destroying it. I felt that if only more people could appreciate Nature's wisdom, if only more people could experience the connection I felt while standing alone in that remote sandy creek bed in the middle of the night in the middle of nowhere, they too would understand how important it remains to every aspect of our lives.

I sat on the cold sand for much of that night just being aware of how perfect the scene was and how important this place had been to my own journey. It was an experience that left me, yet again, in awe of Nature's power and its required presence to living the life of health and happiness I thought lost and now had found. The insights that came at that moment made 'liberation' an act of grace by a very benevolent power indeed. It was in that moment I realised the full cost of staying on the self-destructive path I had unwittingly taken. Knowing what I now knew, the lost salary was a small price to pay for the valuable insights gained during this walkabout.

Glen Annie Gorge, further to the east, is rugged, spectacular, and difficult to access. The rough track along the sandy bed of the Hale River, evidenced by two deep tyre marks that followed a somewhat random and meandering but parallel path, was the only way to access the gorge properly. The track, a convoluted mixture of sand and rocks, with the river hiding various pitfalls, was definitely not the type to take on with an attitude of arrogance.

Be that as it may, and the slow, careful approach I took, I still found myself stuck – hung up on a rock that suddenly shifted leaving my back axle and wheels off the ground with the weight of the vehicle precariously balanced on a slowly crushed exhaust pipe. Not a good place to be with nobody around. And so, as many travellers before me had also likely done, I grabbed the shovel and started digging, piling up the sand and rocks to build enough support under the tyres so the traction would be enough to release the vehicle. It took a lot of patience, quite a few rocks, and a little luck to extricate myself from that quite unexpected predicament.

Yet, just when I thought the track was about to improve, it got even worse. More and bigger rocks, more and deeper sand, and less of a track to follow indicated even fewer vehicles took this route. This meant getting out of my vehicle more often to check the ground to be driven over, which I often had to get right by a matter of centimetres. With patience, and a little luck, I got through the worst of it. Appreciatively, my reward for the effort and patience shown was the allure and serenity of the most remote gorge in the East MacDonnell Ranges with not another soul around.

My camp that night was a veritable paradise. It was another of the inspiring places in the remote Australian inland with which I completely resonated. Gently waving reeds hinted at the soft breeze blowing across an ancient waterhole in the Hale River near where I camped. Broadboughed eucalyptus trees provided a shady respite from what was a hot, dry land while finches and dragonflies playfully skimmed over the waterhole off which the ochre-red gorge walls reflected in the afternoon sun. The soft, sandy beach running down to the river was the perfect foil to the hard, rocky ground over which I had spent so much time driving. It was a vision of paradise. No, it was paradise.

Sitting on my swag on the soft sand, in a remote gorge in a remote part of the continent, the vastness of the night sky mesmerised me. As the moon was no longer rising early in the evening, nothing interfered with the brilliance of the stars at night. Perhaps it was the darkness of the gorge where I camped, but that night I remember as one of the most starlit of my journey. From the historical and spiritual significance of the Southern Cross and its two pointers to the Big and Little Dippers, the night sky was alive with light. It was a most appreciated change from New York where the night sky barely existed – most evenings I was lucky to use both hands in counting the stars. However, here in Central Australia, in the vastness of a clear winter's night, I felt I could see almost to the edge of the Universe itself.

Resting on my swag later that night, completely alone, under the blaze of the starlit night sky with the fire casting its warming glow over all, my former life was as far away as I could possibly imagine. Twelve months previously, my wildest dreams never even contemplated the opportunity for an Australian walkabout. My trust in society, and the efficacy of its beliefs, was the only path and philosophy I envisaged. Yet fate had played its hand in a manner for which I will remain truly grateful for the rest of my life. It forced me to understand how beholden I had become to society's unhealthy beliefs, and how much I had sacrificed quality of life for a path that, without balance, had become a destructive and negative influence on my life.

Surrounded by the rugged grandeur of the ranges, the stark imbalance of being wedded to society's expectations versus a life struck home. I had put complete faith in the belief that achieving the traditional version of success would provide the opportunity to follow my walkabout path. I had lost myself in that murky, unnatural place with the most important goal of all, a life of health, happiness, and adventure, ignorantly and naively subjugated to the whims of others. I learnt this would be our reality unless we ensure our choices work to our benefit rather than becoming beholden to the unhealthy, self-serving needs of others. I learnt our reality could be very different if only we have the courage to follow our own path, trusting the twists and turns we may not expect, which ultimately reflect the journey that is most interesting, meaningful, and pertinent to our core being.

The next morning, I woke early to the multi-toned calls of the avian community for they were clearly early risers in this remote oasis. As I rolled my swag, a flash of colour caught my attention. Looking across the river, to the other side of the gorge, I saw a dingo nonchalantly walking along the rocks as if it did not have a care in the world. To see one unexpectedly, in the flesh, gave me a big thrill. I had heard the squeal of dingo pups the previous evening so knew they were about. The paw prints around my swag from several curious visitors the previous night further confirmed a healthy dingo population in the gorge. Clearly, they had not been disturbed for some time, losing their fear of humanity somewhat, which was a delight to see.

Most appreciatively, the charms of Glen Annie Gorge continued to beguile me with their delights throughout the following days. From the ever-changing colours of the gorge, faithfully reflected off the waters of the river and framed by the cobalt-blue Outback sky, and the flocks of birds randomly skirting its waters, to the cooling breeze that intermittently blew through the day, I felt intimately caressed and nurtured by the abundance of natural pleasures surrounding me.

Walking through the gorge, my path followed ancient and recent tracks. I followed the same path Aboriginal people would have once used on their travels. I followed the same path native animals used, whose activities I was increasingly able to discern through the fresh tracks at the water's edge each morning. In deciphering these tracks along the river's edge, I quickly realised how full of life the gorge was. Kangaroos, dingoes, goannas, lizards, crows, and galahs were just a few of its residents I was fortunate enough to see.

Being part of such a naturally wild place, joyfully living in harmony with the life around me, made it difficult to leave after the several days spent relaxing in its luxurious embrace. Fortunately, it was not as difficult to leave as it had been on arriving as I carefully manoeuvred my 4WD over the rocks and sand. Yet, heading back into the hard and rocky country that otherwise defined this land, it was with a feeling of sadness and awe I left the serenity and magnificence of that rarely visited place.

From Glen Annie Gorge the road now turned west, back to Alice Springs and finally the sanctuary of Ormiston Gorge in the West Mac-Donnell Ranges. Following the familiar path, along the valley floor with the scalloped ranges on either side, I increasingly felt I belonged here and would continue returning now I intrinsically understood this. Seeing the slight opening in the range, my initial glimpse of Ormiston Gorge, it resembled the first grin from an old friend when catching up after too long apart. And like that first grin that slowly grows into a glowing smile, Ormiston Gorge expanded its magnificence, in effect smiling its own welcome return to its cool and appreciated embrace.

Returning to my sacred place at the eastern end of the gorge to watch the sunset over Mount Giles in the distance, its rugged form lighting up and then slowly extinguishing, my only feeling was one of peace. Not surprisingly, the connection I first felt all those months ago was still there: my sense of belonging just as beguiling and just as strong. As the sun slowly set, and the wallabies indulged in their gymnastics across the rocks, I walked back through the gorge to my camp. And there, under its magnificent bluff, wrapped deeply in my swag as the stars pulsated gently overhead, I welcomed the opportunity to return to Nature's soft embrace in this most inspiring of places.

The most cherished aspect of my walkabout was how simple life had now become. It helped me to remember how important maintaining simplicity in our life is to our whole being, how important meditation, exercise, a healthy diet, and sleep are to a life well lived. I now knew these were the only 'meds' I really needed.

Meditation helped enhance my spiritual connection to the Earth while keeping my intellectual capacity clear and balanced. Exercise helped optimise my physical health while enhancing my emotional flexibility. A healthy diet optimised my physical capacity while ensuring greater balance in my emotional state. Sleep was important for all parts of my being though particularly for my intellectual capacity and physical health. It was fascinating to piece together how healthy doses of these individual elements were not only critical to my whole being; they were actually critical to each part of my being.

The simplicity of my lifestyle played a key role in ensuring my whole being slowly came back into balance with these elements. On waking each morning, the first act of the day was to roll my swag, brushing off the leaves and dirt, then wrapping and finally buckling its two leathers straps. I then meditated for 20 minutes or so, just appreciating the peacefulness and harmony of the bush as the sun's early morning rays gently warmed my body and soul. Then I indulged in some basic exercise, just enough to keep my muscles worked and heart rate up, with slow sit-ups and push-ups mainly.

Breakfast was a plate of muesli, a tin of fruit, and a small carton of long-life milk that would survive stuck at the bottom of my tucker bag for months on end, along with a cup of green tea boiled in my quart-pot. In the space of 30 minutes, breakfast was done with everything cleaned and packed away. It was that simple. With the reverse done in the evening, it introduced a symmetry to the day that slowed time down: the behaviour most supportive of the other pieces of the puzzle falling properly into place.

This symmetry particularly helped with the most critical of the 'meds' I needed: sleep. Despite camping on predominantly hard and rocky ground, sleep came increasingly easily, and quickly, without any interruption as I connected with the circadian rhythms of the natural world: eight to nine hours enjoyed before the first hint of dawn woke me completely refreshed and ready for what the day would bring. It certainly prepared me in a healthier manner for a day of intelligent thought, physical exertion, emotional balance, and spiritual awareness than the self-inflicted exhaustion I previously believed was just an unfortunate consequence of living a Western lifestyle. It also helped me to appreciate how destructive my life in New York had become and why it was so important the path of walkabout be taken at this particular time!

It was during this visit to Ormiston Gorge I experienced the most meaningful conversation of my walkabout. One that reinforced, in the most practical way, Nature's soulful teaching over the previous eight months.

The catalyst for this conversation was a chance meeting with two older travellers. They had just finished the difficult walk around the gorge and Pound, and had stopped for a rest. As they sat down near me at the edge of the waterhole, I complimented them on how impressive their feat was and how healthy they looked. We spoke a little more about how much of Australia they had seen on their travels. I commented that, for a 60-year-old couple, their physical prowess was impressive. That was when they left me awestruck – the husband was 86 years old and his wife was 84! It was impossible to believe for their faces radiated an energy and their bodies showed a strength of people half their age.

The thought that flashed through my mind at that moment was I had discovered the elixir of life. What else could it be that made this adventurous couple such happy and healthy human beings? It was their lifestyle and maybe a little in their genes. Their life, based around a small farm in Tasmania, included regular exercise each day while working outdoors. They did not smoke or drink. They ate only the healthy produce their garden provided. They fully connected with the natural world in most parts of their life. That was it. That was their simple secret to a long life of health and happiness!

Listening to the inspiring story of this extraordinary, loving couple, as they spoke unwittingly about how their life mirrored the 'meds' I increasingly realised were a critical part of a life well lived, was one of the most valuable experiences of my entire walkabout. It was the catalyst that helped me to finally understand the critical kernel of wisdom I sought – that Nature will teach us how to live in a way that provides everything we need to be happy and healthy, and all we need do is incorporate that wisdom into our lives.

When it comes to our life, we are what we think. Where we do not take the time to meditate on the important issues of life internally and externally, we are far more likely to be processed by society for its best interests rather than our own. When we ignore the need for exercise and a healthy diet, we cannot then complain when our body does not conform to the healthy, supportive force we expect and need it to be.

Despite the health problems the West is experiencing, we continue to fill our bodies with processed garbage instead of Nature's wholesome nourishment. The quality of our food significantly determines the quality of our life. When we eat processed food, our lives mirror the toxicity of those foods just as they mirror health and happiness when we eat nourishing and sustaining foods. It should be no surprise society's health is failing when our food's nutrition has been replaced with toxic chemicals whose names blankly stare back at us from predominantly plastic packaging. Much of our food, it seems, is no longer a medicine. It has become a poison!

Finally, our sleep patterns have become completely distorted giving our whole being no chance to rest and, more importantly, no chance to heal. Moreover, when any or all of our behaviours are out of sync with the natural world, our life experience can only be sub-optimal at best or dis-eased at worst.

As Westerners, in particular, we have created belief systems that ignore and ridicule Nature's wisdom, replacing it instead with mind-numbing saccharin commentary about the latest miracle health fix or product. We ignore how increasingly toxic our environment has become, and the self-inflicted destruction facilitated by human behaviours under many different guises, which only makes our existence more precarious. We appear to blatantly ignore the simple reality of the environment's health ultimately determining how healthy we can be. We self-righteously expect our companies and politicians to have integrity for their products and policies, yet many have no integrity even for themselves.

With increasing levels of sickness and dis-ease physically today, and the plethora of mental health issues continuing to expand, our denial of Nature's teaching has clearly been to our great disadvantage. And, as I was increasingly coming to understand, we often have nobody else but ourselves to blame for that predicament.

There have been five mass extinctions across the 4.5 billion year history of the Earth. Whatever the Universe has thrown at Nature, it has always evolved in a manner that took advantage of the circumstances affecting it. Nature has always survived and ultimately thrived.

Yet, only 250 years since the start of the Industrial Revolution, we as humanity seem willing to throw away the rules that have taken billions of years to evolve. Eating garbage, drinking poison, and filling our minds and souls with ignorance, we then feign surprise at the mental, physical, emotional, and spiritual dis-ease we directly incur from those choices. We are often directly at fault for we know the outcome of these behaviours is invariably sickness. We cause most of the problems we experience yet refuse to change our self-evidently limiting beliefs and behaviours. There is nothing, and nobody else, to blame for the lifestyle based diseases we inflict on ourselves today.

Unfortunately, humanity, especially in the West, appears to have become more adept at playing the victim card and the blame game rather than taking personal responsibility for the dis-ease now experienced. With the inevitable result these problems have become highly costly and increasingly intractable. We only need look at the leading indicator of our new health reality, the Western healthcare system with its increasing costs and consequences, to understand the damage we have inflicted through our choices. Not only on ourselves, but also selfishly, greedily, and lazily on future generations!

Looking across the grandeur of Ormiston Gorge, I could easily imagine a day when humanity is just another fossilised species scattered across a sedimentary layer awaiting a time when a more evolved civilisation will pick at our bones and societal detritus. A day when our lack of attention to Nature's wisdom facilitates the end of our brief, inglorious reign here on Earth. On that day, I suspect, Nature will still be applying the same wisdom regarding health and happiness it has from the beginning of time. The next evolution of life will probably have a genetically unmodified warning label attached – 'Ignore this wisdom at your own peril!'

Yet it does not have to be this way. After eight months of working horses, travelling through the ranges and gorges of Northern and Central Australia, and living almost entirely on healthy food and water, I felt completely invigorated. My mind and body felt clean and free of disease for the first time in many years. I felt full of energy with my body supporting my daily goals rather than being a tired and lazy impediment to their attainment. My heart and soul felt enlivened and expanded after contracting for many years. Paradoxically, but intuitively, this was achieved through something as easy and simple as incorporating Nature's teaching into my life on a daily basis.

The most important realisation of all was this – that once our health is gone, once our mind and body deteriorate to the extent surgery or drugs are required, most people are on the slippery slope to oblivion. It may be possible to slow this deterioration for a short time, or even undo it to a certain extent. Maybe. Most likely, there will be a high price to pay, as individuals and as a society, for this behaviour, not only in the current generation but also in subsequent generations who become too well versed in the self-destructive behaviours and belief systems of today.

For the most part, drugs and surgical interventions cannot, will not, achieve the same result a balanced, healthy lifestyle would have achieved. Seeing the cost this lack of focus and discipline imposed on the health of many travellers, staring me in the face at various campsites across Australia, truly scared me. The more I saw the results of living a Western lifestyle, and the cost and pain associated with that decision, the more I recommitted to living in harmony with Nature's wisdom.

With this increasing awareness of the importance of Nature's teaching to my life, I came to understand how it would provide humanity with all that is required for a life of health and happiness. Conversely, where we fail to learn and utilise this teaching, where we instead destroy the natural world, so we will ultimately destroy ourselves. That is Nature's blessing and its curse!

My last night at Ormiston Gorge, for the time being at least, was another of those rare, heartwarming times travellers experience when everything pointed to the potential of humanity to live in harmony with not only the natural world but also with one another. The small group cooking around the stoves that night was as diverse as any other I had met during my journey. A student from East Germany cycling around Australia as part of a world trip, an older Australian who had motorcycled across India, Europe, and over the Himalayas, and several others who led equally interesting and adventurous lives were happy to have me bring my swag over and join them.

As we sat around after dinner, talking and reflecting on our respective experiences in life, one of our group pulled out a guitar and started to play folk songs whose stories resonated with our own lives at that moment. It was a humbling and gentling experience to be sitting on my swag, under the brightness of the moon and stars in my spiritual home, listening to those quiet yet moving traveller's anthems wafting among the trees like the smoke from our stoves. It was a moment of pure serenity, of pure bliss, where the feeling of peace and goodwill to all men flowed with the strength of a river and the lightness of a cloud. It was another moment from Ormiston Gorge I will never forget.

The Plenty Highway stretches east from Alice Springs into the Channel Country of Western Queensland: the same braided country I saw when driving the Birdsville and Strzelecki Tracks. It was not difficult to understand why it was named the Plenty Highway – there was plenty of dust, plenty of space, and plenty of time to reflect on where I was going. The highway actually gets its name from the Plenty River it crosses, except the only thing there was plenty of sand. That was it. Similar to most other dirt roads and bush tracks across Australia, the only hint of civilisation across the vastness was the occasional fence and even less occasional windmill. This was cattle country as far as the eye could see.

Travelling east, the suspension working overtime as the corrugations tested the resilience of my 4WD, I crossed the three primary and almost mythical rivers that water the plains of Southwest Queensland when they come down in flood. First was the Georgina River. It was bone dry, its bed a tangle of deep cracks and fissures pleading for rain. The following day I reached the Diamantina River, the same Diamantina River whose waters upstream filled Combo Waterhole and whose waters downstream provided such bliss at Birdsville. It too was bone dry, though it made a good place to camp, among the mulga and gidgee, with plenty of flies to keep me company.

From there, as I headed into the harsh early morning light of sunrise, I soon reached Cooper Creek: the oasis I had been patiently seeking. From the stony, dry gully crossed on the Birdsville Track to the southwest, to the glorious waterhole on the Strzelecki Track and the final resting place of Burke and Wills, it had come to beguile and inspire like no other river. Now crossing it further upstream, just below the junction of its primary tributaries, the Thompson and Barcoo Rivers, it showed me a vista I could never have imagined. This broad reach of water, resplendent in the winter morning sun, to me, defined Cooper Creek and its mythical contribution to the Australian inland soul.

Pelicans, galahs, finches, and corellas floated and darted across the water: their avian symphony a cacophony of screeches, deep-throated calls, and sweetly pitched songs. Wide-trunked eucalyptus trees spread their majestic, gnarled boughs across the river with all the listlessness of a human being stretching as they wake in the morning. Compared to the waterless plains I had spent the previous two days crossing, Cooper Creek was paradise. And, as I had on the bank of the Diamantina River to the southwest, I dipped my quart-pot into its waters and boiled a cup of tea as a sign of respect and appreciation for its bounty and history.

Later that morning, farewelling this most majestic inland river as my path now took me far from the Channel Country, I knew I would never forget its bountiful realm. Cooper Creek remains, for me, one of the most important of all Australia's inland waterways to connect with the delights of the desert country through which it meanderingly travels.

My journey east from Alice Springs, to the next chapter of my walkabout, which initially brought me to the oasis on Cooper Creek, was not the only reason for taking this track. I had wanted to follow its path since childhood to connect with a mentor from my youth, one whose story represents a defining thread in the rich tapestry of Australia's pastoral heritage: Patsy Durack.

Patsy Durack was a remarkable man. He and his family were the first Europeans to settle this part of Australia, arriving on Kyabra Creek in 1868 only seven years after the death of Burke and Wills just a short distance to the southwest. Droving their small herd of cattle from Goulburn, in Central New South Wales, they pioneered a 1,200-kilometre route as the crow flies into the Channel Country of Southwest Queensland. An earlier Durack exploration party had already discovered the attraction of Kyabra Creek. It had a permanent waterhole in even the most oppressive droughts according to local Aboriginal people. Their name for this place was Thillung-gurr: the Europeans called it Thylungra. It was this waterhole, on which I could turn back the dust-lined pages of history to be there on a specific day, I most wanted to visit on my journey east.

Patsy Durack and his clan epitomised the extraordinary resilience and commitment of the pioneering families who opened up much of the remotest parts of Australia. They were among the first to drove cattle into Southwest Queensland and later into the far-flung reaches of the Kimberley: their story as exciting and riveting as that of any tale from across the New World. Like other successful Australian explorers and pastoralists, the Duracks also came to appreciate and rely on the knowledge and experience of local Aboriginal people as they slowly learnt the workings of their new land.

The Duracks' story, a tale of persistence, bravery, and resourcefulness as they built their cattle empire, is one of the most compelling insights into these times. The mistakes made, the lessons learnt, and the tragedies endured as one family's walkabout kept them on the Australian frontier for almost 50 years.

The Duracks learnt to first appreciate and then utilise the unique character of the Australian bush in the development of their pastoral empire. Their respect for Nature's teaching, and an appreciation for the opportunity it represented to those who applied that knowledge, ultimately facilitated their success. Moreover, the Duracks were not the only pastoralists who benefited from this persistence. For the trail they blazed to Thylungra, and ultimately to the Kimberley, became a beacon for many who subsequently followed in their tracks.

In memory of the Durack family and their accomplishments, I wanted to boil my quart-pot at Thylungra. I wanted to see the waterhole and peer back into its history to connect with their exploits that marvel today much as they did 134 years ago. Boiling my quart-pot at the edge of the waterhole, while sitting in the shade of the trees lining its banks, was quite poignant for me. For it was not difficult to peer back through time to the day the Duracks arrived. I could almost hear the shouts and stock whips' cracks as the first cattle were brought to the waterhole, along with their deep, plaintive bellows as they finally smelled and tasted water. I could almost hear the calls of a thousand startled birds wheeling overhead. And I could almost hear the cries of anguish and confusion from the First Australians as their lifestyle was lost forever.

For, as much as this moment represented an exciting new page in the development of European Australia, it also represented a devastating tragedy for Aboriginal Australia. It represented the beginning of the closing of the history of a people who had survived and prospered in that country for at least 30,000 years.

While Thylungra was the Duracks' home for the next 15 years, it was in a sense only a staging point during their much longer journey across the top of Australia as they built and consolidated their cattle empire. Patsy Durack, aware of the vagaries of the Australian seasons, realised that while Thylungra initially offered an exciting opportunity, its remote geography and capricious weather conspired to make it a difficult enterprise. In fact, he commented that his empire was one of grass castles that could be blown away upon a puff of wind. To reduce this risk he expanded into the Kimberley, a region that offered greater access to international markets and their increasing demand for beef.

Fifteen years after arriving at Thylungra with 100 head of cattle, the Duracks were on the road again, this time droving 7,250 head of cattle to stock stations they had chosen in the East Kimberley. This cattle drive succeeded despite the many obstacles fate placed in the path of that small party of men – floods, droughts, sickness, local Aboriginal people defending their land, and the land itself. Their journey took almost two and a half years during which time they crossed almost 5,000 kilometres of some of the toughest country Australia has to offer.

Patsy Durack was ultimately proved right for his pastoral empire was comprised of grass castles that time and the vagaries of the Australian seasons conspired to blow away. Yet this takes nothing away from the Duracks' history-defining accomplishments on the Australian frontier. And while the same spirit of adventure they embodied remains a key part of the Australian Outback's psyche and soul, their remarkable story will never be forgotten.

From Thylungra, and the indomitable spirit of the Durack clan, I followed the road east to Central Queensland, and Clermont, where I planned to spend the rest of the year working as a ringer on several of the cattle stations I had worked when at university. The allure of exploring the remoter parts of the country was now put on hold given my desire to work with horses one last time before my walkabout was completed.

After spending time connecting with the Duracks' story, I was excited to return to the life of a ringer followed during my university holidays. The opportunity to see the bush from the back of a horse was a delight I had thought about for some time. Sitting behind the wheel of my 4WD, I had increasingly reflected on the pleasures that only come from the back of a horse, from seeing those places very few people are fortunate to see, and living a life that had called from my childhood days.

This break from the road also provided the opportunity to reflect on what I had learnt of Nature's wisdom and to think about how I could now incorporate those lessons into my life. Appropriately, at this stage of my walkabout, it was also a chance to return to a place I had first known as a child: a place that had encouraged the following of Nature's siren call when almost everything else stifled that call. It was an opportunity to reconnect with the spirit of optimism and adventure that had diminished on being part of the adult world. Most importantly of all, it was an opportunity to be seduced by the bush, once again, and the many enchantments of the natural world.

7

Wild Cattle

'It is here, in the southward, under
The rays of a sun that fall
Where the stockwhip's gathering thunder
Is music sweetest of all:
Where the 'scrubbers' under the dust-clouds
Are challenged, and caught, and passed,
Though flanks may bleed ere we wheel the lead
At the wings of the yard at last.'

Will Ogilvie – Kings of the Earth

Working as a ringer on a large cattle station is a particularly Australian experience. For many overseas visitors, and coast-bound Australians for that matter, the ringer, stockman, or drover is one of the more enduring and iconic images of the Australian Outback along with that of Uluru, majestic ochre-red gorges, and a remote track leading to a spinifex-clad horizon. It may seem a romantic portrayal of a freedom previous generations once enjoyed, which we no longer do. It may be that ringers, stockmen, and drovers experience a healthier connection with the natural world through an active lifestyle. Alternatively, it may just be that the grass is always a little greener on the other side of the fence and the life of a ringer would quickly lose its appeal given how demanding and isolating it can be. Nevertheless, for those with a desire for hard, physical work, a connection with horses, a need to be part of the natural world, and a sense of adventure, working as a ringer offers a lifestyle lost to much of humanity today. And never will it be more exciting or more dangerous than when wild cattle are being worked. Cattle that can, and will, kill you with the whip of a horn or the kick of a hoof you do not even see.

The gates at Logan Creek looked a little newer than when I had last seen them 12 years previously. The dry, dusty landscape of 2002 was a welcome contrast to the humidity, mud, and flooding experienced following the deluging aftermath of Cyclone Joy at the end of 1990. This is how it often seems to be in the Australian bush. One day parched and dusty, pushing cattle from one muddy waterhole to the next under the unrelenting blaze of a summer sky, the next shoulder deep in water working to keep fences up as wall after wall of water churns down the creek after a tropical cyclone. The Australian bush is certainly far more inclined to show the full breadth of Nature's spectrum than that shown in softer, younger countries!

However, if enjoyment were not experienced across the wide variety of Nature's spectrum, there would be no reason to be out here. Which would mean never experiencing the mesmerising vistas painted across the vastness of Nature's magnificent Australian Outback canvas. Vistas that never failed to inspire whether wet or dry, summer or winter, morning or night.

Driving up the winding dirt track to the homestead, past the dam and small stands of gidgee lining the track, it was more than just a return to an old haunt – it was a journey back to the days of my early adulthood.

And despite the intervening years, much remained the same. It was a gratifying reconnection to those seemingly long gone, carefree days.

Seeing the homestead and ringers' quarters brought back many memories of old friends whose faces now burned a lot brighter than they had for some time. The stockyards were just a short distance away. Nothing had changed about their shape or feel. Even the smell was the same: the pungent, dusty scent of horses and cattle, sweat and blood, the past and present all churned into one. The adjacent corrugated iron saddlery shed looked exactly as it had all those years ago with saddles and bridles hanging from pieces of wire, twisting in the breeze, as the sweet scent of horse sweat filled the room. Odd bits of tack hung from different hooks on the back wall while spurs and boots lay ready for the next muster. It had all the feel of an efficiently run cattle operation, which is exactly what it was.

Logan Creek, named for the creek that runs through the property, a torrent during the cyclone season otherwise a loose linkage of small waterholes, was once part of the earliest station in this part of Queensland – Logan Downs. Like almost every other early station on what were then the fringes of civilisation, its ultimate fate was to be carved into several smaller properties. Interestingly, its old boundary fence can still be seen in a few places today giving the interested observer a brief glimpse into its former grandeur.

Robert O'Sullivan, a tough, self-made cattleman who worked on and managed cattle stations in the Northern Territory and the Kimberley, owned Logan Creek. He was the consummate cattleman and knew his cattle and their history like that of his own family, perhaps even better. When it came to working cattle, Robert had forgotten more than most people would ever know. He had worked them in almost every possible situation, giving him an innate sense of what they were going to do long before, I suspect, the cattle even knew it themselves. He was also a very good horseman having spent as much time in the saddle as he had, though I suspect his real love was the cattle business. He was one of an old breed, one that is slowly being lost as the industry changes and life moves on.

Working with Robert was a unique opportunity to experience station life much as it would have been during Australia's early pastoral history. It was an opportunity to turn the dust-lined pages of history back to the days of the early stockmen and drovers, to see how they lived and worked, and to better understand them despite never having known them. Robert's experiences and stories were to provide a connection to the fascinating history of pioneer Australia in a way few people experience today.

Sitting next to a small gidgee fire during a day of mustering, as our quart-pots quietly bubbled away to provide a welcomed cup of tea, Robert regaled us with stories of his experiences in the Kimberley and The Territory. Stories of large mobs of cattle worked and droved, of wild scrub bulls tossed, of falls taken and accidents survived, of working with Aboriginal people at a time when many still lived the old bush ways, and of living out of a swag with nothing but the sparkling stars above and the hard ground beneath.

At certain times, the past melded into the present so closely did Robert's stories mirror the lives of the mentors accompanying me on this journey. It was through Robert, his many experiences and fascinating stories, I more closely connected with the lives of my mentors who, while their tracks have long since faded, left an inspiring and indelible legacy.

Robert and I first met 15 years previously, on the recommendation of a mutual friend, when he offered me the opportunity to work with him one summer during my university holidays. I remember it as being a hot, dry summer and the work especially tough on a mind previously immersed in books and a body soft from a lack of physical work. It was an incredible experience to spend time with him, to see how he worked his cattle, to see how he rode his horses, and to understand what it took to be a success in what is a tough business.

Working for Robert certainly had its moments. I was expected to know as much as he did and he let me know in no uncertain terms when my performance was not up to scratch; this being done in the colourful language expected from an old-time cattleman with none of the political correctness pervading society today. I quickly learnt not to take anything too personally for, if I had, I might never have believed in myself again! During the time I worked for Robert, and despite his tough, uncompromising nature, I grew to admire and respect him and his accomplishments. Given my desire to return to the life of a ringer, there was no better person for whom to work.

Despite the passing years, Robert was just as I remembered him. The dusty, sweat-lined, broad-brimmed Akubra showed all the wear and tear of a person who takes full responsibility for their own cattle, while the scuffed boots and dusty shirt, sleeves rolled down and open at the cuffs, indicated he had just come back from a full day of work. A slight, toothless grin was the first hint of recognition shortly followed by a firm handshake: the type that leaves you acutely aware of the hard work those hands have seen.

The old homestead smelt the same as it had all those years ago. The aroma of freshly baked cakes, of dust and leather, and the all-pervading smell of the Australian bush confirmed this was indeed the place from my memories of the past. Nothing had really changed. The furniture, curtains, stacks of papers and magazines in the study, and several daunting racks of cattle horns adorning the dining-room walls were just as I remembered.

Speaking with Robert, we began where we had left off 12 years before. It was difficult for both of us to understand where the time had gone. However, that is life and after a short conversation about the work to be done, which is Robert's way, it was time to head over to the ringers' quarters that would be my home for the rest of the year.

Ringers' quarters are somewhat standard Australia-wide – a demountable building with three or four rooms and a communal bathroom at one end. Each room was very basic with a bed, a small cupboard, a splash of material across the window masquerading as a curtain, and an air conditioner that made life somewhat comfortable in the hot summer months. Apart from the communal kitchen, where we ate our breakfast, made our lunch, and socialised after work, that was it.

Our delicious evening meals, prepared by Robert's wife Raye, were enjoyed at the homestead. As would be expected, beef was the food of choice. We killed and butchered a bullock every six weeks or so ensuring the meat was always fresh, lean, and tasty – irrespective of whose property it actually came from! Fresh corned beef with mashed potatoes was my favourite though the stews, roasts, and baked meals were also delicious. I had forgotten how much a ravenous appetite contributed to the taste of a meal. Either way, I never left much on my plate and remember going back for second or third servings as often as I could.

Most nights, I was in my swag shortly after dinner and the washing up, with the hours of exhausting work precipitating a sleep as appreciated as much as the fine dining enjoyed. Our day started just on dawn with the work lasting through to sunset or later depending on what needed completing. Weekends were not something we typically got. For when there are cattle to be worked, it is all hands to the pumps until the job is done.

On arriving at Logan Creek, the work was in full swing as it had been from the beginning of the year. Robert had recently acquired Saraji, another property a short distance away, and was in the process of 'cleaning it up': a euphemism for mustering, yarding, and working 5,000 head of wild, thirsty, and tough cattle. Saraji had become dilapidated over the previous 10 years: its cattle very unpredictable and dangerous. Many had never seen a stockman while most had never been mustered. The country they were running in had almost no feed with the drought further complicating the situation as little surface water remained for thirsty stock.

Parts of the country the cattle roamed were remote ranges. Similar to other regions of Australia, ranges attract dingoes and these ranges were certainly no exception. Many of the cattle showed how close their run-ins with dingoes had been with their partially or fully docked tails reflecting a close encounter at a young age. And as we spent more time in that country, and came across the carcasses of young calves killed by dingoes, it became very clear why the cattle had become as wild as they had. It was either kill or be killed, and that was all these cattle knew!

Mustering cattle on Saraji was impossible in the normal manner unless you were an expert horseman and skilled cattleman. The cattle hurtled off into the scrub and ranges at the slightest hint of danger, that is if they did not charge on first sight. Many were horned with the bulls in particular supporting impressive and daunting racks that induced a well-earned respect for them in all of us. With their thick, wide, curving, and sharp horns, and 1,000 kilograms of pure, unadulterated, testosterone-rich muscle to back them up, only the most experienced cattleman would attempt their mustering with any expectation of success. Or survival. Quite simply, the cattle were too tough, too wary, and too dangerous for successful mustering. To yard them quickly, and with the least possible risk to man and beast, they were trapped instead.

Trapping is a uniquely Australian method of yarding cattle, with a 'one-way' gate, used since the earliest days of European settlement. The best thing about yarding cattle in this manner, versus mustering them, is human involvement is limited to setting the trap along with building the yards behind the trap. And if the yards are built properly, the cattle stayed trapped without the inherent risk of losing them that comes with mustering. The yards Robert built for trapping, holding, and working these wild cattle were impressive in their scale, flexibility, and ability to withstand the onslaught that was brewing.

The main holding yard was built like a fortress. It had to be otherwise it would not have survived the destruction capable of being wrought by the trapped and angry cattle. Heavy wooden posts and rails, using gidgee for the most part given its toughness and durability, defined the structure. Thick, heavy barbed wire, strung eight strands high with just enough space between the strands for a ringer to slowly push between, though not without scratches, ensured the trap was almost escape-proof. Next to the main holding yard, we built demountable steel yards for working the cattle. These yards, assembled with heavy, steel-railed panels fitted together, allowed us to build the most effective structure for the multitude of cattle to be worked.

Constructing these yards was hard physical work given the weight of just one panel. Each panel was carried into position, typically on our backs or shoulders, with several thick steel pins used to hold it in place. Within the yards, we included a round yard for separating cattle into their different classes, a crush where the work on each beast took place, and a number of holding yards. Given it took several hundred panels to build a set of yards, and there were only two or three of us doing the work, the sun had often long disappeared over the western horizon before we appreciatively began our exhausted journey home for the evening.

While building strong yards was critical, the most important stage was setting the trap properly. With the cattle very wary, any mistake would cost us significantly in terms of yield and timing. For, if we did not get it right, the cattle would avoid the yards for some time and we would have to set up another operation elsewhere. It was therefore vital the trap be set properly.

And so, after long, gruelling days of toiling in the dust and heat building yards and watering points, rolling out hay, and getting the cattle less wary of our presence, it was time to close the trap by setting the 'one-way' gate at just the right width. One that would allow the cattle to enter the main holding yard but not leave. This was done by using a set of 'spears'; two panels of long, thick, and straight saplings wired together horizontally, one sapling under the other, hung from an overhead frame in the space where the gate would otherwise have been. It allowed the cattle to push their way into the yard in one direction, to find hay and water, but not return in the opposite direction.

It was not a simple decision as to how wide the spears were set given the cattle came in all shapes and sizes. The good thing about a well-positioned set of spears is it gives larger cattle, with wider horns, the space to manoeuvre their way through while ensuring smaller cattle are not able to double back. With the width decided, the spears were set. There was nothing more to do except head home and wait to see what the following day would bring in terms of the size of the catch.

Returning the following day, the success of the trap was unmistakable. Even before reaching the yards, the thick pall of brown dust rising above the trees indicated a sizeable catch had been made. On arriving at the yards, there were cattle everywhere and all with one intention – getting out!

Many bullocks, some as large as a horse, showed a faint brand indicating it had been at least a decade since they were last worked. There were bulls whose sharp, fearsome horns hacked at anything that came within reach: even trapped they fought one another. There were several hundred head inside the holding yard, of every colour, breed, and size, with many more outside who had been unable or unwilling to go through the spears. Some cattle paced up and down the fence looking for the slightest opportunity to push their way out. Many others, especially the younger, cleanskin calves, walked around aimlessly. Other cattle just stood there, head down in the slightest piece of shade they could find, resigned to whatever their fate would bring. Most looked undernourished which was not surprising given the ongoing drought and the denuded nature of the country where they ran.

Swathing cattle and ringers alike was an almost deafening discordance. From the pitiful, high-pitched calls of young calves to the angry bellows of huge scrub bulls that echoed around the ranges, a blanket of anger and frustration covered us all much like the slowly settling dust. Even though the trapping process initially stressed them, most cattle were subsequently taken to better-watered and grassed country. If only we had been able to communicate this early on, our job may have been significantly easier and safer!

The first order of the day was moving the trapped cattle into the yards where we could work them. As the main holding yard was far too dangerous to be on foot, we used two vehicles, acting in unison, to slowly push the mob off the back fence and forward into the yards. Whenever a beast broke from the mob, the vehicles quickly changed direction, and speed, as we tried to keep the mob together as best we could through our pursuit.

While having many horsepower was extremely helpful, the flexibility to change direction, as on a horse, was not quite there which meant cattle often escaped to the back of the yard. For those of us standing on the back of a vehicle, it was a thrilling, scary, jolting, and dusty ride pushing these wild cattle forward. Once the cattle were finally in the yards, we quickly jumped off the vehicle, at a sprint, to shut the gates before the mob, realising its mistake, wheeled and came straight back at us.

Chaining the gate, all the while ensuring enough time to jump clear if the cattle hit it more quickly than expected, always involved a life-preserving sense of caution. For once the mob made the split-second decision to spin around and charge the gate, it would have been like trying to hold back a river in flood. Accordingly, it was always with a view to preserving life and limb we worked to get the gate locked, and the cattle securely in the yards, as quickly as possible!

The most dangerous time of all involved pushing two very large, very angry, scrub bulls, who had managed to avoid all our previous attempts by using the mob as a decoy, into the yards. Each time we pushed them closer to the gate, they spun around and came straight back at us. As the vehicles slowed or stopped in the chase, the bulls darted around the side, or between them, to the back of the holding yard where we had to start again. For those of us standing on the back of a vehicle, with only the roll bar to hold on to, it made for an exhilarating yet scary ride.

Often reaching speeds of 40-50 kilometres per hour, we barrelled through the dust and around trees trying to push these two bulls into the yards. At times, as the bulls got close to the gate, they stopped, looked, and then charged the nearest vehicle. Sometimes they hit us head-on making the whole vehicle shudder. At other times, they hit us hard, side-on. It even appeared they wanted to jump over the back of the vehicle, which was the last place we wanted them. After half a dozen hair-raising attempts to yard them, one of the bulls put himself at the barbed wire fence and through sheer strength and brute force pulled himself clear – he was the only one of the thousands of head we worked to do that. The other bull, seeing the dust of his companion as he trotted to freedom, quickly lost heart and ran into the yards. Although he was clearly any-thing but defeated as our work soon showed!

On yarding, the cattle became a bellowing, cantankerous mob charg-ing and kicking at will. Working these cattle was as hard on them as it was on us; the scorching summer sun, dust, and toil all conspiring to make us drop our guard just when we needed it most. It was comparable to being in a combat zone with the consequences of making the wrong decision equally deadly. With one eye on what we were doing and the other continually behind us, we had no option but to remain aware at all times should a beast loom up out of the dust with the sole intention of grinding us bloodily into the ground.

Even then, despite my best efforts, a couple of missteps trying to avoid a charging beast resulted in several bruised ribs when I missed my footing and crashed chest-first into the steel rails. While adrenalin helped pull myself out of harm's way, my bruised ribs made working and sleep-ing over the next few weeks a difficult and painful experience as any sud-den movement sent a sharp spasm hurtling through my body!

To draft the cattle into different yards, we first moved them into the round yard. With one foot and one hand on the nearest rail, to pull myself out of danger when required, it was constant action all around. The air was alive with the sound of metal on metal as gates slammed shut, and beast on metal as a bull or bullock tried to jump over a fence or come through one to get us. The swirling dust, choking cattle and ringers alike with its brown, heavy humidity, made things even more dangerous. I lost count of the times a huge shadow loomed up out of the dust to put me back on the rails. Even on the rails, we were still not safe as bulls in the adjoining yards, separated only by the fence, tried to horn us thereby ensuring precious little opportunity to stay out of harm's way.

Once drafted into separate yards, we worked the cattle individually. Bulls were the most dangerous with their horns potentially lethal. One quick sweep could disembowel us or hook us in a way that was going to require a long, painful hospital stay. Therefore, the bulls were first immobilised in the crush with their heads held tightly by a mechanical arm. Well, as much as it is ever possible to immobilise 1,000 kilograms of pure, angry muscle!

When it came to actually dehorning these bulls, things got even more dangerous. Their horns were so hard a set of dehorners would not work. Given how important it was to cut their horns off quickly, for the bull's sake and our own safety, we used a small chainsaw. To make it safer, we first slipped a blunt clip onto the bull's nose, pulling his head tightly to one side while one horn was sawn off, and then to the other side to remove the other horn. It was dangerous and nimble work getting the nose clip on a bull as it bellowed and whipped his horns around as hard as he could to nail us. It was scary how quickly these bulls moved and how close they often came to achieving their objective. Even with the bull firmly held, the shrill sound of the chainsaw in my ear, with bits of horn, blood, and hot oil tumbling down my neck and arms, meant no respite to the continual assault my senses endured.

This work went on for hours under the blazing Central Queensland summer sun, each bull another struggle to subdue and dehorn as we each tried to stay in one piece. On removing the horns, the cattle were then loaded onto several road trains and trucked to the main stockyards at the homestead where our work, once again, began in earnest.

Once drafted into different yards for different classes, bulls, cows, and calves, our work changed to handling these classes though it was just as dangerous and exhausting as when we first trapped and drafted them. The bulls were run into the crush, a little less menacing without their horns, but equally capable of killing us if given half a chance. We branded, ear tagged, inoculated, and finally castrated each bull with a rubber ring doing the job of a sharp pocketknife and disinfectant spray of the past. We branded, ear tagged, and inoculated each cow, tipping its horns if required. Each calf went through the same process with their high-pitched calls a whisper compared to the deep-throated bellows of their testosterone-rich older brethren.

And in the dust of this ancient land, under the same relentless burning sun of those who went before us, we worked each beast through the crush in a blur of motion, colour, and noise, only stopping for the occasional respite of a cool drink or to replace a piece of broken equipment. Once the work was finished, and the yarded cattle given time to adjust to their new surroundings, we released them into several different laneways to find their way to their respective paddocks, and a far easier life than the one previously known back in the ranges.

With the closing of the last gate, we were finished for the day though our work was anything but completed. There were still many more cattle to catch and work. Accordingly, the spears were carefully reset and our work commenced once again. Through half a dozen sets of yards, through the hottest months of the year, the work ebbed and flowed until we had caught and trucked all cattle: a process that ended up accounting for over 1,500 head during my stay.

Appreciatively, as I worked these cattle, so they also worked me: my body slowly regaining its form and health on the back of the prolonged days of exhausting work, fresh food, water, and sleep. Fortunately, during these days, nobody was hurt as a slip or fall at the wrong time could so easily have proved fatal. While we owed our good fortune to intuition and a little luck, I suspect we owed a lot more to Robert given his knack for keeping us out of harm's way. Those days certainly taught me to respect my sense of fear and understand exactly what my capabilities were. It was probably that awareness that helped me come away unscathed most of all.

On my final day at Logan Creek, once we had released the last mob to find its way down the laneway to its new home, I stayed behind in the stockyards. As the other ringers exhaustedly trudged back to their quarters, back to a welcomed shower and a well-earned meal, the dust and quietness of the yards made them the perfect place to linger and reflect on what I had learnt. Sitting on the rails of the now empty drafting yard, as an orange-purple haze spread across the western sky, a deep feeling of contentment washed away the bodily pains and exhaustion that had perpetually raised their voices over the course of the day.

These days really tested my endurance: the heat, dust, flies, and continual exertion driving me to exhaustion. These experiences also reignited my childhood memories of how it felt to be alive, to have adrenalin coursing through my veins in a rush of excitement, and to wake refreshed and ready for what the day would bring. During these halcyon days, I dug deep within myself to rediscover who I was as a human being, who I wanted to be, and how to live happily with nothing more than the contents of my swag and the sweat of my brow. While they were difficult and exhausting days, they were also some of the most rewarding of my walkabout. They were days I will never forget.

There was another experience at Logan Creek I will also never forget; one that poignantly reminded me that another people had once lived in that country and had worked the land, though in a very different manner to that of today. It was a reminder the First Australians had also once made that country their home despite the few remaining signs of their habitation, and had done so for at least 30,000 years.

The catalyst for this reminder was a chance encounter with a throwback to a time when Aboriginal people were masters of this land. Near one of the stockyards we worked, evidence remained of an Aboriginal camp probably from a time long before the first Europeans even arrived. Inside a small cave at the base of a ridge, next to a sand-filled waterhole surrounded by several large eucalyptus trees, a number of ochre-red hand stencils lined the cave walls. They were quite faded and appeared to have been there for some time given the area was well sheltered from the sun, rain, and wind-whipped sand.

I could imagine this was a preferred Aboriginal camp given the abundance of fauna in the ranges and the protection afforded to the waterhole by the shade of its large trees and the surrounding ridge. It would most likely have been an important waterhole and may have even been their last point of refuge during the years of drought that remain a regular feature of the Australian continent.

Yet, that is not what existed today. The waterhole was long gone, filled with the dust and sand that started blowing once the hard hooves of sheep and cattle replaced the soft pads of the native animals from the 1860s onwards. Today, the life-giving role of that waterhole, as highlighted by the faded hand stencils from an ancient time, is no longer. As I sat in front of that cave, it was clear many changes had occurred since Europeans first arrived 140 years previously and completely changed the face of the country. It was also a sad reminder of the changes that land had seen in the short time since my childhood only 25 years previously.

Huge swathes of brigalow country had been pulled and burnt. There was nothing left in some paddocks except a lone tree standing as the last survivor from an ancient civilisation seemingly destroyed by some cataclysmic disaster. The creeks of my childhood, which I fondly remembered as brimming with water and fish, were now bone dry. Nothing remained except a few small, pathetic, dried mussel shells lying on cracked ground.

On a more continental level, the increasing impact of dry land salinity and the desecration of almost all the major river systems highlighted the same pressures. On the coast, the destruction of the Great Barrier Reef, one of the natural wonders of the world, continued unabated with its corals blighted by runoff from agricultural industries and pressure from human-induced climate change. Furthermore, behind this destruction of the environment, the cause remained the same as it always had. More food, more resources, and more consumption.

Agriculture, mining, energy, and the utilisation of the Earth's resources have been the cornerstone of any society from the beginning of human history. Empires have risen and fallen based on how those resources, and more importantly, the environment, were managed. The utilisation of those resources has determined the very quality of our life. Nothing will change this reality as we continue to rely on the natural world to support and sustain our lifestyle, seemingly irrespective of the increasingly destructive impact this has on the Earth.

What can change, however, is how we view the taking of those resources and how we ensure the true cost to the environment is properly accounted for. What can change is our understanding of what we need to consume verses what we want to consume. What can change is understanding that our excessive and unnecessary production and consumption of those resources is what creates the fundamental damage to our environment; particularly their consumption. What can change, most importantly of all, is recognising that there will ultimately be a significant cost to us as individuals, a society, and as humanity where that consumption remains out of kilter with the intrinsic balance of the natural world.

'What you sow, you reap' is a defining proverb from enlightened teachers throughout human history. It is a timeless reminder that where we destroy the natural world, where we rapaciously take all we want with no respect and no thought for the consequences, so we will ultimately destroy ourselves. It is our own choice. The most interesting part of our behaviour is whether that portion of humanity who can currently make a difference, who benefit from the advantages of democracy and education, will ultimately be responsible enough to heed Nature's wisdom and the environment's increasing warnings. Or whether an inherent greed and laziness on their part will instead consign humanity to a path that destroys our very source of life.

After working for several months at Logan Creek, I moved to Robert's property on the Belyando River: Mellaluka, so named for the tea trees that surround the natural spring and waterhole near the stockyards and homestead today. Mustering was in full swing and they needed another ringer to complete the team. As the days were baking hot, with the temperature well north of 40 degrees Celsius in the shade as a heat wave blanketed the region, we started work several hours before the cool of dawn. Given the heat, it was important to start early for the sake of the cattle. It did not make sense to muster them in the middle of the day, especially the younger calves, if we could avoid it.

Each day started the same way: the horses were run into the horse yard where we caught and saddled our respective mounts for the day. Then, with a last tighten of the girth and a foot in the stirrup, we mounted up and headed off for a day of mustering. Most of the paddocks were around 10,000 acres: a good amount of country for the four of us to cover and work. We usually had a fair idea for where the cattle were resting and, with a point in the different directions to take, split up at a quick trot into the scrub to track them down. The first hint of cattle was normally a brown or white blur through the trees. More often than not, one of the beasts would try to break behind us, or off to the side of the mob, and then our work really began.

When a beast broke so did I, at a gallop if I could given the country, on a gentle rein trusting in my horse's skill. In the gidgee scrub of Mellaluka, with its short, sharp branches like daggers and the ground covered in fallen logs, I went as fast as I dared. Riding quickly, out wide of a breaking beast, I worked to push it back into the mob all the while trying to ensure the other cattle did not randomly scatter in a number of different directions at any moment. Some cattle broke with a real desire to escape and it often took a hard, fast chase to return them back to the mob. Letting my horse find its own way through the bush at speed, learning to anticipate how he would react to trees, logs, stumps, and creeks, made the first few chases an interesting time as we both learnt about each other!

Increasingly, as I learnt to trust my horse's intelligence in chasing down a breaking beast, the work became easier than when I tightened the rein and tried to control them myself. It was the same insight I had learnt from working with Can-Can – that when we ask and let our horse react in its own way to our request, we often achieve a far better result with minimal effort than when we try to control them ourselves. Chasing cattle through the timber, weaving between trees, jumping over logs, and pushing them back into the mob was the most fun I had enjoyed in a long time. And more than anything, it was the sure-footed, smart stock horses I rode that made for such an exhilarating experience.

Once the paddock was mustered, and the mob securely held, a quick bite of lunch was taken; the battered sandwiches and fruit from my saddlebag quickly washed down with a lukewarm, though much appreciated, quart-pot of water from a trough or tank. Then it was back into the saddle and more mustering before the slow journey home pushing the mob back to the main stockyards. As the mob moved at the speed of the slowest beast, the journey home was often slow and dusty, especially in the tail of the mob pushing the stragglers forward.

Similar to droving a mob of cattle, one person rode in the lead to control the mob's speed, occasionally stopping to keep the cattle from stringing out too far. Others rode on the side of the mob, on the wing or at point, to ensure the mob stayed together and any cattle that sought their freedom were quickly brought back. Several of us rode in the tail, at the back of the mob, slowly pushing it forward. The tail is not the place to be, especially in the middle of a hot summer day pushing tired and thirsty cattle when all they want is rest, living in the sea of dust that announced our slow journey through the bush. For only once the mob was safely yarded, and settled down for the night, were our horses finally turned for home.

It felt liberating to be working on a horse again. While trapping and working cattle at Logan Creek offered plenty of excitement, I missed the intrinsic joy that came from simply riding through the bush for work or play. There was a regal pleasure that came from simply enjoying the splendour of the natural world with only my thoughts for company. There was something timeless about a long, relaxed canter in the cool of dusk as the sun's setting rays danced in the dust and off the coat of my horse: the sound of his hoof beats a gentling and soothing melody. I felt no greater joy than during those late afternoon rides home, once the mob was settled down, content with the work done and the welcomed rest to come.

It was often dark when we got back to the homestead, horses and riders both covered in dust and sweat, and turned our horses loose. With a quick wash and rub down, followed by a farewell pat on their neck and wither, we slipped their halters and let them go. After their roll in the sand, with its requisite sounds of contentment and pleasure, they slowly wandered over for the feed they knew was coming. It was always with a contented chewing and gentle sighing we left them for the night, back to a warm, relaxing shower, a delicious dinner, and the sleep of the physically exhausted.

Working the Mellaluka cattle was very different to working the wild Saraji cattle. Having been worked as young calves, which helped to reduce their fear of man, they were a lot calmer with the process. We started as early as possible for the days were very hot as the sun beat down with a relentless ferocity, further abetted by a blast of hot air from the west that only increased the furnace-like feel of the day. Adding to the heat was the branding fire with its red coals pulsating like the coals of a blacksmith's forge. With the calf crush and gates leading into it greased, the branding irons red-hot, and other tools of the trade carefully laid out, it was time to start work.

The first calf was run into the crush. Bang! The crush was slammed shut with the calf inside and pulled onto its side. Instantly, everybody jumped to work in a blur of action as I grabbed the calf's back leg tightly to stop it from kicking. Another ringer grabbed the brand and, with a quick flick of his wrist, imprinted its burning mark while another tipped and ear tagged the calf. If it was a bull calf, a quick flick of a knife and a spray of disinfectant relieved it of its manhood. Before the calf knew quite what had happened, and was still a little dazed and unsure of itself, the crush was flicked open for it to regain its freedom, though on somewhat wobbly legs. In the space of less than a minute, an exhausting and action-packed minute, we were finished.

However, that was just the beginning. There were several hundred calves to work and no chance of any respite as the calves kept coming one after another. Our routine was the same for hours on end, working in a blur of motion and noise, all the while swathed in the pungent smell of burning hide, the dust's earthy fragrance, and the tangy smell of eucalyptus smoke.

As the sun crawled higher into the sky, and the dust got heavier and thicker, it felt like working in a furnace as the heat from the branding fire added to the intensity of the natural cleansing process. Our shirts were soon soaked with sweat as were our arms and faces; the dust hanging in the air quickly changing our complexions from a healthy brown to a dirty brown. My arms and back ached from the continual exertion of holding kicking, straining calves as tightly as possible; calves whose power was sometimes greater than mine leaving me flailing like a fish on a line as they thrashed away.

My mouth, dry from the heat, dust, and smoke, tightened with a clay-like taste down the back of my throat. And, as the calves kept coming, so the temperature kept rising as it reached close to 45 degrees Celsius that day. In all likelihood, given the lack of shade, it was probably quite a bit hotter for the four sweat-stained ringers in that yard. After a brief respite for lunch, relished in whatever sliver of shade was available, we slowly returned to the yards and the work of the crush until the last calf was through. Only then did we head home at the end of the day to a most welcomed shower, a most delicious meal, and a most exhausted and appreciated sleep.

This routine, of very early starts and working until the dusk appreciatively arrived, went on for weeks without a break. Once we finished mustering and working cattle in one paddock, we moved straight into the next paddock and started all over again. This was my life until, somewhat thankfully, the Christmas holidays finally appeared on the horizon and the mustering season slowly drew to a close.

It was fascinating to reflect on the transformational impact this work had on my body as I followed the lifestyle most consistent with the essence of Nature's teaching.

My eyesight improved significantly with the previous long-sighted blurring from my career days almost gone by the end of my stay. The cure was not glasses or surgery. It was something far more basic. It was simply working my eye muscles to reinvigorate them. The weight and lack of tone that previously defined my physical being had vanished, replaced instead with lean muscle that now made the exertion of everyday living significantly easier. My practical aerobic capacity had dramatically increased from both chasing calves around the stockyards and being chased by their older brethren. Far better exercise than pounding the treadmill without the likely damage to my tendons and ligaments. I felt stronger and cleaner physically, which had the same effect on my mind, heart, and soul.

Fittingly, this transformation had not required drugs, surgery, or a radical change of lifestyle. All it had required was embracing Nature's teaching and living a simple, healthy life. It taught me, once again, that we alone control our health. The elements for a healthy, happy lifestyle are all around and it is our responsibility alone to make that choice. Where we instead chose less disciplined approaches to attain our health and happiness, such as drugs, alcohol, processed food, surgery, or consumption, we debase Nature's wisdom and that is our loss alone. Given we are each a child of the natural world, it is difficult to see how ignoring Nature's teaching could ever be to our benefit!

Unfortunately, given how corrupted much of the Western food, pharmaceutical, and lifestyle industries have become, it not only makes that choice more difficult. It makes it even more imperative. Our desire to control and perpetually take from the natural world has led humanity to a state of mind that does not serve us. Instead, we incur significant, self-inflicted consequences reflecting how destructive our beliefs and behaviours have become, and will continue to do so as individuals and as a society until we change those ways.

It was ultimately to be the totality of these realisations, the opportunity to regain my health, and the getting of wisdom around what was required to maintain that health, which made my time on walkabout the life-changing gift it turned out to be. If being 'liberated' and not earning a salary for several years was the price required to reconnect with the innate wisdom of the natural world, and the fundamental role its teaching will play in the quality of our life, it was a small price indeed. And, as I approached the end of my first year of walkabout, it was these insights that came to define the benefit of Nature's teaching most succinctly of all.

Unfortunately, like everything else on walkabout, what has a beginning also has an end. As Christmas 2002 slowly rolled around, it was soon time to head back to Sydney and a well-deserved holiday by the beach. In too short a time, my swag was rolled for the last time and I farewelled Mellaluka and the allure of its country. While this marked the end of my time as a ringer, and working with horses, it would only be a short walkabout hiatus for Nature's siren call remained loud and strong.

On my last evening at Mellaluka, I stayed by the horse yard just watching the bush come alive as a cool wind blew gently through the trees and the rustling leaves reflected the silvery glow of the full moon.

As I rested on the smooth, wooden rails of the yard, several of the horses we had ridden earlier that day slowly made their way to the trough for a well-earned drink. Their gentle whinnies and snorts, as they drank and splashed in the water from the trough, brought on a feeling of contentment for my life with them. Watching their muscle-bound forms as dark, dappled shadows slowly amble towards the gate, I realised how much I appreciated being part of their world. Listening to the soft plodding of their hooves in the sand of the yard turn to a canter, and then to a drum-roll as they galloped out the gate, I followed their progress until it was lost in the night.

Resting on the yard rails at that moment, there was one thing I knew with absolute certainty – Nature's teaching would always be my guide and Outback Australia would always be my home.

8

Anzac Day

'The skies that arched his land were blue,
His bush-born winds were warm and sweet,
And yet from earliest hours he knew
The tides of victory and defeat;
From fierce floods thundering at his birth,
From red droughts ravening while he played,
He learned to fear no foes on earth–
"The bravest thing God ever made!"'

Will Ogilvie – The Australian

Travelling the vastness of the Australian continent, there was one defining geological and cultural thread binding the myriad of diverse scenes together. It is to Australian society what basement rock is to the continent's integrity. That thread is granite, marble, and sandstone; its form the plethora of war memorials lovingly built in every city and town in memory of Australia's war dead. These tall, proud sentinels maintaining their eternal vigil deeply move me whether at a remembrance service or simply passing them by in daily life. The starkness of their shape against the azure-blue Australian sky is as haunting as the tales of slaughter in their scroll of names is tragic. Passing by the Clermont War Memorial, after leaving Mellaluka to return to Sydney, memories came flooding back of an Anzac Day Dawn Service on a cool April morning in 1977. As a Patrol Leader in the local Scouts, I lay a remembrance wreath in front of the simple sandstone octagon in what I remember as a very solemn occasion: an occasion I was not to know would play a key role in how my own life philosophy evolved. Reflecting on that particular Anzac Day, as I stood next to the same memorial in December 2002, my mind took me back to a small, nondescript cove on the other side of the world. The very place from which Anzac Day originated all those years ago.

The Dawn Service at Anzac Cove, on the Gallipoli Peninsula in Turkey, is one of the most profoundly moving experiences I have ever had. Listening to the Last Post played over the hallowed ridges and gullies of Anzac Cove in April 1995, as the sun's first rays silhouetted the craggy horizon, I could not hold back the tears. As the last melancholy notes faded into the cool ocean air, and the first seconds of a minute's silence slowly ticked past, my thoughts turned back to the moment 80 years before when the first Australians jumped from their boats onto that same sandy shore under Turkish fire on 25 April 1915.

What they found was an almost impossible task. For rising above them in the gloomy dark was the first of many ridges, an almost vertical slope covered with thick scrub barring their way. Everything was in chaos for they had been landed on the wrong beach. There was nothing to do except head off into the unknown hinterland much as their forebears had done on the Australian frontier the preceding century. It was the inspiring yet sorrowful events on this small, narrow stretch of sand, and in the surrounding scrubby acres, which came to define a key thread of the fabric of Australian society today. It is the names of those killed at Gallipoli, and subsequently in France and Flanders, and Palestine, which now grace those tall, proud granite, marble, and sandstone memorials half a world and many lifetimes away.

Today, though the bodies of Australia's war dead lie in many countries across the world, it is Gallipoli, and Anzac Cove in particular, which has come to symbolise the Anzac story. Our reverence and respect for this day, and its history, is felt from the first Dawn Service attended as a child, when, in the autumn chill of the early morning air, the notes of the Last Post hauntingly echo over the memorials silhouetted against the Australian sky as the sun's first rays light the eastern horizon.

Visiting Anzac Cove today is a unique form of pilgrimage for Australians and New Zealanders. The country is striking in its similarity to many parts of the Australian Outback. A dry and dusty land with little surface water except for what remains in small puddles after a passing storm. Much as it does the Australian Outback, geology essentially defines the character of Anzac Cove with the stunted trees, scrubby bushes, and grasses more of a biological afterthought. The heat, especially during summer, and the tired, worn look of the country gave it a feel many Australian troops would have deeply resonated with given the rural backgrounds from which they came.

I undertook my pilgrimage to Gallipoli in April 1995 for the 80th anniversary of the Landing. Shortly before my visit, a fire had swept across Anzac Cove completely burning back the vegetation that had salved the country in the intervening years. It appeared the clock had been turned back to December 1915, when the Australian and New Zealand troops were finally evacuated from the Peninsula, so thorough had the fire been.

What the fire had done was lay bare the soul of Anzac Cove. I could see the terraced ridges with the faint outlines of paths still visible. I could see slight depressions in the ground where men had dug possies into the ridges and gullies, when sandbags and a sheet of canvas or tin provided the only shelter against the weather and the rain of shrapnel from Turkish guns. The smallest pieces of evidence from those days were again revealed to the world after their burial by the vegetation for the best part of three quarters of a century. It appeared the men had left only yesterday so visible was the evidence of their stay.

From water bottles and mess tins rusted to their bare skeletons to pieces of shrapnel, ammunition, and unexploded shells, the ground was alive with the remnants of that time. Everywhere I looked was a reminder of those days: a knife here, a fork there, a bone next to me with its stark whiteness gleaming in the midday sun. It was a poignant journey back in time given how much of the past was revealed before me. It gave the Anzac story a closeness in time and spirit that would never have been otherwise experienced given how quickly the land reverts to its former scrubby state.

The Anzac story starts at the beach; the waves of the Aegean Sea lapping the sandy shore a reminder of Nature's gentleness in contrast to the destruction humanity was to brutally inflict on itself. The beach was very peaceful in the early spring sun of April 1995: its azure water a reminder of picturesque beaches half a world away. It was this peaceful and nondescript beach that became the crucible into which men from around the world were thrust. It was this nondescript beach, on a nondescript coast, which marked the beginning of the core thread of what would become a significant part of the fabric of Australian society today.

Two blunted, sandy headlands envelop the beach at Anzac Cove: Ari Burnu to the north and Hell Spit to the south. Both contain cemeteries with the multitude of white gravestones reflecting not only the glow of the midday sun but also the reverence every Australian feels for these men. It is in the quiet, almost serene, cemetery on Hell Spit one of the most sought after graves of the whole campaign is found: that of John Simpson Kirkpatrick, the man with the donkey, who became immortalised as few others were but who equally deserved to be.

On arriving at Anzac Cove, it was the cliffs that first caught my eye. They rose sharp and straight up, off the beach, into the wild heights of the First Ridge, silhouetted against the azure-blue sky with the same starkness as the memorials that rise into the Australian sky today. You quickly realise the land dictates the history of Anzac Cove: its geography determining the subtle underlying themes of this most inspiring of places. Ridges and gullies dictate the path of visitors today just as they governed the movement of men and the sway of battle in 1915. It is the land, personalised by the names now attached to its features, which defines the physical character of Anzac Cove.

There is no other way to start a pilgrimage here than walking out of the cold waters of the Aegean Sea; the shingles slipping beneath your feet much as they did for that earlier generation of Australians all those years ago. From the narrow, sandy beach, enveloped by its two blunted headlands, there is only one direction and that is straight up. It was this path and direction those first Anzacs took, up through the thick, dirty-green scrub that pulled at their clothes and entangled their rifles, as the shouts and screams of men, the whine of bullets, and the crashing sound of exploding shells urged them on.

It was quite a scramble getting to the top of the First Ridge, pulling myself up with whatever vegetation I was able to grab hold. The soil was loose and rocky: I felt that for every three steps I took up, I slid back two. It was a difficult enough proposition with two spare hands. Yet in 1915, men weighed down with their packs and the accoutrement of war had only one spare hand, the other tightly grasping their rifle. Following this path of the original Anzacs, as they made their way up and over Plugge's Plateau into the gloom of the valley below, is one of the most meaningful climbs I have ever undertaken. It is not often the opportunity arises to follow in the tracks of those whose valour, enterprise, and fidelity created one of Australia's most meaningful and enduring legacies.

Plugge's Plateau is the highest part of the First Ridge, which starts at Hell Spit as the steep slopes of MacLagan's Ridge and ultimately runs back to the northern end of the beach at Ari Burnu. On reaching the top, the plateau panned out before me much like many views in the Australian ranges today. A gently rising slope with its edge silhouetted against the sky; its stunted vegetation suggesting how difficult it remains for the flora and fauna to get a firm footing in this land.

Some of the earliest photos of the Landing show men moving across Plugge's Plateau under fire, their slouch hats pulled low as if trying to stay dry in the storm of lead bursting above them. Today, fortunately, the scene is one of peace and serenity. Looking west down over the beach, the Aegean Sea sparkled a cool, refreshing welcome. Looking east over the ridges, their rugged wildness inspired an awe and respect that made their exploration impossible to resist.

On Plugge's Plateau today, a small cemetery is found: its crop of white, rectangular gravestones in stark contrast to the natural dullness of the surrounding vegetation. On each of the small, white gravestones, sprouting from the ground as if they were a common shrub, the name, age, regiment, and date of death of the entombed soldier was carved. At the bottom of most gravestones was a quote, the last gift bestowed by a grieving family from throughout the British Empire, whose words reached into the depths of my soul crying out against the brutality of war and the tragedy of young lives cut down in the prime of their great adventure.

My most poignant moments were spent reading these remembrances for the dead; the pain and pride of their loved ones palpable as they tried to make sense of what had transpired on this rugged coastline so far from Australia.

From a gravestone in the Beach Cemetery on Hell Spit, the parents of a 22-year-old soldier reminded passers-by of the reason for their tragic loss: *He Gave His Life That Others May Live.*

On a gravestone in the Ari Burnu Cemetery, the respect of his parents for their 17-year-old son shone through in their remembrance of him: *He Died a Man & Closed His Life's Brief Day Ere It Had Scarce Begun.*

On a gravestone in the Lone Pine Cemetery, the parents of a 28-year-old soldier reflected on the reality of his sacrifice: *He Died In A Far Country Fighting For His Native Land.*

On a gravestone in the Walker's Ridge Cemetery, a Light Horseman's final words before the charge at the Nek reminded passers-by of his breathtaking humanity: *His Last Words 'Goodbye Cobber God Bless You'.*

And on a gravestone in the Shell Green cemetery, the parents of a 23-year-old soldier eloquently expressed their tragic insight into the feelings of all parents who lost a child in that place: *We Take Our Saddest And Happiest Walks Along The Sands of Memory.*

Every grave moved me deeply so loudly did its underlying message resonate. Each grave held a story that would make any parent, any society, proud to call them their own. Yet, despite the cemeteries, it was difficult to appreciate the violence that had claimed so many lives. Each cemetery was such a peaceful location it was almost impossible to grasp the brutal struggle that had once unfolded among the surrounding gullies and ridges.

Moving outside the manicured serenity of these cemeteries, however, the intensity of the struggle quickly reasserted its grip on my consciousness. For all around, even after 80 years of Nature's slow cleansing of this battlefield, the scars of war still lay visible. On the inland edge of Plugge's Plateau, I could still discern the remains of an old trench with its sides reinforced with rocks much like the ruins of an ancient fort. Around this trench, the relics of war still lay everywhere – spent .303 cases green-black and half buried in the dirt, sharp and rounded pieces of shrapnel, and other bits of steel that could have been the shoe from a donkey or the reinforcement to the heel of a man's boot.

From the edge of this trench, overlooking a broad valley, the heights of Plugge's Plateau afforded a majestic view over the battlefield, with the vast expanse of the Second Ridge and its heights clearly stamping their authority over the whole landscape. It was from the heights of this First Ridge, just like those first Anzac soldiers, I followed my momentum over the top of Plugge's Plateau and down into the valley that became their home for eight months in 1915.

The valley between the First and Second Ridges, which winds its way up from the beach as Shrapnel Valley, diverges into a number of smaller gullies beneath the Second Ridge. Of these, the most important was Monash Gully, which joined Shrapnel Valley just beneath Braund's Hill. This path was the primary route to and from the front line.

Shrapnel Valley got its name from the ever-present shelling men endured while traversing its length: hailstorms of lead and iron that regularly and randomly burst with a ferocity unmatched by Nature's storms. It was in Shrapnel Valley that Simpson was fatally shot while bringing down a wounded man from the ridges above. Today, from the surrounding heights, it looks like nothing more than a dry, shallow creek, which is exactly what it is. It looks the same as a thousand dry, shallow creeks from across Australia.

As I walked down the steep, rocky slope of the First Ridge into Shrapnel Valley, I could have been walking through the Australian bush. The hot sun beating down, its heat making me tired and thirsty as I tramped through the rising dust, was no different to the reality of working cattle or putting up a fence somewhere across Australia's vastness.

Yet, unlike Australia, the feel of Shrapnel Valley today barely masks the carnage once incessantly plied along its path, with its cemetery providing an understated hint into its macabre past. Today, when walking up Shrapnel Valley, it is the fragrance of rosemary and flowers, not the stench of death, which greets the visitor. The masses of flies that fed off the carnage of war are now replaced with insects and birds; their chirping and humming a soothing melody as Nature shows its true face when not forced to submit to the ugliness of humanity's violence on itself. In many ways, it was impossible to imagine what Shrapnel Valley was like all those years before.

Men were killed walking along its path every day from the direct shot of a Turkish sniper or a more random, less personal piece of shrapnel. Not surprisingly, the Shrapnel Valley Cemetery is one of the largest at Anzac Cove: the white gravestone for each man killed solemnly marking the violent passing of a generation. Sitting among these gravestones, in the quiet of the afternoon sun with nobody else around, I could almost hear the voices of the dead in the breeze that occasionally blew. Or was it the voices of the living, the mothers and fathers, wives, sons and daughters, brothers and sisters, whose last gift to their loved one was the heart-rending quotes carved into the stone all around? Thoughts and words that always deeply resonated, crying out in anguish for the loss of such potential to both their family and their country.

Walking up Shrapnel Valley to connect with Monash Gully, the Second Ridge quickly reimposed itself on my consciousness. To the right, to the left, and straight ahead, all I could see was azure-blue sky and the ridge. The Second Ridge was the front line for most of the campaign with its crest today dotted with cemeteries and memorials to the fallen: the white gravestones glowing in the sun with serene repose in the stunningly azure-blue days that still smile on the living.

At the Landing, the troops were told to get off the beach as quickly as possible and to head inland as far and as fast as they could. The nature of the terrain made the carrying out of these orders with any form of coordinated precision almost impossible. The ridges broke into spur after spur, the valleys and gullies often ending up against the sheer face of a ridge. Combined with the increasing shrapnel, and Turkish rifle and machine gun fire, that first day was as tough and brutal as can be imagined.

Yet several men did glimpse their final objective. From the Third Ridge, the waters of the Narrows glistened steel-blue and bright in the mid-morning sun. That same narrow stretch of water that has played its part in many of the adventures and misadventures of humanity since the dawn of Western civilisation. Most men were pinned down and fighting on the Second Ridge, which is where they stayed. Walking up Monash Gully with the Second Ridge on my right, the names of those positions, etched into my memory as they were carved into the ridge, came flooding back with the same certainty as the names of my own family. Steele's, Courtney's, and Quinn's Posts, and Pope's Hill, all named for the officers originally tasked with their establishment and, most importantly, their defence.

Walking along Monash Gully was in effect walking through a cemetery. There were bones everywhere. I could barely walk more than half a dozen paces and not see the glint of a jagged whiteness sticking out of the dull-brown sand with a shape not of that land. Many bones were lying in a small, dry creek bed, bleached clean and white. Large bones and small bones, straight bones and curved bones lay both in the creek and higher up the ridge. In the early days of the campaign, many men killed in the open were left where they fell. It was simply too dangerous to retrieve and bury them. Other men who were killed later in the campaign, attacking Turkish positions on the heights of the Second Ridge, were also left where they fell; their bones slowly washed down into the gully below by 80 years of intermittent rain.

Reflecting the personal nature of the fight at Anzac Cove, it was not just bones I found. Water bottles lay baking in the sun, their sides ripped apart by bullets and shrapnel: the rust marks of other indentations showing they had been hit more than once. Mess tins, some with their handles still attached, others blown apart, were found regularly. At the top of Monash Gully, at the bottom of Pope's Hill, I came across a pile of ammunition from the last attempt to wrest control of this part of the frontline from the Turkish soldiers 80 years before. It lay there in the sun, welded together by rust and dirt. Clips of five rounds ready for charging the magazine: their colour green and black compared to their former brassy glory. And as always, another steep gully leading up though I never knew quite where to.

It was a poignant and sobering experience to walk the length of Monash Gully. It was equally impossible to stop the tears. For here were the bones of my countrymen, here were the bones of men who had come from the town of my birth or the towns in which I had lived. Whose remains had lain undisturbed since their death 80 years before. Whose name was now a carving on a memorial but who had once lived and breathed as I now did. Whose sacrifice had allowed me to follow opportunities they never had the chance to explore. Whose friends I had come to know in the dawn of my life and the twilight of theirs. And whose actions were the first step in the creation of a national identity that would strengthen their country's cultural fabric more tellingly than any other would.

I felt a great responsibility to lay as many of those remains to rest, spending much of the afternoon doing just that. The least I could do was bury their bones a little deeper, a little more gently, so they could finally enjoy the peace they so richly deserved.

While Shrapnel Valley and Monash Gully represented the main thoroughfares at Anzac Cove, the Second Ridge defined the Anzac position: its heights today still providing the same majestic view over the Australians' position as it did for the Turkish soldiers in 1915. It is by following the Second Ridge north, from the southernmost Anzac defensive position at Chatham's Post to the heights of Chunuk Bair, the stark reality of the campaign plays out before your eyes like an exciting drama, only the tragic outcome is already known. This is the only way to really see the country and understand its history in a most profound and poignant way.

Walking the old trench lines and cemeteries that mark the front line, the years fell away as their story came alive. The history of Anzac Cove describes how the Australian and New Zealand troops were pinned down, barely able to show their heads over the top of the parapet for fear of being instantly shot. Once the Second Ridge is walked, it is easy to understand why. The Turkish positions overlooked almost every part of Anzac Cove. There were few places the Anzac troops could not be seen by the Turkish soldiers squinting over their rifle sights.

The southern part of the Australian line was defended from Chatham's Post, a small position dug into a lesser ridge coming off the Second Ridge. After 80 years, all that marked its existence were a number of slight indentations in the ground that had been rifle pits and communication trenches. Apart from that, there was nothing. Nothing except for its place in a few old history books and a few equally old photos showing the grinning faces of its defenders under their slouch hats as their rifles rested on the parapet.

From Chatham's Post, the gently rising slope of Bolton's Ridge was followed north along the front line towards Lone Pine. For most of the front line, it was easy to determine which trenches belonged to whom: Turkish trenches were on the right with the Australian trenches on the left for the length of the Second Ridge. Often the trenches were almost touching with barely a few metres separating the two armies. It was easy to see how difficult it would have been for the Anzac troops to break out of the 150 acres they had been able to wrestle from their tough and undaunted Turkish foe.

Visiting the memorials dotted along the Second Ridge, the last remaining physical manifestation of the Anzac achievements, further strengthened the respect I felt for the men who had fought there, and the dead who remained. Shell Green was one such place. It was also the location of one of the largest cemeteries at Anzac Cove. It lay just behind the Second Ridge but close enough to have been constantly under fire: its name reflecting the incessant shelling applied to the relatively flat and wide expanse of what had been a small cotton field. The gravestones here dated from the Landing to almost the last day of the campaign; the mix of battalions and regiments further testimony to the closeness of the men and the randomness with which death could strike.

Shell Green was also important for another reason. For it was at this location one of the most remarkable photos of the campaign was taken. A photo of a cricket match played shortly before the troops were finally evacuated from Anzac Cove. The game was part of a larger effort to convince Turkish soldiers the Anzac troops were settling in for the winter when it was actually planned they be evacuated over several days towards the end of December. It was said there was as much chance of a lost life as there was a lost ball in that particular match.

Walking among the gravestones on Shell Green in 1995, I realised that particular game of cricket was far more than just a game. It was, in fact, a significant insight into the nature of the men who had lived and died across those very acres. Men who gave everything they had to win, but who also found time to make the most out of the hand they were dealt during their time on the Peninsula. Cricket games have been played in some unique places – this one surely ranks towards the top of that list!

Heading further north, along the slight incline of the Second Ridge, Lone Pine was finally reached: another of those locations that reaches from the history books to grab at your gut and twist. Although now just a place on a map, it is a name that sends a shiver of recognition through those who know of its bloody past. Lone Pine, another small natural feature over which the Australian and Turkish soldiers continually spilt their blood for eight months, became renowned as a byword for the fierce and brutal nature of the campaign. It was the scene of the most intense bayonet and hand-to-hand fighting experienced by either side. In its maze of blasted trenches, thousands upon thousands of Australian and Turkish soldiers killed one another over a few days in August 1915. It was said the only way to respect the dead was to avoid stepping on their faces. Today, it is a very peaceful place with the old trenches now part of an evocatively sculptured cemetery.

It is at Lone Pine, over its maze of trenches where so many men died or simply disappeared, the Australian memorial to the missing was consecrated; the monument with the names of those men whose bones are still found across the ridges and gullies of Anzac Cove today. Similar to other Anzac Cove cemeteries, traces of the carnage from that time can still be found once outside its manicured lawns. Broken rum jars, their corks still firmly in place, lay on the ground among pieces of shrapnel whose sharp shape willingly defined their destructive intent. The indentations from other trenches also remained as if to remind passers-by of the tragic reason for the existence of the otherwise serene and well-tended cemeteries.

From Lone Pine, as I headed north following the windy, narrow road that used to be No Man's Land, more evidence of the scanty hold Australian troops maintained along the Second Ridge was found. Steele's Post, Courtney's Post, and Quinn's Post, all named for their respective commanding officers, were just that – a small outpost dug into the seaward side of the Second Ridge that, if captured, would have given the Turkish soldiers a clear run down to the beach.

Nowhere was this clearer than at Quinn's Post where a perpetual bomb fight engaged both sides for the duration of the campaign. The history books record how often weary and troubled eyes turned towards Quinn's Post as yet another of the titanic bomb duels erupted, flames and explosions lighting up the night sky. Today, it is a serene and peaceful place with only its small cemetery and the remnants of old trenches evidence of the horrendous duels that once gave it a reputation for swift and brutal death. Its natural rebirth an important reminder of how often Nature has to rehabilitate what humanity has brutally and ignorantly rent asunder.

Following the names of different battle honours, now more meaningful as contours on a map, I advanced up the Second Ridge across Baby 700 to the highest point at Chunuk Bair. It was here, with their heroic advance in August 1915, the New Zealand troops almost won the heights, so desperately sought, with a determination and steely resolve that defied ferocious Turkish counter-attacks for several brutal days.

Below the New Zealand memorial on Chunuk Bair, on the slopes of Rhododendron Ridge, I found remnants of those days 80 years later. I was sitting under a shady pine tree, as grateful for its shade as I was for the chance to reflect on the New Zealanders' magnificent bravery. Just beneath my boot, a white glint among the dirty-green leaves caught my eye. As I brushed the leaves and dirt away, it became clear it was a bone. As I slowly brushed away more dirt, I saw it was not one bone but several bones still joined.

The New Zealanders killed on Rhododendron Ridge still lie where they fell; their remains today barely covered by a thin shroud of dust and leaves. Next to me, another white glint caught my attention. Scraping away the dust and leaves, I found a jawbone, complete with its teeth, and a little further away a fork and more ammunition. I could barely touch the ground without disturbing the final resting place of another unknown soldier whose name is today carved on a memorial in the Land of the Long White Cloud.

While Anzac Cove is hallowed ground in every sense of the word, there is one particular place forever etched into the consciousness of the nation. That is the Nek, a narrow sliver of land, several tennis courts wide, whose sides fall abruptly away into deep valleys either side. If the Australian troops were ever to secure control of the Second Ridge, they first had to control Baby 700. Which meant taking the Nek from a determined and entrenched Turkish foe.

The views from Baby 700 are spectacular in all directions. It is easy to understand why the Allies vested so much in its capture, and the Turkish in its defence, should you sit on its summit today. In that sense, it is similar to the battlefields of France and Flanders. Names of places in history books mean nothing until they are actually seen. For only then do you realise it was not just a town or hill on a map. It was actually the highest local ground whose strategic importance fatally drew competing armies to it like moths to a flame.

As the New Zealanders scaled the slopes of Chunuk Bair, so the men of the 3rd Light Horse Brigade were given the supporting task of attacking one of the most fortified positions on the Turkish front line. In the space of 15 minutes, almost to a man, their courageous, self-sacrificing charge was obliterated under the withering fire of the Turkish machine gunners. Reflecting the brutality and confusion of that day, almost all the 234 men who died charging the Turkish lines have no known grave. Their remains, not recovered until after the Armistice, were buried where they fell, in 1919, with the Nek Cemetery today positioned on the very ground over which they so unflinchingly charged and died.

As I quietly reflected on the story of that place, the paucity of gravestones giving the Nek Cemetery a quite different feel to the other Anzac Cove cemeteries, it was almost impossible to imagine the carnage those Light Horse troopers so recklessly endured so serene was the cemetery 80 years later.

Charles Bean's recording of that tragic event was particularly poignant, especially his recitation of the actions of Trooper Wilfred Harper. As he dutifully recorded, Trooper Harper *was last seen running forward like a schoolboy in a foot-race, with all the speed he could compass.* It was this action, so movingly recorded in the closing scenes of the movie, *Gallipoli*, which has come to define the bravery and commitment of those men. And why it still resonates with another generation of Australians almost a century later.

Captain Charles Bean is one of the least known, but certainly one of the most important, figures from Australian history. He dedicated his life to observing, recording, and writing the story of Anzac. In essence, he created the defining Australian narrative whose threads bind the fabric of Australian society today more strongly than any others do. His focus on honestly recording all aspects of the Australian experience across the tragic battlefields of Gallipoli and the Western Front created and inspired a legacy never to be forgotten. He created a belief that still influences how Australians define themselves. He created a pantheon of achievers, saints, and sinners whose lives became beacons for future generations of how to live with a sense of commitment to any task. He crafted the story Australians often turn to when disaster strikes, whether natural or man-made.

His humility at accurately recording the words and deeds of the great-hearted men and women of the First Australian Imperial Force was commensurate with the true nature of their sacrifice. Bean actively turned down any attempt at recognition, including twice declining a knighthood recommendation, despite dedicating his life to the completion of his works. In addition to writing the first six volumes of the *Official History of Australia in the War of 1914-18,* and jointly annotating the final, twelfth *Photographic Record of the War* volume, he played a critical role in building the Australian War Memorial in Canberra; one of the most recognised war memorials in the world today.

Bean was the consummate war correspondent. Not only did he live in the trenches with the men, he dealt with the same miseries and took many of the same risks. He was a courageous, considerate, and inspiring man, being recommended for the Military Cross after rescuing wounded soldiers under fire during the Second Battle of Krithia; a joint Australian and British assault on the Turkish lines at the bottom of the Peninsula in May 1915.

Late at night, when most other men were resting or asleep, Bean sat in his cramped dugout, with nothing more than a smoky candle, pencil, and notepad, writing the detailed notes and observations he subsequently crafted into one of the most exhaustive and inspiring histories of an army ever written. If the history of Anzac has a father, it is he alone; the 5,600 pages and 2.2 million words he wrote a lasting tribute to his sense of purpose and integrity. It was his single-minded dedication to this task, over the course of his life, which ensured Australians retain such a strong sense of connection to the people and events of 1914-18, and their resonance for the Australia of today.

Importantly, a significant part of that history reflects how fundamentally the men of Anzac Cove, and their subsequent achievements during the First World War through France and Flanders, and Palestine, were shaped by the experiences and hardships of the Australian bush. It is especially through the words of Bean, and the inspiring story of Anzac, the importance of the teaching of the natural world to the story of Australia is intimately and comprehensively understood.

Bean spent his years before the war working as a journalist focused on the lives of those living and working in the far-flung regions of the Australian Outback. He came to understand, better than most, how the challenging environment in which those men and women lived and worked significantly influenced the Australian character of those days. Bean intrinsically understood it was Nature, it was the bush, which melded the poorest of the British Empire's citizens, who had arrived from its prisons, factories, and farms barely a hundred years before, into one of the finest armies to take the field in the tragedy of the First World War.

Given his insights, Bean's works speak volumes to the influence of the bush on the Australian soldier, and their skills, from the first days of the war and the battles at Gallipoli to the final days of the war and the battles in France and Flanders. It was his insights into the Australian soldier, how their experiences in the Australian bush uniquely created the skills best suited to the profession of soldiering, which are among the most critical truths we have into the role of the land itself to creating a core piece of the Australian identity.

My last connection to Anzac Cove was in the cemetery at Lone Pine where I returned for one final act of remembrance before leaving the Peninsula. That evening, at the going down of the sun, as the western horizon blazed in a magnificently layered radiance of orange, purple, and pink, I lingered in the cemetery for some time. The sky appeared to ignite, a reflection perhaps of the eternal flame from memorials scattered across a similarly dry and rugged land half a world away.

The Lone Pine memorial, standing tall over its cemetery of manicured gravestones, reflected the soft pastel hues of dusk: the marble reflecting the light like a smaller, equally sacred version of Chambers Pillar. It was the most peaceful of scenes I could imagine with Nature once again showing it can create places of sanctity in places of such tragedy. The air was cool with the sound of insects on the breeze; their harmony a poignant requiem for the surrounding souls lying in both marked and unmarked graves. As the dusk slowly turned to night, and the strong fragrance of pine from the surrounding trees lingered in the air, I could have been in the Australian bush as the insects slowly quietened and the leaves returned to rest leaving nothing but an absolute silence.

Sitting among those gravestones, with not another soul around, the quiet allowed my mind to wander back to those long gone days and the men who had originally tramped the surrounding gullies and ridges. Many, a significant proportion, had been born in the bush, had lived or worked there, had learnt its ways, and had been toughened and strengthened by its many trials. It was the bush that forged and ensured the mettle and philosophy of those men. In this manner, Nature's hand played a significant role in weaving one of the most important parts of our cultural fabric. For this reason alone, Anzac Cove remains a core pillar of our heritage. Not only as a fitting memorial to those first Anzac troops, but also as a powerful reminder of Nature's role in creating a legacy that will in some way always define who Australians are.

Standing silently in front of the Clermont War Memorial, as I had done 25 years previously, I realised it was Charles Bean's life that had the greatest impact on mine. My favourite life quote is his definition of Anzac. As he insightfully and respectfully articulated in his book, *Anzac to Amiens*, Bean stated that *'Anzac stood, and still stands, for reckless valour in a good cause, for enterprise, resourcefulness, fidelity, comradeship, and endurance that will never own defeat.'* It is these words, from one of the bravest men in the First Australian Imperial Force, which represent a most worthy life philosophy.

Propitiously, these words also defined the philosophy of my other mentors whether they spent their lives exploring and understanding the Australian continent, building its cattle and mining industries, or writing the poetry and stories that inspire their readers even today. And in each case, it was the bush that shaped their lives much as it had the men at Anzac Cove as Bean so adroitly recorded.

At that moment of realisation, I felt an even deeper connection to Charles Bean and my other mentors. I had knowingly embraced their life philosophy with my decision to go walkabout, trusting in the goodness of its cause, and had respectfully received its life-changing wisdom in a most appreciative way. Not only had I connected with Nature's soul, embracing the teaching it had shown in a multitude of places in a multitude of ways, I had trusted its siren call from the Western Australian Pilbara over 30 years before. A call that resulted in one of the most important relationships of my life.

I felt connected to the natural world in a profound and intimate manner, trusting its power to transform my whole being if only I embraced the lifestyle and discipline such a choice entailed. Even though I sensed there was more to glean from my walkabout, my gratitude to Nature for its teaching was as overwhelming as my appreciation to the legacy of the men whose lives inspired mine. In hindsight, I could not have asked for more perfect mentors. Moreover, with their tracks still to be followed, I looked forward to my return to walkabout and the wisdom its path would surely teach.

9

On The Wallaby

'Let us steer to the Northward, comrades!
To the Bush with her witching spells;
To the sun-bright days and the camp-fire blaze
And the chime of the bullock bells!
Down the long, long leagues behind us
The rain shall cover our track,
And the dust of the North shall blind us
Or ever we follow it back.'

Will Ogilvie – Beyond the Barrier

The road still called. Nature's exciting, mesmerising siren call had not yet released its gentle but firm grip on my soul. Despite having spent 2002 travelling and working in the vastness of the Australian Outback, my feeling of not having fully experienced everything Nature had to teach was still there. I felt an apprenticeship had commenced though it had yet to finish. There was still much to see and many lessons to learn before

Nature, and Odin, would release me from the walkabout path I had chosen. It was a journey requiring a dedication to its completion before moving to the next stage of my life; a journey I had to trust was leading me in the right direction, down the right path, at the right time. This need to travel to those places not yet experienced, not yet seen, was a difficult feeling to throw. Accordingly, with Nature's stirring whisper still urging the journey's completion, I returned to the 'Wallaby Track' to complete my walkabout around Australia. It felt very natural to roll the swag and head back to the bush, back to the majesty of the natural world. Especially as this would be the last opportunity to enjoy such freedom, for a while at least, and the life-changing wisdom it would no doubt impart.

Leaving Sydney on walkabout once again, the feeling of stomach-churning excitement was as intense and intoxicatingly heady as when I first started the engine 18 months before. In that moment, I felt there was nothing more important than finishing this journey before I could move onto the next stage of my life.

My plan for the rest of the year was deceptively simple – to travel to those regions not yet visited and to savour their beauty and charm in whatever way felt right in that specific place at that particular time. I had no other agenda, just the knowledge the magnificence of the Australian continent lay before me. A magnificence that had called and inspired since my first memory.

I had only one obligation in those months of travel: my promise to Mum to be home by Christmas Eve at the latest, which meant Christmas Eve at the earliest for me. With that promise, and the strong, slightly teary hug I always got from her before undertaking a long journey, it was time to start the engine. And excitedly, with a last wave, my focus returned to the road and completing the adventure of a lifetime.

The morning I left Sydney, immersed in Nature's surrounding beauty, was another I will never forget. The sky was a dazzling azure-blue with not a hint of cloud: the bush alive with the calls of galahs and kookaburras, cockatoos and currawongs. Spring was in the air with Nature's creations all displaying the requisite enthusiasm for learning and discovery expected in this time of life's fresh blooming. The joy of learning, exhibited in many ways by the natural world, further confirmed my need to continue this journey of discovery and teaching under Nature's expert tutelage.

The rustle of leaves as a cool breeze wafted gently through the bush, the tangy smell of eucalyptus trees providing their familiar springtime blessing, and the ranges in the distance enticing me with their unexplored treasures magnified my happiness at leaving Sydney and returning to Nature's sanctuary. As the city's outskirts slowly shrank in the rearview mirror, it was time to leave the unnatural order of society's rules and unhealthy beliefs behind, instead trusting in the wisdom of the natural world with which I now increasingly resonated.

From the rugged and chiselled sandstone ranges outside Sydney, and their rolling western foothills, to flatter plains of grass then saltbush heading inland, Nature's ever-changing panoramas passed by with the regularity and precision of an engaging play: each scene an act where only part of the final story was revealed. It felt liberating to be back in the calm embrace of the bush, enjoying Nature's genetic diversity, and returning to a life lived in accordance with the nurturing circadian rhythms of the natural world.

Initially heading west, I followed the narrow strip of bitumen to the rippling, muddy waters of the Darling River at Bourke; the same Darling River whose ancient course has marked the beginning of the Outback in Western New South Wales from the days of the earliest pioneers. As the towns quickly passed, each a little smaller and less developed than the last, the bush slowly reasserted its presence with little of humanity's impact to be seen except for the narrow strip of bitumen and requisite parallel fence leading to the horizon. Everywhere I looked, it was the natural world and its resonating beauty that defined the vista spreading to all points of the compass.

On returning to the road, one act always signalled the journey's beginning – the first time I unrolled my swag. Even though every night spent under the stars and canvas was one to remember, my first camp back within Nature's realm always felt special. It represented a unique opportunity to reconnect with Nature's spirit in a respectful manner, one that created the right relationship for the rest of the journey. After my time away from Nature's soft touch, my first night back within its embrace was always a most appreciated return.

Sitting on my swag that evening, as the sparks from the fire drifted into the night sky, the enveloping peace and quiet was a reminder of the subtleness of Nature's moods. Despite my time away, Nature's underlying essence continued to make its presence felt whether in the glory of a sunset reflected off a creek's gently rippling waters, the wheel of a galah as the evening light glinted off the grey of its wing, or the lowering of Nature's cool curtain of relief at the end of the day. I always felt intensely nurtured after reconnecting with the resonance of the natural world following a few days on the road and a few nights in my swag.

After several days driving north from Bourke, heading towards the natural bounty of Cape York Peninsula, the opportunity to pursue my fascination with Australia's gorges presented itself once again. It was the first of many that remained to be explored across the enchanting vastness of the continent.

Porcupine Gorge is a small, quiet gorge carved from a sandstone plateau on the western edge of the Great Dividing Range: the rocky spine that runs the length of the Australian east coast. It is a modest place in the Dry with its small waterholes clean and inviting after a long trudge through its sandy creek bed. It did not have the exquisite grandeur of other gorges visited though its subtlety and shade gave it an appreciated, relaxing feel. Its most prominent feature was a large rock pyramid jutting out into the river, carved from the torrents that run during the Wet.

The pyramid stood proud and tall, a sedimentary version of its Egyptian equivalent, with the fractures creating the perception of a structure created by humanity. And it could well have been. For at dusk, as the sun's golden rays struck its angled sides turning it into a glowing beacon as the bush darkened all around, it resembled the tomb of an ancient Aboriginal pharaoh given its pyramid form surrounded by a bed of shining sand.

Sitting on the bank of the creek, the quietness only disturbed by the gentle hum of butterflies, bush flies, and dragonflies flittering across the small rocky pools, the symmetry of Nature's reflection off the water was perfect in every way. Not one line, not one aspect, of the delightful scene was out of place. It was a welcome reminder, as I returned to Nature's sanctuary, of the harmony and pleasure that comes from simply being part of its exquisite domain.

Further down the track was Cobbold Gorge, a less rugged and more serene gorge with a very different form. It was almost the opposite of Porcupine Gorge: long and narrow with the sun barely able to pierce its depths even in the middle of the day.

Cobbold Gorge can only be fully explored from a small dinghy; the gorge so narrow and sheer in some places I could touch both walls simultaneously with outstretched arms. The gorge owed its existence to a small creek whose waters had carved their path down into the soft stone creating its long, narrow form. It was so quiet I could hear my own breathing and the water lap against the gorge walls and the dinghy. Spiders had spun their webs across the gorge high above my head creating several fragile, narrow silver bridges: quite a contrast to the heavy eucalyptus branches sometimes also seen overhead.

The gorge walls were smooth to the touch and cool like the water. The rock was a conglomerate with the larger, rounded pieces of white quartz, embedded like plums in a pudding, contrasting exquisitely against the darker hues of the sandstone host. The creek emptied into a river downstream from the gorge: a broad, wild river during the Wet and a broad stretch of sand in the Dry. At this junction, most appreciatively, a clear waterhole was found, dappled with the shade of several large-boughed eucalyptus trees that spread their canopy over all. It was the ideal place to wash off the sweat and smoke from days of living on a dusty track.

The country around Cobbold Gorge was quite intriguing as Nature's diverse vistas highlighted the different stages of the landscape's evolution. Volcanic rocks defined much of the country, directly through the darker soils and indirectly through the floral species taking root in the richer ground. Outside the areas of volcanic influence, the rock was sedimentary sandstone and limestone whose lighter soils reflected different floral types. The land had seen many stages of geological and biological change in its history as set out in the rocks before me. Even in a small region such as this, Nature had clearly worked the land many times to create the vistas of today.

The eastern ranges of Australia are particularly interesting in this manner. Being geologically much younger than the country to the west, the nature of the land's origin was easier to discern than older parts of the continent where eons of erosion had slowly obliterated its ancient geological history with only billion-year-old basement rock or sand-draped lands remaining today. Reflecting the continent's ancient geological age, and the numerous stages of its development, it would intriguingly show me many more sides to its character as the vistas continued to unfold through the dirty haze of my windscreen.

Heading further north, my objective was Cairns and its location as the gateway to Cape York Peninsula. Much of the coast, from Cairns to the tip of the continent, is covered by an ancient rain forest reflecting a time when Australia was a much wetter place. To drive through it was one thing. But to see it from the air, in all its grandeur, was entirely another. Having seen much of the country through my windscreen, and on foot, I decided to see this part of Australia from the air. Not only to discern the overall lie of the land better, as it was often covered in jungle, but also to appreciate the intriguing impact of Nature's intelligent design on this part of its canvas.

Leaving my 4WD in Cairns, I joined a safari group travelling across Cape York. Our trip involved flying to Horn Island and returning by ferry to Seisia on the mainland, before driving back along the Telegraph Track and the Bloomfield Track to Cairns. It was a welcome relief to have someone else take charge of the driving for it gave me far more time to take in the country than I had when travelling alone. It gave me a chance to relax for most of the trip and let someone else take care of the logistics. It gave me an appreciated opportunity to focus on what I was seeing without having to keep one eye on the road at all times. And in no way did it detract from connecting with another part of this captivating, fascinating, and intriguing continent.

My trip to Cape York, and the northern tip of Australia, started on the flight from Cairns to Horn Island. Flying out over the ocean, following the coast to the north, the colours of the ocean and beaches glistening in the sunlight were unlike any I had experienced during my journey.

The Pacific Ocean was crystal clear along the coast: the jungle-clad islands and coral reefs easily discernible from the white sand underlying the azure hues of the ocean itself. Sunlight, intermixed with light cloud, cast shadows across the waves gently dappling the shallow sea floor with a patchwork of light and dark. The coast was a narrow strip of lightly coloured sand bound by the verdant green of the rainforest to the west and the azure of the ocean to the east. At some points, given the vertical drop of the ranges into the ribbon of breaking waves along the ocean's edge, the forest met the sea in a clash of green, white, and azure.

Even from the plane, the ruggedness of the coast was easily discernible. Nature had created a wild and pristine environment that evoked instant respect for its capacity for life. The wildness of the land resonated strongly as there was no sign of its subjugation by humanity: no tracks, no buildings, nothing. Here, the open, more developed country to the south had returned to its naturally pristine state as humanity had yet to make its mark in the thickness of the jungle unlike many other places I had seen.

On landing at Horn Island, we boarded a ferry and began the slow, choppy trip back to the mainland and Seisia, the Northern Cape York port. Arriving into port was similar to going back in time. Everybody was waiting for the boat, the lifeline to the outside world. It represented an important means of entry to, and exit from, this part of Australia.

As the human cargo disembarked, so possessions of all types were disgorged from the hold. From suitcases and bags to food and mechanical equipment, it was clear the ferry played an important role in the day-to-day life of the area. The crowd on the wharf was equally interesting. From small groups of talkative Aboriginal people and busy local port personnel, to rambunctious shopkeepers seeking their packages and quiet tourist groups awaiting direction, it was a unique insight into the cosmopolitan make-up of Cape York. Young and old were there to meet friends, pick up cargo, or just watch as a new group of visitors came hesitatingly off the boat.

The wharf was very much a working place with no pretence at meeting the tourist need for glamour and cleanliness defining other places across Australia. Watching the red dust of the ancient, oxidised soils blow across the wharf, coating everything in a gritty, ochre-red film, reminded me of a Central Australian roadhouse. Except it was now a ferry bringing in the supplies, not a road train.

Reaching Cape York was also important for me personally. For it was here, and on the journey south back to Cairns, I was to cross the tracks of another mentor and a most impressive Australian adventurer: Sir Hubert Wilkins.

Hubert Wilkins was a great Australian in much the same way as Essington Lewis and Charles Bean were, living as an adventurer on the intellectual and physical frontiers. He was Australia's pre-eminent battlefield photographer across France and Flanders under Bean's guidance, earning the Military Cross and Bar for conspicuous bravery under fire. Following the First World War, he explored the wilds of Northern Australia at the behest of the British Museum, and undertook several gruelling scientific expeditions to both the Arctic and Antarctica. For his success in completing the first flight across the Arctic, from Alaska to Norway, and his other scientific work in the Polar Regions, he was knighted and received the Patron's Medal from the Royal Geographical Society.

Hubert Wilkins lived his life as one long adventure. Similar to my other mentors, he too was a child of the bush, growing up in the South Australian Outback, before a run of bad seasons forced his family to move to Adelaide. Yet his desire for adventure kept returning him to the frontier in some of the most inhospitable environments on Earth.

It was his time in Northern Australia and the realisations he made regarding the natural environment that define him as one of the far-sighted visionaries Australia has produced. Not only did he actively highlight the unnecessary destruction of the bush, and its Aboriginal people, he actively railed against their ruination hoping Australians would heed his insights into the cost of their behaviour. Unfortunately, for the most part, it was to no avail with the same behaviour, and its many destructive consequences, remaining an unfortunate and disappointing blight across the continent 80 years later.

In 1921, the British Museum received an urgent wire – the native fauna of Northern Australia were under significant threat as reflected in their increasingly rapid diminution. Given this reality, there was an urgent need to collect as many different species as possible for the benefit of future study, before they too became extinct.

Reflecting Wilkins' previous success as a collector, combined with the self-reliance he had shown on prior expeditions and during the First World War, he was chosen as the leader to undertake a scientific expedition across Northern Australia. While its primary focus was the collection of mammals and birds, in particular, he was given free rein to collect other items that would be of interest to the Museum, including those related to the local Aboriginal people on both the mainland and the Torres Strait Islands.

Over the course of two years, from 1923-25, he travelled over 4,000 kilometres, primarily alone, through the wild and uninhabited country of Cape York, Arnhem Land, and the Torres Strait Islands in his quest to identify and collect the specimens he sought. His conclusions from this time were tragic for the environment as its native fauna were being decimated at rates that were some of the highest in the world, even though much of it remained unknown to Western science.

And, as the environment was slowly being destroyed through European actions, so Aboriginal society was equally affected. It was during this time, working closely with Aboriginal people, that Wilkins courageously noted Aboriginal civilisation was often of a higher state than that of Europeans given the mutually supportive nature of Aboriginal culture and the manner in which they lived in harmony with the land.

To his credit, Wilkins was one of the few Australians at this time who took a stand against the increasing destruction of the environment and Aboriginal culture. His honest depiction of the damage being wrought, without fear or favour, mark him as a far-thinking environmentalist at a time when his views were very much in the minority. Moreover, his concerns were ultimately well founded for much of Northern Australia, and the continent in general, has suffered greatly because its newly arrived European inhabitants failed to heed his objective and perceptive insights. A small change in society's behaviour 80 years ago would likely have resulted in a meaningful difference to the needless cross-continent destruction unfortunately seen on walkabout today.

From Seisia, the track headed northeast into the Lockerbie Scrub: an isolated remnant of rainforest across the top of Cape York. It was only when I got into the scrub I realised how ancient and rare this place was compared to most of the flora of the region. Whether it is Palm Valley in Central Australia or the Lockerbie Scrub on Cape York, subtle clues remain as to how much the Australian continent has changed as it slowly desiccated over the last five million years and drought-resistant trees, shrubs, and grasses replaced its previous forest coverings. The Lockerbie Scrub is one of those clues.

Walking through this ancient forest on Cape York, a botanical time capsule in the otherwise scrubby country typifying much of the region, I appreciated the cool relief from the heat of the day. It was similar to being inside another of Nature's cathedrals with the canopy of leaves and vines an extended roof the thick trunks and branches held far off the ground. Unlike the clean, fresh air of the open plains and ocean, however, decay was the overarching smell with the rotting, dank vegetation reminding me as to the reality of our own bodies from the moment of our birth if we do not live in accordance with Nature's teaching.

Decay in the natural world is something we rarely notice outside a forest – the erosion of mountains or the rifting of continents is not on a scale that typically resonates. However, in the forest, with the smell of decay all around, it was a constant reminder that we too spend much of our lives in slow decline unless we actively slow, halt, or reverse the process. It was another important reminder of what our reality will be unless we actively keep it at bay through 'meds' that serve us rather than through lifestyle beliefs and behaviours that destroys us.

On the edge of the Lockerbie Scrub, to the east, the ruins of the first European attempt at settling Cape York can be found: the original Jardine homestead at Somerset. The view from the Somerset ruins, out into Albany Passage, was breathtaking as the azure hue of the water almost matched that of the sky. In the heat of the day, it was the perfect place to swim except it was also the undisputed domain of salt-water crocodiles, not to mention sharks and sea snakes.

That is the fascinating reality of Northern Australia; the delights of its beaches and rivers are only matched by their lethalness to humanity given the fauna that call it home. Even walking along the beach, there were plenty of indications humanity was not even close to the top of the food chain here. Whether it was the bush signs highlighting the dangers, such as crocodile drag marks up the beach, or the overt human signs, it was clear we needed to be careful and aware at all times.

As I discovered during much of my journey across Northern Australia, being lower on the food chain gave me a very different, more realistic perspective of humanity's place on Earth. It was this increasing awareness that reinforced how Genesis is fundamentally wrong, and actually quite dangerous, in its assertion that humanity has dominion over every other species.

Nature did not singly create the Earth of today for humanity's benefit alone. That is just hubris, ignorance, and an out of control ego speaking. Nature, the plants and insects primarily, created the environment of today over 3.5 billion years for all its beings, of which we are only one species, with each having a unique role to play in the planet's health. This obvious reality, sitting on the beach at Somerset, played a key role in my increasing awareness of my true place in the natural world, and my appreciation for the simplicity and reality of that place.

From the physical and philosophical insights of the Lockerbie Scrub and Somerset, the track headed north to our primary destination: the northernmost point of the Australian mainland. Walking across a rocky headland, leaving the cool shade of the forest behind, I followed a winding, greasy path down over ancient, weathered rocks being careful not to slip as the breeze and sea spray had covered everything in a fine layer of salty mist.

After a short climb down several steep, rough-hewn rocky steps, I reached the tip of Cape York with its somewhat nondescript sign telling me I was now standing at the northernmost point of the Australian continent. It was actually something of an anti-climax given how easy its accomplishment had been compared to the challenges endured in reaching other parts of the continent. However, as a location, it was very important.

To the west, just a short distance away in Torres Strait, lay Possession Island where Captain James Cook planted the Union Jack thereby claiming the east coast of Australia in the name of King George III. While the Chinese, Portuguese, Dutch, and French had also previously visited the Australian continent, it was this act in 1770 that resulted in Britain playing the primary role in the founding and development of a new society. Standing on the tip of Cape York, I felt a surge of respect for the accomplishments of the small band of convicts and soldiers who hesitatingly followed in his wake 18 years later to establish the first British colony on Sydney Harbour.

Yet, I also felt a deep sense of pain, a deep sorrow, for the First Australians whose way of life was slowly destroyed from that moment, like the land itself, with minimal concern. It was a bittersweet moment given the increasing paradox it represented for me, one I had unwittingly inherited on being born as a non-Aboriginal Australian in a land where the First Australians are still not fully recognised and respected. A land they transformed into a natural paradise before its ignorant and wanton destruction at the hands of its supposedly more civilised, newly arrived European inhabitants.

Hopefully, with a meaningful, long overdue reconciliation with Aboriginal Australia, and a stronger spiritual connection to the land itself, my children and grandchildren will not have to live with that same unfortunate, and ultimately unnecessary, paradox.

Having reached the tip of Cape York, there was only one direction to travel and that was south. The best way to do that, in fact the only way to do that, was via the Telegraph Track: Cape York's equivalent of the tracks of Central Australia.

The Telegraph Track is exactly what its name implies: a track following the path of the telegraph line that was initially built in the 1880s to connect the northernmost parts of Queensland with the state capital, Brisbane. While the track today has lost much of its originality and some of the challenges its earlier route provided, it still represents the best way to access Cape York and gain unique insights into the many geographies of the region. From pockets of ancient rainforest and thick eucalyptus scrub to wide-open grasslands with termite mounds stretching to the horizon, the landscape was a geographic mosaic where Nature seemed to have developed many of its regional ideas for other parts of the continent.

For the most part, it was wild, rugged country. This was particularly appreciated when its pristine rivers were crossed, though only a few were safe enough to swim. Fruit Bat Falls, on the Jardine River, was one such place. Resting under its gently massaging waterfall, as the humidity first started to make its presence felt, or swimming in the clear and refreshing embrace of its pools, was a most luxurious experience after days on the dusty track.

As the track headed south, the country continued to transition from dense scrubby forests to eucalyptus tree plains to open grasslands and back. For the most part, it was dry for the Wet had yet to arrive. Nevertheless, the build-up of clouds over the course of each day indicated it would not be too long until the dust turned to mud and the brown tinge across the land once again returned to a verdant green.

While the country continued to call and cajole, it was not until reaching Lakefield National Park I finally connected to Cape York and the allure of its land. Lakefield National Park, known as Rinyirru to Aboriginal people, was breathtaking in the range of flora and fauna across the rugged topography of the country. From numerous waterholes and low-lying lakes to the purple-blue smudge of distant ranges on the horizon, it was a microcosm of everything spectacular Cape York has to offer.

It was at one such place, Low Lake, I was completely enthralled by Nature's ability to create vistas of such enchantment I did not want to leave. Low Lake was just that: a natural depression into which water from the surrounding country slowly drained making it a haven for local bird-life. From leggy egrets, storks, and geese to parrots, falcons, and cockatoos, the flapping of wings and the calls of its avian symphony perpetually filled the air as I appreciatively rested on the soft, cool bank of the lake.

Long stemmed waterlilies protruded from its rippled waters, their white and yellow flowers gently resting on green pads open towards the sun, providing a luxuriant mat for the avian community to wander as they undertook their daily forage. Layered over all was an insect concerto as the sounds of cicadas and wasps, dragonflies and grasshoppers filled the air. Their more nuanced, vibrating tones resembled a gently hummed didgeridoo that never fully waned until Nature's cool curtain of relief finally settled in the dusk of another hot, humid day.

To rest in that place, to soak up Nature's bounty, was the perfect antidote to the increasing tiredness I felt from long days on the move. The chance to lie on the ground, to reconnect with the circadian rhythms of the natural world, recharged my body with an energy I was increasingly appreciative of and respectful for. While travelling with a group allowed me to see far more of the country than I could have done alone, it did not provide the opportunity to facilitate a more intimate connection with the land. My time at Low Lake provided that opportunity, reminding me, yet again, that it is only when we stop to appreciate a particular place can we fully connect with, become part of, and learn from, it.

Lakefield National Park was my last chance to appreciate the inland regions of Cape York fully. For the journey back to Cairns now returned to the coast and the Bloomfield Track into Cape Tribulation National Park. From the flat, dry, and brown-tinged Cape York landscape where rain had not fallen for some time, we were soon back among the ranges and forest environment where rainfall is a perpetual part of the seasons. And in a blur of green and azure, with the forest on one side and the ocean on the other, the track was followed through the salty humidity until first the bitumen, and then finally Cairns, was gratefully reached.

By this time, I had seen enough of the coast for the time being. I had seen all the forest I wished to see. It felt too closed-in with the vast sweeping vistas to the horizon blunted and tamed by the trees and clingy damp of the ever-present humidity. I missed the vast, dry, soul inspiring regions of the Australian Outback I had come to love. I missed the interplay of space and sun, and the dappling of the clouds across the land, which make the deserts, ranges, and plains such an uplifting place to be. It was time to return to my 4WD and leave the forest behind. It was time to head west into the wide-open spaces of the Gulf country, and the interplay of dazzling azure-blue and dusty brown I enjoyed most of all.

Before leaving Cape York, there was one last experience I sought. That was the chance to walk with Aboriginal Australians across their land to better understand what it was to see the country through their eyes.

Unlike many other parts of Australia through which my walkabout had taken me, where it was often difficult to find a way to connect with

Aboriginal culture directly, here in Cape York it was almost the opposite. From the many caves of rock art visited on the journey south to the proximity of Aboriginal guided tours, this country offered a unique opportunity to walk their land and learn their perspective. Given Aboriginal Australians have lived in this part of Australia for at least 40,000 years, and their art has been dated as being at least 25,000 years old, I could not imagine a better place to connect with their culture and wisdom.

The Quinkan rock art site at Split Rock, just outside the small town of Laura, the southern town from which the track first heads north, was the perfect place to start. On an ancient sandstone escarpment carved by the Laura River, three galleries existed with rock art that was a unique insight into the respect Aboriginal people had for this land and their appreciation for its fauna. While the underlying themes of the rock art made it similar to other places visited, with kangaroos, wallabies, emus, dingoes, snakes, crocodiles, turtles, and fish painted on the walls, the inclusion of a broad range of distinct figure types differentiated it from any other art styles previously seen.

Human-shaped spirit figures, with curved heads, large sexual organs, and knobbly elbows and knees covered the walls along with many human forms. Women figures, many with enlarged breasts, represented a particularly important insight into the respect they clearly held in Aboriginal society. In a separate gallery, quite different from the first two, tall, elongated figures showed the shadowy form of the Quinkan ancestors who give their name to this art. Across the galleries, there were also many hand stencils: these ancient marks of Aboriginal people the common thread from their civilisation across the continent. Here, the primary material used was red ochre with a limited amount of white, yellow, and black ochre also seen.

While the Split Rock galleries introduced me to the art of the region, it was not until I visited the Nagul rock art sites outside Cooktown that I gained a better appreciation for the cultural nuances of the First Australians on Cape York. Here, an Aboriginal ranger walked us through his country explaining the different sites and rock art, most of which was painted on the walls of caves and overhangs: the strangler figs pushing their roots down through and over the entrance to these caves making them even more difficult to randomly find.

Kangaroos, turtles, fish, and flying foxes adorned these walls along with a rainbow serpent, Quinkan figures, and the stencilled hands of people who initially left their mark hundreds or thousands of years before. We visited a birthing cave where pregnant women were cared for in the presence of other women, before and during childbirth, and then supported until mother and child returned to their community; a wise, nurturing practice the Western healthcare industry could well learn from today.

As the Aboriginal ranger explained the story of his people and their connection to this land, with a glint in his eye and a perpetual smile across his face, it appeared quite a few of us yearned for a similar life with its simpler rhythms. Fortunately, I was able to connect with this feeling somewhat more strongly as I looked forward to resuming my walkabout and a life more intimately connected to the resonance of the natural world.

Heading west from Cairns, after several days spent organising my supplies, I felt happy to be behind the wheel once again. Crossing the Great Dividing Range and heading west into the setting sun, I felt unshackled being back on the road. With open plains rolling to all points of the compass, and the clear azure-blue sky the perfect complement to the brown flatness stretching to the horizon, I headed for Normanton and the start of my journey west.

Normanton is a small town just off the Gulf of Carpentaria. Its claim to fame is the giant saltwater crocodile shot nearby, memorialised today in a concrete statue which is the closest I would ever hopefully come to seeing one of the Mesozoic Era's creatures in the flesh. From memory, the crocodile was almost nine metres long with a set of open jaws that could fit any part of my body, almost my whole body. It certainly made an impression and kept me well away from the waters of the Gulf's rivers and creeks for the rest of my journey west despite the slow, continued increase in humidity and temperature!

Before leaving Normanton, however, fate had one more surprise in store for me. For it was here I randomly met the first of two travellers whose memory I will never forget. Lars, a very tall, tough, enduring, and sincere fellow, was German. He spent over a year cycling not only around Australia but also across it. He carried all his gear on his bike and had no other support. Nothing. He battled the heat of summer and endured the chill of winter willingly. He accepted the loneliness and danger of cycling across the vast, daunting space of the Australian Outback with an attitude of nonchalance rarely seen these days. He took everything in his stride. Not only that, he was a real ambassador for his country. Lars was a true gentleman.

Lars and I met in the Normanton caravan park. He crawled out of his little tent about the same time I crawled out of my swag that morning. In his best German-English, I heard a quite distinctive *"G'day mate."* He was covered in dirt. I was covered in dirt. And he was tall, somewhere north of six feet. He mentioned he had been having a lot of difficulty on the roads, as his tyres kept puncturing, and he only had one spare tyre left to reach Mount Isa where he hoped he could buy more: a distance of about 500 kilometres.

As I was already heading south to Lawn Hill Gorge, I offered to extend my journey and drop him off at the Burke and Wills Roadhouse where he could find a lift to Mount Isa. It was fascinating to hear his story for he had seen quite a bit of the world having always had the desire to travel. The caravan park at Normanton just happened to be where he was at that particular moment.

As the kilometres passed, in a blur of sand and scrub, we soon discovered we had much in common. Not only from an ancestry perspective, both having Nordic genetics that was interesting to say the least, but from a life philosophy perspective as well: we both appreciated the importance of walkabout to understanding our role in the world. Our lives had been different in many ways, yet we were quite similar in our approach to what makes life worth living. We spent several hours chatting on the drive south, each relishing the chance to connect with a fellow traveller, with much laughter as we joked about leaving our former lives behind for the benefits of time on the track.

I can still see Lars waving goodbye from the Burke and Wills Roadhouse – his tall, brown, muscled body rolling his heavy bike loaded with packs into the shade as if it were a child's. His arms and legs a mass of sinews and muscles that rippled with each step: his blonde goatee and long blonde hair blowing in the wind as they would have done for our Viking ancestors when they headed off into the wilds of the North Sea a thousand years before. Lars did finish his cycling adventure around Australia before returning to Germany and his life there. I am not sure the wilds of Australia have seen the last of him if our conversation was any guide!

Before heading west across the Gulf, towards Katherine, there was one remaining gorge to visit. The most magnificent gorge in Queensland and one of the most spectacular across Australia: Lawn Hill.

The road into Lawn Hill National Park, known as Boodjamulla to Aboriginal people, was rough, jolting, and jarring; its corrugations and washouts the perfect excuse to slow down and watch the seemingly never-ending plains roll by. There was a harmony to this country with the willowy scrub and grass covering the rocky foreground, towered over by sharp, angled ranges in the distance, presenting a perfectly proportioned Australian landscape. This relationship came to define how I saw and understood the allure of the Gulf country. The other thing I noticed were the cattle. The Gulf is cattle country. Most tended to stay in small mobs a little off the road with their sleek white shapes, heads down grazing or heading to or from water, matching the leanness and brightness of the land itself.

Most cattle were of the Bos Indicus breed, Brahman and Brahman-cross, given their ability to survive and prosper in the tropics. Their sleekness was quite a contrast to the rounder, heavier Bos Taurus breeds such as Hereford and Angus, and their respective crossbreeds, commonly seen further south. In the vastness of the Gulf country, the mobs were few and far between reflecting just how far off the road most watering points tended to be. In addition to the cattle, my other memory of the track was the never-ending corrugations as my vehicle shuddered and bounced its way towards the purple-blue smudge in the distance that barely hinted at the stunning natural jewel it contained.

Lawn Hill Gorge, an emerald-green oasis in an otherwise brown sea of grass and dust, is an unlikely haven as I ever expected to find. In the dust and heat of the Gulf in the Dry, I would never have believed such a wonderful natural jewel could exist. As I relaxed into its refreshing waters, my appreciation for Nature's propensity to create places of such natural splendour reminded me it was the most natural occurrence. Yet, even then, it was almost impossible to believe the sumptuous delights created in the otherwise dry, hard, and rocky land.

The waterhole at the front of the lower gorge was one of the most enrapturing I enjoyed on my journey across Australia. The water was crystal clear, its freshness and purity the ideal tonic for the aches and pains willingly endured in reaching its sanctuary. There were fish every-where: I felt I was swimming in an aquarium. From the pandanus palms, eucalyptus trees, and grasses thickly lining its banks, an almost impen-etrable forest of green, to the plethora of insects and birds flying across the waterhole, there was life everywhere. Swimming felt like an intimate massage with the cool, caressing touch of the water appreciatively dis-solving the gritty feel of dirt, smoke, and sweat, banishing it back to the land from which it came. Looking into the azure-blue sky, while lying on my back treading water, there was no other place I would rather have been.

Lawn Hill Gorge is carved through the Constance Range; a range formed from sandy sediments deposited on the edge of the North Aus-tralian Craton around 1.5 billion years ago and subsequently uplifted in an ancient orogeny: the degree of uplift clearly visible whether canoeing the gorge or walking the land today. The diversity of Lawn Hill's gorges reflected Nature's geological, biological, and zoological DNA: their combined influence the reason for a place of splendour in this otherwise dry and rocky land.

While much of the gorge walls remained hidden by a thick, green leafy screen, the tough, scrubby nature of the country quickly reasserted itself above the waterline. Here, the flora appeared as sharp and stunted as the land from which it grew. For this was generally a hot, dry place with Nature's balm primarily limited to the waters of the gorge itself. Walking across the sharp, baking rocks to the top of the gorge, I could see how the river had changed course many times over the countless millennia suggesting it was not always the luxuriating presence enjoyed today. And how the quiet, gentled place I now rolled out my swag was only a very recent stage in the long geological history of that ancient place.

Canoeing through the gorge, on the other hand, felt similar to entering another of Nature's cathedrals. The ochre-red gorge walls, baking in the hot midday sun, rose directly from the rippled, glistening emerald-green waters: the uplifted sediments showing exactly where they had been cleaved from their original position. The sweet fragrance off the water picked up whenever the breeze did: the wind grabbing the bow of my canoe like a playful spirit and trying to turn it in the direction of my camp. At the top of the lower gorge was a small waterfall, the perfect place to relieve myself of all clothing in the heat of the day and sit under its cool, refreshing, tumbling waters. With a quick portage past these falls, fully clothed once again, the upper gorge was finally reached. And what a place of equal allure it also turned out to be.

The upper gorge was more open than the lower gorge for the walls did not rise as high and were further apart. The wafting, enveloping natural fragrances, including a tangy eucalyptus smell in the heat of the day and a sweet, refreshing fragrance off the water in the cool of dusk, were intoxicatingly heady. Canoeing through the gorge, I felt surrounded by life as the bush pulsated in the heat of a summer day with the gentle didgeridoo-like hum of an insect concerto. Yet, just a few metres above the water line, it too became a rocky former shell of itself. Which is why the campsite on the lower gorge waterhole was such a delight.

That campsite at Lawn Hill was one of the most relaxing and well kept I found on my journey. Plenty of shade, warm showers, and several fire pits made it a place to stay and relax for some time. Even more appreciated was the sandy softness of the ground which made it the ideal place to rest under the magnificence of the starlit night sky. Like other similarly appreciated campsites on my journey, it engendered a feeling of peace and harmony for all irrespective of our backgrounds or nationalities. The distances travelled and the days spent enjoying its quiet luxury encouraged friendships in a way other remoter campsites did not. It even included a friendly camp kangaroo who drank wine from my cup if given half a chance!

Given these influences, I was not surprised to experience another memorable night on the road at Lawn Hill, with a simple "*G'day*" and an offer to share a bottle of wine around a fire the perfect catalyst for another remarkable evening. Under the stars of the Southern Cross, in a fascinating group of travellers from Germany, Switzerland, Britain, and Italy, our conversation was as wide ranging and insightful as the land itself.

From Western history and Eastern philosophy, to Aboriginal culture and the state of the global environment, our conversation flowed freely and uninhibited until the fire and bottle of wine had long been consigned to the past. It was another of those times I never wanted to end, when I realised how much we have in common with all human beings, and how much we could learn if only we would listen. It did not appear anyone had an agenda to push or an argument to win that night. It was simply a free flow of ideas that were treated with equal respect and equal time, with everybody leaving that fire more educated than when we arrived.

Nevertheless, despite the fascinating ebb and flow of that conversation, as is the way of walkabout, we were never to return to that special place as most of the group left the following morning. Yet the insights of that evening are with me still, as are the faces and voices from all those years ago. Most of all, I remember the handwritten note I found on my vehicle's windscreen later the following day, after coming back from another canoe trip through the gorge, which quoted several lines from Frederick Nietzsche regarding the importance of a soul connection to the natural world to truly understand ourselves. A philosophy we unfortunately seem to need to relearn as a society once again.

What made Lawn Hill even more fascinating as a campsite was that we were merely the most recent in a long line of travellers across the millennia to have enjoyed its bounty and pleasures. For it is estimated that Aboriginal Australians previously lived in its sanctuary for at least 30,000 years: that is for at least six times as long as the history of Western civilisation.

Overlooking the gorge in the evening light, I found it intriguing to think back to those long gone days and how different yet satisfying life would have been for the original inhabitants of that place. With an abundance of animal, bird, and fish life in and around the gorge, and a smorgasbord of plants, it must have been an epicurean delight with minimal work required to prosper, let alone survive. Every now and then, I sensed voices from the past as a light breeze brought a strange yet happy sound to my ears. It would not surprise me should the spirits of those people continue to return to this magnificent gorge and its multitude of delights, even after all this time.

And while Aboriginal history is ancient from a humanity perspective, it is actually relatively recent in terms of the gorge's other previous inhabitants. For, just to the south, at the Riversleigh Fossil Site, Nature has tantalisingly revealed its history from the last 25 million years. Here, evidence of a time when marsupial lions, carnivorous kangaroos, and giant snakes roamed this region is found. So far, over 200 previously unknown species of mammals, reptiles, birds, and fish have been unearthed that show over 20 million years of evolution for some species.

It is a history that shows humanity is a very recent branch on Nature's evolutionary tree. Not that I needed much convincing given how many other times a similar reality had played out before me!

My last experience at Lawn Hill was a quiet, secluded, early morning swim on the day I left. The sun had barely risen as I gently immersed myself into the waters of the lower gorge; the golden rays across the tops of the trees a visible reflection in the still waters below. The moon was full: its round, white shape reflected in the waterhole as a small pearl high in the early morning sky. Swimming out into the dawn's reflection across the gorge, I felt completely accepted by the natural world. I was part of it. It was part of me. I could never feel lonely surrounded by its living beings for I was one with them and they were one with me. It was a moment of pure rapture with Nature on all levels. Everything I needed to be happy and healthy was around me or within me.

With that last swim, and final insight, it was time to leave the majesty of Lawn Hill and its ancient history. It was time to leave its recharging oasis and return to the track for other alluring delights that would inspire and entice as much as the charms of its gorge had soothed and succoured. It was time to travel into the vastness of the Gulf country. It was time to follow the Gulf Track and its 1,100 kilometres of dust, rocks, and corrugations across the long, wide curve of the Gulf of Carpentaria.

10

A Vision Splendid

'Their tents in the evening would whiten
The scrub, and the flash of their fires
Leap over the shadows to brighten
The way of Ambition's desires;
By the axe-marks we followed their courses,
For scarcely the ashes remain,
And the tracks of the men and the horses
Are hidden by dust-storm and rain.'

Will Ogilvie – The Men Who Blazed the Track

The Great South Land is an extraordinary continent. It is a place of such enchantment and ancient beauty it perpetually amazed and awed, succoured and sustained me during my two years of walkabout. In every sense, its lights, colours, rocks, plants, and animals were elements of alchemy that combined to inspire my fascination for, and connection with, so much of the country travelled through. And the Gulf country was no exception. Following the long, wide curve of the Gulf of Carpentaria to the west, it was a land of big skies, big rivers, and extremely big and lethal saltwater crocodiles: those ancient denizens from the distant age of the dinosaurs. It was a country of broad, sweeping vistas from the brown, dry plains stretching to the horizon under the azure-blue sky to the welcomed forests of paperbark trees and waterlilies lining its many rivers and billabongs. Unexpectedly, one of the most remarkable visions I experienced during my journey across the continent was seen here. Remarkably, it was not a place but rather a person. An Aboriginal gentleman who was the perfect example of who we can become when we learn to live in harmony with the teaching of the natural world. So mesmerising was his presence, so inspiring was his physique, and so integrated was his being, I will never forget him.

Driving west across Northern Australia, after leaving Lawn Hill, I felt I was heading back to where my heart truly belongs – the wide-open spaces of the Australian Outback. While the Gulf Track was the only path to follow geographically, its route was far more important personally. For its path traces several of the most exciting journeys of exploration across Australia's north: its history resplendent with both adventure and misadventure unlike any other.

Augustus Gregory blazed his trail across the Gulf during his heroic journey from the Victoria River District to the settled regions of Queensland in 1856. It was the track used by pioneering drovers, led by Nat 'Bluey' Buchanan two decades later, when cattle were first overlanded to stock newly established cattle stations in the Northern Territory and the Kimberley. It was the track used by the Duracks when taking cattle from Thylungra to their newly acquired Kimberley stations.

The Gulf Track today mirrors a fascinating history, one that is almost as forgotten as the many graves that line the track of those who did not make it through. Driving its length, I was literally following in the tracks of the early explorers and drovers whose determination and resilience I increasingly respected as one dusty kilometre vibrated into the next.

While the Gulf Track today follows the path of several of Australia's most admired explorers, it also crosses the path of perhaps the best known. Just outside Normanton, the northernmost camp of Burke and Wills is found: Camp 119. It was from here these two explorers made their final push into the mangroves of the Gulf of Carpentaria, achieving their goal of being the first Europeans to cross the Australian continent from south to north, before attempting their arduous return journey to Cooper Creek 1,500 kilometres to the south. Camp 119 was another chance to reflect on the saga of Burke and Wills. There was virtually nothing remaining of their camp: just a few blazed trees and the requisite memorial cairn.

Yet knowing how close they came to achieving their objective, knowing how much an eight-hour difference was going to determine their legacy, I wanted to somehow leave a message for them. A message to hurry, a message to go like the wind. You can survive, you will survive, but you need to hurry. Unfortunately, that message cannot be delivered. They were as subject to their fate as we are each to ours. I felt a certain sadness while visiting this camp, from knowing how close they came to succeeding yet how tragic their failure would be. It was another place in Nature's realm to reflect on how much a twist of fate can impact humanity's grand plans.

From Camp 119, the Gulf Track headed west into the scrub that defines much of the Gulf country today. While geology's role in the creation of this land was always present, it initially played more of a secondary role. It was the flora and fauna that stood out most on passing through this part of Nature's domain. The scrub changed often from broad, sweeping grasslands, dry and brown awaiting the next Wet, to open forests with lush, verdant fern-lined floors. The one constant was the dust. It trailed my vehicle much as it had every other time I ventured onto the dirt. Mind you, I think the dust and corrugations were there for a reason. For they encouraged me to turn off the track and enjoy various campsites along the banks of different rivers, each of which had a unique feel and a distinct pleasure.

My first night travelling the Gulf Track was spent at Kingfisher Camp; a small oasis 40 kilometres off the main track named for the birds that woke me the following morning with their engaging, energetic, raucous calls. This camp on the Nicholson River was the perfect location to unwind after a day spent absorbing the dust and corrugations, with its cool, refreshing waters and grassy shade the perfect tonic for any travelling ailment. The opportunity to sleep on the soft, sandy ground in my swag, enveloped by the all-pervading smell of eucalyptus as the stars mirrored the sparks from my fire, was an experience that never lost its appeal.

Camping on the Nicholson River was also important personally. For it represented an opportunity to cross the long-forgotten tracks of one of my earliest mentors: one whose adventures had stirred and enthralled from the moment I first heard his name many years before. For it was at Turn-off Lagoon, on the Nicholson River to the east, one of the most successful and quietest achievers in the pantheon of Australian pioneers, Nat 'Bluey' Buchanan, commenced his epic cattle drives west along the Gulf Track.

Buchanan was the Gulf Track's droving pioneer, initially taking 1,200 head of cattle across in 1878-79; a journey on which Aboriginal people determined to protect their land killed one of his small droving party. Two years later he used the same track as the last leg of one of the largest and longest cattle drives ever undertaken in Australian history – 20,000 head of cattle were walked over 2,500 kilometres from properties in Southwest Queensland to their new home on the Daly River in the Northern Territory.

It was cattle drives like this, undertaken across the tough and unrelenting country of Northern Australia, which have come to represent the foundation of Australia's pastoral and pioneering heritage. To follow his tracks, to see the land as he had first seen it, was a great privilege given how much his remarkable story had enthralled me for a long time.

Buchanan was an extraordinary Australian, in a pantheon of remarkable achievers, whose pioneering successes warrant far greater recognition than he receives today. He was the consummate bushman and horseman, opening up more of Australia's frontier than probably any other person. His ability to guide and drove large mobs of cattle through the largely unexplored Australian bush, his significant feats of solo exploration across some of the most trying environments on the continent, and the humility he brought to his achievements made him one of the most respected Australians of his time. Even into his seventies, Buchanan continued to explore parts of Australia that previously defeated men half his age.

Most importantly of all, he was highly respectful in his contact with Indigenous Australians. He appreciated and understood their walkabout lifestyle and how valuable their experience and knowledge was. His respect for Aboriginal people, and his inclusion of them into his droving plants and station stock camps, placed him in high esteem among the First Australians in the country he worked. Even today, Buchanan is spoken of with respect amongst Aboriginal Elders for his compassionate and fair ways in an otherwise quite brutal time for Aboriginal people.

And this was just the start of his impact. Before my journey was over, I would cross his tracks many more times so prolific was his drive for pioneering the country. His respect for, and achievements across, the rugged frontier of the Australian continent remain an inspiration for those who seek to live with as much of a sense of adventure and connection to the bush as Nat Buchanan had.

Heading further west, faithfully following the tracks of the early explorers and drovers, the country continued to change. One of its more interesting features is Hell's Gate, an oval pile of sedimentary rocks, one on top of the other, like large dumplings. In the track's early days, police escorted westbound travellers as far as these rocks. After that, they were on their own for another 1,000 kilometres until reaching Katherine. This meant surviving the ever-present threat of local Aboriginal people defending their land, fever, starvation, and thirst, not to mention the deprivations of their fellow travellers. Fortunately, my list of concerns was a lot smaller. It was only Nature's impressive power and predators I needed to be concerned with!

Nature's power was most exemplified by the many rivers crossed that, while they breached the track regularly, were anything but monotonous. Most rivers here were very wide compared to those in the south of the continent, with the volumes of water churning down their course during the Wet mind-boggling. It was through noting the dead grass, sticks, and branches high in the trees I realised what a powerful, uncontrollable force Nature was in this part of the continent during the Wet. Yet, in the Dry, those same rivers showed vistas of luxurious beauty with their waterholes an appreciated, shady oasis from the dusty, jarring experience that was driving the track.

The Wearyan River was one such place with the peacefulness of my camp another reminder of Nature's propensity to provide for our physical and spiritual nourishment at all times. The camp I chose that evening, upstream from the main crossing, was just off the Gulf Track. I had noticed an overgrown path meandering roughly through the bush and followed it more out of curiosity than anything else. To my complete surprise, the oasis created by Nature on this river astounded me. Even if I had conjured up a vision of the perfect camp during my long days on the track, it would not have done this particular place justice.

The sun was slowly setting when I arrived; the cool curtain of relief at dusk a most appreciated respite from the tiredness that had set in after another long day's driving. Yet, on arriving at this magnificent waterhole, the stresses and strains of the day quickly melted away. The waterhole stretched out before me across the width of the river like a rippled mirror. The golden glow of the sun's evening light, with just a hint of an orange-purple shading on the horizon, and the pale greens and whites of the surrounding trees and grasses were faithfully reflected across its surface. The soft gurgling of a small waterfall was the only sound I heard except for the lazy rustle of leaves as a slight breeze gently massaged all living things.

I also remember this camp with particular fondness for there were no mosquitoes and, accordingly, the mosquito net was appreciatively not required. Over the next four months, when in Northern Australia,

I fastidiously tucked its edges under my swag each night otherwise my sleep was of a most disturbed kind!

The natural allure of the waterhole was particularly enticing for a quick swim. It was such a peaceful and relaxing location: just the place to cleanse myself of the dust, smoke, and aches of long days on the track. There were no crocodile marks in the sand along the edge of the water-hole and, as I watched the sunset over its waters, nothing stuck its head up for a look. Yet this was the Gulf and I could not take that chance, especially where it was just the crocodiles and I. Instead, I revelled in a bucket shower, the first of many for the course of my journey west, high in the rocks away from the water. It was just as refreshing as taking a swim without any of the inherent dangers.

Sitting on the smooth, worn rocks overlooking the waterhole, refreshed once again, I gratefully indulged in my favourite dusk ritual of simply watching the splendour of the sunset unfold. And what a unique indulgence that evening turned out to be. For that sunset over the Wea-ryan River was truly magnificent. Light clouds had rolled in from the west, which was like adding fuel to the fire. The western sky exploded in a blaze of colour; the light clouds a canvas on which the intensity of the slowly changing orange, pink, and purple contours of dusk were captured then lost. It was a sunset watched in perpetual gratitude as the light transforming the sky was perfectly reflected across the waterhole. It was another time I felt intimately connected with the bush and its moods, and inspired by how each scene nurtured and enraptured my whole being.

Intriguingly, as if to remind me of Nature's ability to induce different moods and feelings during the course of the day, I woke to a quite sober-ing view of the waterhole the following morning. Instead of the strong early morning light, with its chorus of birds to wake me from the depths of my slumber, the dawn was grey, damp, and very still. A fog had qui-etly closed in during the night covering everything in its light grey blan-ket of moisture. The landscape from the previous evening looked and felt completely different. Even the waterhole looked smaller, somehow shrunken and degraded, from the mesmerising vista it had been the previous evening.

As the sun strove to break through, its rays weakly attempting to penetrate the gloom, my overall feeling was one of lethargy. The magnificent waterhole that inspired and awed me with its delights the previous evening had become less welcoming in some manner, less hospitable. The uplifting feeling previously enjoyed had completely changed for the waterhole now looked somewhat sinister with no reflection off its surface. And perhaps appropriately given the predators likely resting in the murky depths below.

It was the only time during my travels I encountered such a significant change in the look and feel of a particular place overnight. In hindsight though, I suspect Nature was just resetting my perspective given the vision splendid it was about to reveal. One of the most magnificent of my journey!

Nature's ability to create scenes of untrammelled beauty each day was a constant theme throughout my journey across the Gulf, and Australia. From spectacular gorges to ancient weathered ranges, the underlying geological base defined much of the country travelled through. Wherever I looked, scenes of sculptured geological perfection existed across Nature's broad canvas that inspired and uplifted me on every level. And incredibly, it was not just its geological sculptures that astounded me. For Nature was equally capable of creating biological sculptures of such magnificence, such beauty, they appeared so much a part of the country they could have been carved from the land itself.

It was during my travels along the Gulf Track I experienced a striking vision that will remain with me always: one of the most physically impressive human beings I have ever seen. This particular Aboriginal man, so well proportioned, defined, and beautiful he could have been a modern-day warrior, appeared sculpted from the land through which I passed. He was a monument to the underlying dignity of the human body as built by Nature's hand: one of pure health, pure muscle, and pure life. He represented another of Nature's core lessons – the DNA that created stunning natural vistas was equally capable of creating perfect human beings to wander over, and wonder at, those same vistas.

Most of the travellers I passed were of European ancestry, with the latest 4WD and gadgets, yet unhealthy and unaware of the beauty surrounding them given how disconnected they had become from the natural world. Yet, this Aboriginal man, walking along the side of the track, seemingly oblivious to the impact of modern-day living, fully embodied the physical and philosophical attributes of his country. Attributes many in the West increasingly seek today.

I stopped to offer some assistance but it was not required. I do not think he knew much English though his body spoke volumes for the benefits of a natural life. He was about my height and pure, lean muscle. He was wearing a pair of jeans and a broad brimmed Akubra. That was it. His chest was covered in tribal markings with the deep gouges creating a unique tartan pattern with the special mark of his clan. His stomach muscles rippled like the ancient rock laid down when much of this land was a shallow sea floor. His back and arms were pure energy, radiating power and strength when he made even the most gentle of movements.

In fact, so closely did his body resemble the country, he appeared carved from the land itself. He was perfectly proportioned and perfectly built. Everything was as Nature intended. Everything about his life and physical prowess spoke to the benefits humanity could also achieve if only we lived as he did. In accordance with the teaching of the natural world.

Watching him walk slowly, but proudly, through the light red dust thrown up by the passing parade of 4WDs was to witness another example of Western society's failure to see the reality. Most people drove by without even noticing him; their air-conditioned, bull bar wrapped vehicles insulating them from the hot, humid reality of the country much as their lifestyle of pills and myths insulated them from the short-term cost of dis-ease. It was living in the natural world, in this tough environment, that had created a human being whose physical prowess exemplified all we can achieve when not ignoring the reality of our evolution.

Despite his lack of material possessions and the hard country where he lived, this gentleman had the one critical attribute many people in Western society desperately seek today – complete health and the physical prowess to match. Despite his supposed lack of education, from a European perspective, and the simple life he lived, my intuition told me we still have much to learn from the knowledge held by this Aboriginal man, and his people, regarding the importance of Nature's teaching to the health of both the individual and our society.

Even today, 15 years later, it is the vision of that gentleman I look to most of all as the perfect example of the health possible when we live with respect for the wisdom of the natural world. While it was Nature who taught me the fundamental importance of meditation, exercise, a healthy diet, and sleep to achieving the level of wellness I sought, it was this Aboriginal gentleman, and the older, inspiring couple I met at Ormiston Gorge, who exemplified, most of all, what was possible when these elements were incorporated into a life well lived.

Aboriginal Australians represent one of the most impressive societies on Earth: a society whose forebears survived across countless millennia while many others failed. In fact, their society is the oldest, continual civilisation known to exist. Aboriginal people are estimated to have lived in Australia for at least 65,000 years following their arrival from South East Asia: a period at least 12 times the duration of Western civilisation. Tragically, when Europeans discovered Australia, Aboriginal people were treated with brutal disdain at best and brutal destruction at worst based on their lack of the thin veneer of European civilisation.

Unfortunately, men who recognised and respected their intelligence and aptitude, men like Will Ogilvie, John McDouall Stuart, Ernest Giles, Charles Sturt, Patsy Durack, Hubert Wilkins, Nat Buchanan, Augustus Gregory, and John Eyre, were in the minority. Accordingly, much blood was tragically spilt as Aboriginal people sought to protect their land, and culture, from the ravages of fast encroaching pastoralists and miners.

While the pioneering history of Australia is one to be proud of in many respects, it is also important to recognise the appalling treatment of Indigenous Australians during this period: a treatment based on an ignorant view of how their society functioned. For, as we have subsequently learnt, a comparison of pre-European Australia to the development of European, Middle Eastern, and Asian civilisations highlights why Aboriginal Australians did not develop their civilisation in a similar manner. And accordingly, how wrong initial European views of Aboriginal society, and its true worth to a broader Australian society, actually were.

It is only quite recently we have come to appreciate Aboriginal Australians actually enjoyed a quality of life that was significantly better than that of most Europeans at that time, in terms of both the control they had over their lives and their standard of living. Given their stewardship of the land, and how well they understood its bounty across the regions and seasons, they did not have to live the grinding life of poverty most Europeans were forced to endure at that time.

When most Europeans were peasants, working perpetually under various forms of servitude, Aboriginal people were instead relatively free. They were able to harvest the resources they needed, and prepare for subsequent needs through their judicious use of farming and the firestick, in far less time than Europeans could at that time. Incredibly, it gave them a freedom of lifestyle only the European landed gentry also enjoyed.

Unlike most Europeans, who primarily lived on the plot of land they were born, Aboriginal Australians' connection to their land meant it did not make sense to stay in one place for all the resources required. Instead, they moved across their land to be there when it produced its bounty: an approach that provided the nourishment required using far less effort. Additionally, Aboriginal lore, and people's respect for that lore, provided a very different protection for their country and resources compared to the overt, legally based violence Europeans used. Reflecting these physical and philosophical differences, Aboriginal people did not develop the same attachment to a particular place whereas most Europeans had no choice. Instead, Aboriginal people developed a connection to all the land, even that outside their direct control.

The one factor that appears to have enabled Aboriginal Australia to live this way, and never required they take their society to the next level of organisation, was the low level of population they maintained relative to the land they managed. As they cared for the land and its resources, so they managed their population to ensure they stayed in balance with the land's capacity for supporting their people: an approach Europeans never considered given their different religious and economic beliefs.

This fundamentally different life philosophy encouraged Europeans, and many other civilisations, to develop their society in a manner that supported and took advantage of their increasing population density instead of harmonising their lifestyle and society with the resources of the land as Aboriginal society did.

The state of Aboriginal society when Europeans first arrived did not reflect a lack of intelligence or work ethic. Instead, it reflected a very different developmental trajectory given Aboriginal people's diametrically opposing views on how they should interact with their environment. Aboriginal Australians sought to live in harmony with their land, seeing themselves as part of it, and only took what they needed to survive. Whereas Europeans took the opposite view, particularly under their religious and racial beliefs they were the superior, entitled species and the environment was there to serve them. Moreover, if it did not, they would find a way to make sure it did whatever the cost.

This simple difference, of choosing to belong to the Earth versus choosing to see yourself as the superior species granted some mythical right to take and destroy, was the fundamental reason why Aboriginal and European societies developed so differently. And why Europeans could not even fathom, let alone understand, how the people on this most ancient of continents were in many ways the more evolved human beings as Sir Hubert Wilkins so intuitively recognised.

Moreover, a review of the destruction wrought on the global environment today highlights how damaging the European approach has been. And, while it may have moved humanity more quickly along its developmental trajectory, in some ways, it appears the ultimate cost may be quite high given the significant environmental problems experienced today and the increasingly difficult problems to be experienced tomorrow. If anything, the extent to which the Australian continent has suffered at the hands of its supposedly more enlightened European inhabitants seems further proof of the importance of Aboriginal wisdom to the healthy functioning of this land. And accordingly, the importance of the wisdom of all nature-based peoples to the healthy functioning of the Earth!

Heading west, my journey continued with the dull roar beneath my 4WD a sure sign the never-ending corrugations were working the suspension as only Australian dirt roads can.

My next stop along the track was the Towns River, another enjoyable location for an overnight camp. Or so I thought from my time on the Wearyan River. However, this time it was clear from the outset why it was so important to stay out of the water in this part of the country. For, in the middle of the river, the tell-tale signs were seen – the rectangular, rounded snouts resting just above the water along with the hint of a body and tail. There were crocodiles everywhere, at least half a dozen or so in front of my camp, with a very loud splash at sunset further reminding me that humanity was nowhere near the top of the food chain here. In fact, we were quite a few links down. I made sure to sleep well away from the water that night, well into the bush, with my vehicle and fire between my swag and the river.

A scan of the water with my torch later that night revealed the full extent of its crocodile population. At least a dozen sets of red eyes stared back at me, occasionally blinking, as I swept the beam over the water. A crocodile's eyes glow red in the light so night was the best time to count how many were out there. Nevertheless, when the torch remained on for too long, the crocodiles slowly submerged with barely a ripple into the inky blackness that was the river at night.

On leaving the Towns River, it was only a short drive to Roper Bar, and the end of the Gulf Track, from where I planned a quick drive through to Katherine and the delights of Edith Falls. However, I had not expected Nature to provide one last example of its ability to create a vision of perfection with its biological DNA.

Lomarieum Lagoon lies to the west of the Towns River. Originally, I had planned to visit the lagoon quickly and then leave, but, on arriving, its splendour touched my soul; its charms so compelling I could not continue until I had spent time savouring its beguiling natural beauty.

The lagoon was surrounded by a forest of paperbark trees with their rough white trunks glowing gold then pink as the sun's march across the horizon slowly came to a close. The banks were lined with waterlilies whose wide-green pads contrasted exquisitely with their stalk-topped snow-white flowers. The breeze off the water was certainly appreciated as the increasing humidity announced the Wet's imminent arrival. I unrolled my swag under several paperbark trees and rested there, just appreciating the day as it unfolded over the lagoon.

It was one of those times that took me back to the slow, halcyon days of childhood. It was one of those times when life slowed and Nature's voice came through loudly and strongly, cajoling me with the simplicity and wisdom of its message. Resting on my swag as the cool of the encroaching dusk gently descended, several realisations pushed their way into my consciousness further realigning my whole being connection with the wisdom of the natural world.

The most important realisation was this – that how we treat Nature is how we treat ourselves… how we treat ourselves is how we treat others… and how we treat others is how we are treated. Ultimately, how we treat Nature plays a significant role in how life treats us. In essence, the quality of our connection with the natural world defines the quality of our experience in life.

This distilling of the most basic tenet of Nature's wisdom was the most profound realisation of my journey. It was the one equation that allowed me to finally piece every thought and feeling inspired by the natural world, since my first memory, into a coherent and simple life philosophy. Most importantly, it is a wisdom that Nature makes available to every living being, including every human being, within its realm.

It is a wisdom found in the harmony of a sunrise or a sunset.

It is a wisdom found in the balance of a natural vista whether the shifting sands of the desert, the structural wonders of a gorge, or a galah on the wing.

It is a wisdom found in all of Nature's creations whether geological, biological, or zoological.

It is a wisdom found in the insights from nature-based peoples across multiple cultures and multiple continents since time immemorial.

It is a wisdom, able to be learnt and applied by every human being, which shows no favour to rich or poor, believer or atheist, capitalist or communist, or anyone in between.

It is a wisdom we can learn to decipher and apply irrespective of education.

In essence, it is the key by which Nature provides all humanity with the same opportunity to reach their full potential despite the fact some people are seemingly born into a life of opportunity while others are seemingly born into a life of poverty.

As I thought back through my own life experiences, I realised it was actually society, not the natural world, which places the most limitations on our ability to live the life of health, happiness, and adventure many intrinsically seek.

Sitting alone by the splendour of Lomarieum Lagoon, a reject from the destructive society I had previously considered myself a part, I realised that as humanity destroys the natural world so it is slowly destroying itself. From human-induced climate change to the increasing destruction of the oceans and forests, from the poisoning of our food and health systems to the sixth mass extinction now underway, humanity is slowly destroying the very habitat that gives us life.

Seemingly, in tandem, we are destroying ourselves with the increasing incidence of cancer, obesity, heart disease, depression, autism, memory loss, uncontrolled drug use, violence at an individual and societal level, the rise of celebrity culture, and the ignorant preaching of so-called religious leaders across all faiths just a few of the leading indicators of this new toxic reality.

Our current choices, and the increasingly self-inflicted consequences of those poor choices, only serve to highlight how much modern-day society has fundamentally lost its connection with the essence of Nature's teaching. Despite all our advances as human beings, despite how proud many feel at the 'accomplishments' of humanity, we remain locked into many of the original sins that have bedevilled society from the dawn of time. Yet, where we live in harmony with the natural world, where we trust in its teaching and the inherent goodness of its wisdom, we can achieve a far healthier state for our whole being with the balance and awareness such insight brings to our lives.

In reality, living in harmony with the natural world, living with humility as a branch on its magnificent tree of life, is the only way to mitigate the small and large problems we face today. For, as I learnt, until we incorporate the benefits of Nature's teaching into our lives, we can never, we will never, find true balance and happiness in our lives. Until we resonate with the rhythms of the natural world, we can never fully align with Nature's power and all that we can be as part of its magnificent domain. And that is our loss alone!

It was difficult to leave Lomarieum Lagoon given its physical charms and philosophical insights. Nevertheless, the road still called as the Wet was building and this was the last place I wanted to spend it. The end of the Gulf Track was reached a short distance away, at Roper Bar, where a rocky path across the Roper River was the only place to cross it safely more than 80 kilometres upstream. The Roper River was a mighty expanse of water:

its banks thickly lined with trees, bushes, and grasses sprouting a plethora of insect and bird life. In fact, of all the rivers crossed during my trip across the Gulf, it was the most impressive. It must surely be a fearful sight when it comes down in full flood during the Wet as evidenced by the grass, sticks, and branches high in the trees overhead.

From Roper Bar, the road led past the oasis of Mataranka to where all roads eventually lead in the Northern Territory – the path of that indomitable explorer, John McDouall Stuart: the Stuart Highway. From there, it was a short drive back to Katherine and Edith Falls to enjoy its charming waterfall and gorge. It was just the haven in which to savour a few relaxing days before, once again, resuming my journey west.

Leaving Edith Falls, I followed the road west into the Victoria River District, so named for the spectacular Victoria River whose meandering path carved the many panoramas of magnificent grandeur seen today. The long, deep valleys, their walls a deep ochre-red with the many sedimentary layers clearly visible, showed in spectacular detail how the country had evolved. The panoramas of valley and range ran one into the next as I followed the narrow strip of bitumen along an ancient valley floor. To fully appreciate the splendour of these ranges required pulling over to the side of the road and exploring the country up close.

Experiencing the ranges in this way was to see them in their hereditary uniqueness. It was only then I came to appreciate the surprising lack of tectonic influence unlike most other ranges seen. Not for these ranges the difficult birth endured by many others across the Australian continent. There was not even a hint of uplift so parallel to the horizon were the different sediments lying flat today. This became clear on their summit, as I looked over the panorama before me, for the flat-topped ranges were all the same height and it was the creeks and rivers that had carved out the valleys and plains seen below.

Yet, it was not just the underlying geology that defined the Victoria River country. Its unique and startling flora played an equally important role. It was here the boab tree first impinged on my consciousness: the tree Aboriginal people believe was pulled out by an angry deity and jammed back upside down. Looking at several large boab trees, it was hard to argue with this description for their tangle of leafless branches in the Dry looked exactly as a root system would normally look. Furthermore, it was not just the boab trees that made the scene different to anything seen before.

New, intriguing species of palm, eucalyptus, and acacia trees grew randomly across the ridges and gullies with their contrasting colours and shapes further enhancing the region's unique appeal. Most welcome of all were the tell-tale clumpy, spiky plants that dotted the ranges with a far greater regularity, and whose presence always spelt Outback: spinifex. Since last seeing this plant in Central Australia, I had missed its rounded, bushy shape and the smoky-honey smell of its sticky resin. That was until I walked through the ranges and its spiky barbs pierced my jeans and legs making my meandering path much slower, longer, and more painful than would otherwise have been the case!

While I was intrigued and inspired by the rugged yet nuanced beauty of the Victoria River country, it was not the primary reason I chose to travel this road. For, on the bank of the Victoria River to the west, an ancient boab tree survives that provided a connection to another mentor whose life had inspired me from childhood. An explorer whose path I had earlier followed on the Gulf Track: Sir Augustus Gregory.

Augustus Gregory, another member of the pantheon of great Australian explorers, was a man of the Enlightenment with an extraordinary ability to operate on the intellectual and physical frontiers in all respects. One of the few early explorers who took the time to learn the country, working within its natural rhythms, he opened up some of its most remote regions. He was a man of science, a man of Nature, a man of great action and achievement, and a man today hardly remembered compared to many of his lesser contemporaries.

Gregory came to understand and appreciate the ways of the Australian bush, much of it learned from Aboriginal people as a child, as he was unwittingly trained by the land itself for his future surveying and exploration achievements. Like John McDouall Stuart, his exploration was undertaken entirely on horseback; his success across the rugged country he traversed highlighting an extraordinary level of practical horsemanship. This was not the only distinction he shared with Stuart, however, for he was also not to lose a single man during his numerous expeditions. Reflecting his extensive exploration success across both Northern and Western Australia, Gregory was awarded the Founder's Medal from the Royal Geographical Society. Additionally, he was subsequently knighted for his significant contribution to Queensland society in a number of roles, with his services to exploration a key part of that recognition.

The principle camp for the expedition Gregory led into the Victoria River District, the North Australian Expedition 1855-56, is found on the western bank of the Victoria River – an ancient boab tree, with the dates 'October 13th 1855' and 'July 2nd 1856' carved across its weathered, bulbous trunk, marking the camp's location. Standing next to that same boab tree, on a warm October day in 2003, looking across the vastness of the Victoria River, I felt a strong connection with the life of this great Australian explorer. It would not have surprised me if Gregory himself had walked out of the scrub at that moment, much as John McDouall Stuart could have done at Chambers Pillar, given how little the land had changed since he had first seen it.

Thomas Baines, the artist on the expedition, painted many scenes from around the camp with a pair of boab trees often in the background. Impressively, even today, those same boab trees remain exactly as painted all those years ago. It appeared the clock had been turned back 148 years so faithfully did his paintings reflect the reality of those long gone days.

It was from this camp Gregory explored the unknown regions further to the south and west, spending almost nine months continuously in the saddle. Much of the country driven through today shows how challenging his work must have been as the broad, rocky ranges that regularly rise above the rivers and creeks are hard and rough. It was difficult enough moving through this country with minimal gear compared to the full expedition accoutrement Gregory and his men had to carry. Walking through the ranges in 2003, I could only imagine how challenging their expedition was and how capable those men were to achieve the success they did. Given the craggy nature of the surrounding country, it was also no surprise that places of natural wonder were found across this land.

Limestone Gorge was one such place: its form, a refreshing waterhole carved from an ancient limestone reef, another reminder of how Northern Australia was once covered by an ancient shallow sea. The chiselled gorge walls rose vertically over the mineralised waters while pandanus palms and tall grasses grew thickly to the water's edge: a similar backdrop to most other rivers across the Gulf. With tall eucalyptus trees branching over the water, covering the waterhole in a dappled shade, it gave the gorge a slightly sinister feel. It seemed the perfect place to find a crocodile. Fortunately, with no drag marks seen in the sand along the waterhole's edge and no snouts resting above the water, it appeared safe for swimming with the cool, refreshing mineralised water the perfect tonic for the roughness of the drive in.

Swimming out into the middle of the gorge on my back, looking into the splendour of the azure-blue sky as the cool waters caressed my body, I felt pampered by the natural world in a most gentle way. Overhead, insects and birds darted in and out of the leaves and branches; the beating of their wings and the cacophony of their calls a wonderful chorus further uplifting my spirit. It was in places like Limestone Gorge I came to appreciate, once again, how fuller and healthier our lives would be if only we respected Nature's unique, time-tested ways. Not to mention how much we could evolve as a species if only we learnt to live in harmony with the underlying wisdom of the world around us: our ultimate creator.

While Gregory initially explored the Victoria River region, it was to be pioneered by cattlemen. In many cases, it was the same drovers and stockmen who initially pioneered Western Queensland and the Gulf who then pushed their mobs west to the Victoria River District and finally into the Kimberley. To travel through this country today is to follow in the unique tracks of those early pioneers. And like much of Northern Australia, the same names kept appearing from the dust-lined pages of history. Nat Buchanan played a significant role in the development of the region as a drover and subsequently through his ownership and development of Wave Hill Station: the station's name derived from the wave-like form of the ranges overlooking the homestead.

The Duracks also played a significant role with their contribution recognised for all time by the bronco panel memorial seen alongside the main highway as it crosses into the East Kimberley. Yet, a little closer to home, just down the track in fact, the Durack saga was to become even more real and personal. I felt the history books were pried open, once again, to allow me to meet the men and women who inspired from such a long time ago. It was another of those times when the connection to the past was so strong I almost felt part of those long gone days.

Bullita Outstation, once owned by the Durack family, lies to the south of Limestone Gorge. The property can be visited today, complete with a Durack 'D' carved on an ancient boab tree outside the old homestead itself. Driving up to the homestead, the old buildings provided a welcome relief to the rigours of the track. It appeared the family and station hands had only recently left, with the saddles and other equipment lined up against the wall and hung from the rafters ready for another day's work. The homestead looked just as I knew a well-run cattle station would look.

The old stockyards were still there and it was not difficult to imagine cattle being worked all those years ago. The yells and grunts of working men, the whinnying and snorting of stock horses as they pulled a calf to the bronco panel, and the bawling of young calves thrown and branded all returned to that place as my experiences reminded me of what a tough place this used to be. Standing alone in the stockyards, I could look back through the distant past and see the smiling, healthy faces of those who had once lived and worked in that place peer back from old photos faithfully remembered.

Fortunately, this was not the last time my path would cross the tracks of these epic pioneers; tracks I had first picked up at Thylungra and then followed across the Gulf. The road west into the Kimberley, ultimately followed to Broome, the Gibb River Road, would provide an opportunity to experience the country just as they had first seen it over 120 years before. Not only that; it would afford an even greater insight into the inspiring successes this intrepid pioneering family achieved.

Telegraph Track through thick scrub, Cape York, QLD, 2003

Low Lake serenity, Cape York, QLD, 2003

Lower gorge magnificence, Lawn Hill, QLD, 2003

My kangaroo friend, Lawn Hill, QLD, 2003

Wearyan River reflections, Gulf Track, NT, 2003

Wearyan River at dusk, Gulf Track, NT, 2003

Nicholson River reflections, Gulf Track, NT, 2003

A magical place, Lomarieum Lagoon, NT, 2003

Kimberley dawn, Gibb River Road, WA, 2003

Manning Gorge at dusk, Gibb River Road, WA, 2003

Dimond Gorge at noon, Gibb River Road, WA, 2003

Sir John Gorge at dusk, Gibb River Road, WA, 2003

Desert sands meet the ocean, Cape Leveque, WA, 2003

A river's reflective beauty, Ord River, WA, 2003

A perfect sunset, Ord River, WA, 2003

One of a kind, Bungle Bungle Range, WA, 2003

Some of the oldest country on Earth, Pilbara, WA, 2003

Dales Gorge at dusk, Pilbara, WA, 2003

Kalamina Gorge in afternoon sun, Pilbara, WA, 2003

Storm gathering over the ranges, Pilbara, WA, 2003

Reflective beauty of Hamersley Gorge, Pilbara, WA, 2003

Yardie Creek Gorge, Cape Range, WA, 2003

Walkabout end in sight, Murchison River, WA, 2003

Last walkabout camp, Lake Hart, SA, 2003

Railway line at dusk, Lake Hart, SA, 2003

Salt lake from Stuart Highway, Lake Hart, SA, 2003

Heading east to Sydney, Great Australian Bight, SA, 2003

11

The Last Frontier

'Two worlds there are for mortal men,
As far apart as pole from pole,
Each lifted from the other's ken
To solace each a separate soul;
The world of bustle, cramp, and crowd,
Of clanking wheels and clanging bells—
And a dear world of wind and cloud,
And fenceless plains and open fells.'

Will Ogilvie – Two Worlds

The Kimberley region of Western Australia is one of the last frontiers, not only in Australia but also on Earth. Its ancient sandstone and quartzite ranges, untamed rivers, and awe-inspiring opulence make it one of the few truly wild places humanity can still enjoy Nature's pure embrace. From the spectacular, chiselled escarpment of the Cockburn Range to the plethora of magnificent gorges carved through the ancient King Leopold

Ranges, the panoramas were never-ending. The sapphire-blue of the sky, the rich ochre-red of the rugged landscape, and the emerald-green of countless waterholes inspired perpetual wonder at Nature's capacity for untrammelled beauty. It was a place deep within Nature's realm where I never forgot how untamed the Australian continent intrinsically remains. From bushfires and crocodiles to vast expanses of country barely touched since the dawn of time, the Kimberley defines the wildness of what little remains of the Australian frontier. Of all the regions visited across Australia, it was this rugged, fascinating land that mesmerised and awed me at every turn. The everyday showing Nature's capacity to create works of such splendour as to humble those who experience their majesty.

The best way, the only way, to fully experience this country is to drive the Gibb River Road: the track that runs through the heart of the Kimberley. Including the many detours to its spectacular gorges, the track was almost 1,000 kilometres of dust and rocks interspersed with millions of corrugations of which my vehicle and I felt every one!

Heading west, the Gibb River Road started under the majestic ramparts of the Cockburn Range whose imposing grandeur is the gateway to the East Kimberley. Much of the East Kimberley region is an ancient sea floor, like the Victoria River country to the east, with its sandstone and limestone sediments eroded over the countless millennia to create the plethora of ranges, plains, and gorges seen today. Further west, evidence from the formation of the early Australian continent defines the landscape with uplifted, folded, and faulted ranges showing where ancient sedimentary layers were forged into the most brilliant of natural sculptures.

Nature's DNA defined this country in every respect. From the cliffs and gorges creating its rugged character to the diverse flora and fauna gentling the plethora of idyllic oases of today, there was barely a hint of humanity. While every type of gorge and range I wanted to explore was found here, it was the wildness of the country that transformed the landform into the physical and spiritual sanctuary I had been seeking on my

Australian journey. And, as if to set the Kimberley standard at the same level as that of Northern and Central Australia, the first gorge along the track was one whose beguiling nature astounded me from the moment I stepped into its welcoming embrace.

Emma Gorge, in the El Questro Wilderness Park, is just one of the many splendid gorges that grace the East Kimberley. It pampered and delighted me in a way impossible to experience within humanity's artificially created places today. The slow walk into the gorge wound up a small creek, over and around large boulders, and through lush vegetation. The palms, ferns, and tall eucalyptus trees inside the gorge starkly contrasted with the scrubby, stunted trees and spinifex surviving outside its oasis. It became clear very quickly most plants had learnt to survive in a land that was dry for much of the year unlike those who were fortunate to live within the watery confines of its gorges, rivers, and creeks.

One of the more interesting rocks I came across on my walk into the gorge, and throughout Northern and Central Australia, was ripple rock: its undulating surface like the beach at low tide a hint of the role ancient seas played in creating the sedimentary blanket covering much of Northern Australia today. Walking into the gorge, following the flowing creek back to the liquid motherlode, the air was alive with the sounds of insects and birds. It was also full of moisture as the humidity slowly built. There is nothing quite like humidity, exercise, and drinking plenty of fresh water to cleanse our bodies as my shirt quickly showed!

Then I reached it, the shallow pool at the bottom of Emma Falls. With its full, round, sumptuous form hidden in the shadows, it took a little time for my eyes to adjust to the lack of light and fully appreciate its unique enchantment. The gorge itself was quite deep: the sunlight only reaching into its depths for a short time each day over the chiselled walls that stretched high into the sapphire-blue sky. And when the sun surmounted those walls, its golden touch slowly worked its way across the shallow pool turning the water a lavish emerald-green. The gorge walls were covered in a luxuriant foliage of ferns and mosses off whose leaves water gently dripped like a million tiny waterfalls into the pool below. It was a scene of geological and biological nuance as only created by Nature's hand.

The pool at the base of the falls was appreciatively refreshing with its cool, delicate touch more than worth the effort involved in reaching its sanctuary. Slowly relaxing into its watery depths, I was caressed in a most sensuous manner. I had no desire to splash or dive in. It was enough to slowly sink and be enveloped with all the tenderness Nature was capable. It was deep and relaxing enough that I could leave the heat, dust, and humidity of the outside world behind for as long as I stayed within its cool, nurturing embrace.

Emma Gorge was a most appropriate welcome to this part of the country. For, from the moment I arrived until it was nothing more than a receding vision in the rear-view mirror, the East Kimberley seduced and inspired me on every level. It was resplendent with natural jewels barely touched by humanity allowing Nature to surprise, beguile, and inspire those who sought its natural treasures.

El Questro Gorge was another such place. It was quite a bit smaller and simpler than Emma Gorge with its narrow walls permitting only a hint of light on what was a slightly cloudy day. The walk up through the foliage-swathed interior required I first earn the right to access its sanctuary with its luxury only on offer to those who overcame its challenges along the way.

What pleasure, what sensuousness, awaited my arrival. The cavern-encased pool, with only a small opening to the sky, was among the most intimate of all the gorges I visited across Australia; its deep, cool, and pure water taking my mind off the long, hot walk in. Swimming within its cool, soothing embrace, I felt nothing could hurt me. I felt all was right with the world and my post 'liberation' walkabout was the most natural path to follow. On leaving its waters, my whole being felt completely relaxed: the most luxurious of feelings. While this gorge did not have the stunning grandeur of many others visited, it had something even more special – a nurturing and enveloping caress that made me feel completely safe within its sanctuary. It was a most remarkable place.

While its gorges were spectacular and captivating, the geographic scope of the country intrinsically defined the Kimberley for me. Especially the breathtaking manner in which Nature's hand had carved and moulded the landform into a plethora of exquisite rock sculptures. Whether it was the towering sandstone ramparts of the Cockburn Range, whose soaring conformity revealed its gentle geological beginnings, or the actively created King Leopold Ranges to the west, the character of the Kimberley was defined by the land most of all.

This realisation was first appreciated in the wilds of El Questro, at Branco's Lookout. Perched high atop the ranges, it looked over the Pentecost River, just below its junction with the Chamberlain River, and the meandering course its waters had slowly carved through the underlying formations over millions of years. While spinifex and small, stunted eucalyptus trees registered in my appreciation of the vista, it was the scale and grandeur of the ranges across the horizon that most awed and inspired. And to show the Wet was slowly building, a light squall scudded across the land with its misty droplets barely registering on that hot, humid day.

Fortunately, all Nature requires to create a rainbow is a few drops of moisture, and that is exactly what it did. First, one rainbow appeared: its fleeting form reflecting the reality for most living things in the Kimberley. Then a second rainbow appeared, in tandem, both arching over the ranges and reflecting off the waters of the Pentecost River below. This double rainbow, spreading its delicate colours across the hard, rocky land, completely humbled me. It was another reminder that a harsh geography can be gentled in an instant by a touch of Nature's hand; another reminder an indifference to Nature's teaching can be overcome with just one conscious moment within its exquisite domain.

The East Kimberley is Durack country and it seemed there were as many examples of their pioneering achievements as there were Duracks themselves. Whether it was the Durack Range to the south, the Durack River whose dry, sandy bed I would cross further west along the track, or the Durack 'D' carved into a number of boab trees, the family's contribution to the region's development was seen everywhere. Like other explorers and pioneers, the Duracks regularly carved their initial into the trunk of a tree as a means of marking a boundary or mapping the country.

On El Questro, there was a particularly special connection to those long gone days: another personal link to this most intrepid of pioneering families. For a Durack 'D' is today found at the junction of the Chamberlain and Pentecost Rivers, carved on an ancient boab tree in 1882 while the Duracks were exploring the region after landing on Cambridge Gulf to the north.

A fascinating aspect to the Durack story is that modern-day travellers can experience many of the sights the Duracks first saw all those years ago. As I read the definitive narrative of their exploits during my walkabout, its pages took me back to those pioneering days. They even took me back to the very day that particular tree was marked. History does not get much better than that. Moreover, a look out from the base of that particular boab tree reminded me that not much had changed since it was first marked. The Kimberley is still the frontier. It remains one of the few places globally humanity has been unable to tame.

Hopefully, it will remain this way for a long time to come.

Immersed in the inspiring Durack story, my camp that night was in the bush, just off the track, where I unrolled my swag next to a small, sandy creek. Reflecting a number of fires seen on the horizon through the course of the day's driving, there was a slightly acrid smell of smoke on the breeze as its welcomed arrival cooled my camp. As I boiled my quart-pot, the fire throwing its light to the edge of the creek, I had a sense that evening was not to be like any other. Perhaps it was the spirit of those long gone pioneers, or perhaps it was the wild, untamed nature of the land itself, but my experience that night spoke to the uniqueness of this country far more than at any other time.

As I rested on my swag that evening, I noticed a slight red tinge atop the Cockburn Range: its dark silhouette easily discernible against the brightness of the starlit night sky. The smoke from fires burning across the range had been visible for several days, but not the flames. That night, however, as they reached the edge of the range, their red glow lit the night sky. It was a stunning light show, this fiery gift from Nature. Sparks and embers fell from the cliff top, floating to the ground hundreds of metres below, in a blaze of red and orange. It was captivating to watch the line of flames as it danced across the horizontal range before cascading over the edge in a magnificent waterfall of light.

Yet the flames on the Cockburn Range that night were not the only flashes of red. For a quick sweep of the creek with my torch revealed further flashes of red as the eyes of several freshwater crocodiles stared back at me. Crocodiles and bushfires; that about sums up the Kimberley. Resting on my swag as my fire burnt low, relishing the softness of the sand, I felt enraptured by the light from the sky, the land, and the water. I felt completely seduced by the wildness of the surrounding country. There was no other place I would rather have been, at that moment, than deep within the Kimberley's embrace.

Next morning, with the swag rolled and a quick quart-pot of tea, I returned to the track. This became my routine on the Gibb River Road. Long jolting, dusty drives towards the horizon interspersed with days of relaxing pleasure within the waters of the numerous gorges along its path. Fortunately, there were quite a few gorges to explore. And whether it was their refreshing waters, their appreciated shade, or the many intriguing Aboriginal rock paintings often found close by, each left a lasting impression. Propitiously, there were several gorges whose pristine luxuriousness and natural resonance enticed me to spend more than a morning or afternoon indulging in their splendour.

One such place was Manning Gorge in the Packsaddle Range. Its enchanting natural delights and serene, peaceful feel made it one of the highlights in a region of beguiling natural treasures. To slip into the coolness of its waterhole, the dirt and smoke of the road lost to a slightly dusty film on its rippling surface, was pure pleasure. The water completely invigorated me on all levels: its sweet fragrance as unique to the Australian bush as the tangy eucalyptus oils wafting invisibly overhead. It was another of those special times I felt enveloped by the all-encompassing bounty of the natural world. And, as I swam deeper into the gorge, towered over by its increasingly rocky ramparts, I soon discovered there was another gorge further upstream.

The walk to the upper gorge took me far from the pandanus palm and tree-lined waterhole I first enjoyed, up into the range: the rocky ground reinforcing the underlying impact Nature's geological DNA has in the Kimberley. The soft, green grasses lining the lower gorge quickly gave way to yellow-brown spinifex whose sharp needles reminded me of their determination to survive in what is essentially a waterless land for much of the year. The underlying rock, fractured along its horizontal and vertical axes, created the impression of a roughly hewn carving from the Earth's crust.

Walking through the bush, as the sun's intensity continued to strengthen during the day, the humidity increasingly made its presence felt. In the morning, the sapphire-blue Kimberley sky was free of clouds. There was typically not even a hint of what was building to the north. Then, over the course of the day, billowing clouds like roll after roll of a grey cotton wool slowly built on the northern horizon. As the day wore on, the humidity only increased. Yet it was too early for the storms so there would be no rain. Instead, the intensity drained away over the course of the night only to start building the following day. Fortunately, there were two benefits to this increasing heat and humidity – not only did it act as a whole body purifier, it made a swim even more enjoyable.

Walking through the scrub, all I could initially see were the rocky ridges tumbling over one another to the horizon. As I worked my way over small gullies and across the tops of ridges, there was not even a hint of water. Then suddenly it appeared before me – an emerald gem, glistening in the hot summer sun, held fast within the range as a jewel is held tightly in a ring. It was a mesmerising vista, another example of Nature's intriguing capacity for creating natural jewels of beguiling charm in the least likely of places. From the top of the ridge, a narrow path led down to the waterhole with the fracturing and faulting of the rocks providing a challenging, rough-hewn staircase down into its realm.

There Nature's pièce de résistance was revealed in spectacular glory
– a tumbling waterfall cascading into an emerald-green pool whose
waters contrasted exquisitely with the ochre-red of the gorge walls and
the sapphire-blue sky. The waterhole stretched out before me: its surface
rippled and glistening as a small breeze played its way across. I could easily recognise the shallows as the sand underwater reflected a golden tinge
that slowly disappeared into the depths where there was no reflection of
anything. At least not until the afternoon light faded into dusk and the
geological and biological nuances of the gorge were intimately reflected
off the watery canvas stretched out before me.

Slipping into the golden shallows had all the feel of the perfect massage. Every part of my body tingled and came alive as a chill moved up
from my toes. And with a last deep breath, and dive, I was no longer part
of the regular world. I was instead part of a place whose overriding feeling was one of quietness, harmony, and peace. Swimming deeply within
this waterhole, the sunlight barely registering in its slow, sparkling dance
across the surface, I felt completely relaxed by the water's invigorating
caress. I swam as a platypus would swim. I swam as a dolphin would
swim. I swam with all the power I could muster until the bursting pressure in my lungs returned me to the surface. And with a deep breath and
another dive, I returned to the marvellous new world I had discovered.
This went on for hours with the exhilaration I felt at being alive converted into the adrenalin coursing through my veins.

With nobody else around, my paradise was complete. These were the
times I swam naked with every piece of clothing thrown onto a rock or
left hanging in a tree. These were the days I remembered from childhood
when every waking moment enthralled me. Then, following another
brief rest on the bank, I returned to my new watery home and similar
childhood memories from many years before.

While the upper gorge awed me during the day, so it mesmerised
me into the dusk. As the sun set, the gorge came alive with colour as the
rich ochre-red of the quartzite walls during the day transformed into a
lighter yet equally intense hue in the evening. As the breeze stopped its

mischievous ripples across the watery canvas, it was impossible to tell where the gorge reflection ended and the sky began. The waters of the gorge mirrored the chiselled intricacy of its walls, the wistful grasses and gnarled trees lining its banks, and the broad expanse of the sky. Each reflected colour was true to the original from which it came. Nature was in perfect symmetry. There was no need to improve this vista to make it more exquisite. It was simply perfect.

Sitting on the edge of the waterfall that evening as the western sun ignited the land in a fiery blaze, I felt pure gratitude for the natural beauty laid out before me during my time on the track. My feeling of connection to the land was absolute and humbling. And the only word that came to mind to describe the power that created one perfect vista after another, whose teaching had been a constant source of learning and succour, was Nature. Nature was the power who created every vista of physical and spiritual magnificence I saw. It was Nature, working with its basic elements of earth and fire, wind and water as it had from the beginning of time, who had created the natural sanctuaries in which I was able to rediscover my health and happiness.

There was a full moon that night lighting the rocky path back to the lower gorge: its silvery glow making the journey downhill relatively easy. The bush was resplendent in the moon's radiance with the shadows cast during the day similarly cast at night. And what a sight met my eyes on reaching the lower gorge. For its waters rippled like waves of silver while the flora along the banks were as visible as during the day.

Slipping into Nature's soft embrace, slowly swimming out into the middle of the gorge, the moon's light caressed me from above as the waters of the gorge massaged me from below. The path was clear. If I could only swim to the end of the gorge, I could climb the lighted path into Nature's silvery embrace. It did not require dying or anything so final. All it required were two strong arms and legs to swim and climb. However, it was not yet time to follow that path to where it would take me. It was not calling. It was just showing, as a gentle but firm reminder, that one day it would.

Being part of Nature's moonlit realm that night was the most inspiring experience in a day of enchanting experiences. It reinforced how honest and supportive Nature is, how maternal and paternal it can be. It underpinned and increasingly confirmed my developing belief that when we chose to be part of its domain, when we chose its teaching over the perpetual deceit we now find ourselves immersed in as a society, we will always find similar moonlit oases to be embraced by its inspiring magnificence.

Sitting on my swag later that evening, I realised it had been two years since being 'liberated' from my career in New York. It had been two years of embracing a completely new life philosophy. It had been two years of experiencing how much more there was to life by following an adventurous path, of appreciating the benefits that came from simply being willing and prepared to jump at the right time, and trusting the changes experienced represented a better life path than the one previously tramped.

Reflecting on what I had learnt since my quite unexpected 'liberation', the questions continued to bubble up like the steam from my quart-pot. Even though I had been asking, and answering, these questions for two years, I felt there was still more to learn before my next life stage would emerge from the dust, heat, and vibrations of the track that was my path at that moment. Nature, and Odin, it seemed, were not quite finished with me for the questions kept coming.

How had I become so blind to Nature's powerful life force that provided everything I needed? How could I have instead trusted in a society that not only destroyed Nature but was equally destroying me? What was the point of living in this manner when its essence required the destruction of the natural world for the most meaningless of wants? What was the point of slowly destroying myself to support and sustain the sick, self-destructive society I had previously considered myself a part?

For, it was instead Nature, and its life-giving wisdom I had previously ignored, who had succoured and supported me in my critical time of need. Who had provided me with everything I required to reclaim the life of health and happiness I sought. Bathed in the light of the full moon and my fire, as the sound of cicadas wafted up from the waterhole, the importance of Nature's teaching to a life well lived increasingly crowded into my consciousness. I realised that no matter what the future held, I was now certain of one thing. Nature's wisdom and teaching would be the foremost compass for navigating my life from that moment on. It was a very different mindset to the one I remembered at the moment before my 'liberation' occurred!

Driving the Gibb River Road was not only fascinating from a natural history perspective. It was equally fascinating from an Aboriginal history perspective as I came to appreciate the rock art seen alongside many of the gorges and waterholes through the region today. Yet, unlike the x-ray style from the Top End, the Quinkan style from Cape York, or the paintings of Central Australia, two distinct rock art styles are found in the Kimberley today.

Gwion Gwion rock art, also known as Bradshaw paintings, is the older of the two styles. It is estimated this art is at least 17,000 years old, although it could be up to 60,000 years old, with the most recent paintings determined to be 7,000 years old. The more recent form of rock art, known as Wandjina paintings, are estimated to be only 4,000 years old at most. Not only are the painting ages quite different, which is interesting to say the least, but the styles also appear to reflect two distinctly separate cultures. Fascinatingly, science is still trying to understand the reasons for the timing and cultural differences to determine how Aboriginal society evolved in this part of the continent.

The Gwion Gwion style of rock art shows tall, lean figures painted in a monochrome dark-red ochre with all the trappings of a developed society. From multi-layered hairstyles to complex body ornaments and accessories, from dancing, leaping, and playing figures to leaner body shapes, the art suggests a people who were different physically and culturally from those who subsequently painted the later Wandjina figures. The Wandjina rock art, painted in a broader array of red, white, yellow, and black ochre, does not show a people but rather the spirit figures they associated with the Wet and the regeneration of the land. Spirits who, before they died, painted their image on a rock near a gorge or waterhole before returning to its depths.

With their round faces, eyes representing thunderstorms, and a body covered in dots representing rain, they were a fascinating representation of the season they sought to bring. Interestingly, I saw them in several forms at different gorges: their head alone indicating they were in the clouds while their full body indicated they were instead walking the land. To see a Wandjina figure painted near a gorge or waterhole confirmed it was a very special place indeed. It was another reminder of how much insight there was to be gained from a people who had lived in relative harmony with all facets of the natural world for a very long time.

The distinctly different painting styles have raised the fascinating question of whose culture the Gwion Gwion paintings actually represent, and what happened to that culture given the Wandjina paintings are so different and often painted over the earlier paintings. They may have been a different people from before the last ice age, subsequently leaving the area as sea levels dropped and a mega-drought occurred around 5,500 years ago. Alternatively, they may have been an advanced people who arrived much earlier, survived, thrived, and then declined for today's Aboriginal people have no memory of them.

Whatever the answer, the Kimberley has clearly seen different cultures walk its land and leave their mark on its rocks, by its gorges and waterholes, and in its caves. It was another reminder of how ancient this land is from both a geological and human history perspective.

Mornington Bush Camp, on the Fitzroy River, is another of those unique places that define the Kimberley. It is off the Gibb River Road, about 90 kilometres of corrugations to the south, with the track passing a mini version of the Cockburn Range with small, flat-topped jump-ups the defining feature on the otherwise unremarkable ancient sea floor.

Mornington used to be a working cattle station with the bronco panels from those long gone days now scattered across the landscape as a reminder of the land's commercial use before tourists became the economic motherlode. The campsite here was particularly enveloping with the shade of pandanus palms and small eucalyptus, fig, and tea trees particularly welcoming as the warm summer days increasingly made their presence felt. A small creek on one side, complete with its own freshwater crocodile, and ochre-red quartzite ranges on the other side bounded the campsite. It also had its very own bush symphony with cockatoos, finches, corellas, and friendly larrikin galahs making plenty of noise, particularly in the morning and evening. It was the ideal place to rest out the day's heat unless enticed to visit the spectacular beauty of Mornington's two gorges: Dimond Gorge and Sir John Gorge.

Dimond Gorge took a bit of getting to – a rough bush track twisting and turning through one dry, rocky creek bed after another the only path in. It was worth the effort for, as I swam in the sweeping reach of water, its beauty left me enraptured.

Dimond Gorge owes its existence to the Fitzroy River, known as Bandrarl Ngadu to Aboriginal people, which has slowly carved its way through the King Leopold Ranges. Reflecting the age of the Kimberley region, these ranges were uplifted around 560 million years ago during the King Leopold Orogeny. They were another reminder of the plethora of geological events that went into creating the Australian continent of today. Events that each left their own unique tectonic scar as also seen in the Petermann and MacDonnell Ranges in Central Australia and the Flinders Ranges in South Australia.

It was clear from the beginning this was not some ancient sedimentary range like many of the others passed on the Gibb River Road to the east. It was instead a range whose original sandstone sediments had been heated and fractured, folded and faulted to form the quartzite ranges of today. Some had been folded upwards into perfect anticlines while others were uplifted 90 degrees to the vertical. Several large scars in the walls of the main gorge, old fault lines, were expanding into younger, smaller gorges showing that Nature had yet to finish its work here. Everywhere I looked, the land had been altered in some way. Nature had clearly toiled long and hard in this place to create the breathtaking allure that captivated and humbled me from the moment of its first sight.

The sweeping expanse of the gorge waters, matched by the sweeping sapphire-blue expanse overhead, represented another of Nature's cathedrals where meditation and reflection on Nature's work became as fundamental to the everyday as breathing. Worn, rounded rocks jutted out from the water's edge providing the ideal platform for a diving, seamless entry into Nature's cool, welcoming embrace. Fig and eucalyptus trees lined the banks: their leaves providing a welcome, dappled shade as the temperature and humidity slowly climbed over the course of the day. Pelicans paddled their way across the gorge as eagles soared gracefully overhead. Crocodiles also plied these waters: freshwater only or so the literature said.

Sitting on the river's edge, surrounded by the rocky vastness of Dimond Gorge, I felt intimately connected to the natural resonance all around. I felt I was part of it and it was part of me. I could not imagine a stronger feeling of connection to the land than what I experienced in that moment. My increasingly symbiotic relationship with the land, and the succouring feel of its rocks, plants, and animals, now defined the connection that was most important to me.

Despite being completely alone in a remote gorge, with no career or relationship to return to, I felt as happy as I ever had surrounded by the land and its creations of which I was one. Feeling aligned with Nature, being part of Nature, I felt whole, energised, and complete. I felt the natural world would be my guide, my inspiration, and my sustenance if only I returned its love through respect for its role in my life. For, as I had come to learn, Nature will always provide humanity with everything we need to be happy and healthy when we align our whole being with the inherent goodness of its teaching and the depth of its wisdom.

While Dimond Gorge was inspiring in its vastness, Sir John Gorge was relaxing in its intimacy. It was smaller and had a more serene feel, with a number of high-pitched dingo pup squeals at dusk suggesting several of its other inhabitants also felt the same way. The gorge walls, rising straight out of the river, faced west with the carved quartzite eroded smooth by waters cascading through the ranges for millions of years. All along the river's edge were places to dive into its welcoming embrace with its rocky ledges barely hinting at the depths below. It was just the natural elements and I, conversing between ourselves as we had from the beginning of time, in another of the many different forms and roles we had taken.

The sunset at Sir John Gorge that evening was another inspiring, mesmerising light show from Nature's hand. As the breeze rippling the water dropped, the surface of the gorge was transformed into a virtual mirror. As the setting rays struck the gorge walls at dusk, their glowing brilliance suggesting the gorge was about to ignite, the reflection off the water rendered the whole gorge ablaze. It reminded me of the Central Australian gorges and the interplay of ochre-red and cobalt-blue that always captivated my heart and beguiled my soul in a way few other places do. The reflection caught every detail, even a small eucalyptus tree high on the gorge rim, in the waters below.

It was the type of flawless scene humanity's best painters have so often tried to capture with minimal success. The dynamic interplay of light and colour across the land giving the impression it was spectacularly alive.

From the gorges of Mornington Bush Camp, it was quite a long drive back to the Gibb River Road and its path west. I remember the road here as being especially rough given the corrugations that reduced my speed to about 10 kilometres per hour unless I wanted to destroy not only the suspension but also the vehicle itself. Even then, the corrugations were enough to shake everything loose that was not tightly battened down. No matter where I went on that particular stretch of road, onto the shoulder, the left hand side, or the right hand side, there was no escape. It was just a matter of feeling the vehicle bounce across and down the track in a never-ending experience of violent shaking. To go faster was to put all the tyres at risk, not to mention spraying passing cars with rocks and dust. But of course, as was sometimes the case, some drivers did not bother to read the road and treated it like a highway instead.

On the track into Bell Gorge, another spectacular Kimberley gorge, that is exactly what happened. A couple of 4WDs flew past on the narrow dirt track spraying my vehicle with rocks and dust. As they went by, it sounded like a hailstorm except there was not a cloud in the sky. It was one of the less intelligent things I saw done out there. Yet Nature saw to it they experienced the error of their ways, though whether they learnt their lesson I have no idea. For not more than a kilometre or two down the track, both vehicles had pulled over with each removing a flat tyre that had succumbed to the roughness of the track and the foolhardiness of their behaviour.

The road into Bell Gorge was rough. There was no other word for it. Similar to other gorges visited, the roughness of the track seemed to correlate directly with the opulence of the gorge itself. And Bell Gorge was no exception. It was as spectacular, inspiring, and breathtaking as any other gorge visited. Like many of its peers, even the most profound superlatives were never sufficient to fully describe the spectacular and rough-hewn beauty laid out before me.

Carved from the King Leopold Ranges by Bell Creek, Bell Gorge is really a series of waterholes, bounded by tall, ochre-red, quartzite cliffs, running one into the other over a waterfall. Each waterfall had a different feel, a different experience, Nature offered to those who sought its particular caress. Some were more of a gentle incline in the rock where I could lie and let the water gently wash over me. Others were more vertical where I was splashed and tussled by the strongly flowing water. These were the falls I gravitated to in the heat of the day.

Quite literally, there was profound wonderment everywhere I looked in this most remote of places. Whether it was the uplifted and fractured quartzite ranges through which the gorge had been carved, the flora softening the toughness of the land, or the stark sparseness of the waterless country to the horizon, Nature's ability to create a sanctuary in an otherwise barren landscape was again displayed perfectly.

Bell Gorge was not an easy place to explore. It was quite a difficult climb down into its depths for the rocks created a barrier as much as a rough-hewn path. The spinifex and boab trees lining its edges, clinging to the barest of walls, gave this place a true Kimberley feel. Once I navigated the rocks and spinifex, and made my way down into the gorge, the sight that awaited me was truly captivating. The gorge was much deeper once inside compared to looking into its depths from above. It felt like a cavern with only the roof open to the sky; the exquisite contrast of ochre-red and sapphire-blue giving the land a unique beauty of which I never once tired.

To slip over its smooth rocks and into its watery realm, with no human distraction from the all-encompassing grandeur, I felt intimately part of Nature's intrinsic harmony. Resting under the cascading waters as they washed over me, surrounded by the splendour of Nature's inspiring sculptures, my feeling of connection to the land was complete and total. Experiencing these feelings of belonging, I came as close as I could to how Aboriginal people felt about their land. The land now owned me. I had become as much a part of it as the rocks, plants, and animals. I had become as much a part of it as it had become part of me.

Heading west into the setting sun, I followed the track into the rocky ramparts of the King Leopold Ranges. Here, the metamorphic and volcanic rocks were a geological testament to the tectonic forces that have shaped and reshaped the Kimberley since it first became part of the North Australian Craton around 1.8 billion years ago. The view from the top of the ranges was spectacular. The dry, rocky, spinifex-covered land stretched to the horizon with the only hint of water a green, meandering tinge showing the existence of creeks that only ran during the Wet. As the sun sank below the western horizon, and the shadows slowly lengthened, the vista transformed into one of light and dark until the land was lost to sight as the ranges' shadow inexorably reached the horizon.

Coming down out of the ranges the next day, I was met by a vast plain stretching to the horizon at all points of the compass. I had returned to Kimberley cattle country. Yet, in earlier geological times, this country had been covered by a vast shallow sea in which a great barrier reef had formed, part of which is visible today; its grey limestone elegance stretching across the plain as Napier Range just as it stretched across the sea floor as an ancient reef around 350 million years ago.

The range atop the plains today, weathered and eroded into a plethora of vertical, tubular-like carvings, represents only a fraction of the reef for almost a kilometre remains buried beneath the sand. It was a range whose similar presence in other parts of Northern Australia reminded me that sea levels had been much higher in the past and, accordingly, there was no reason why that should not be the case in the future. And like other ranges in the Kimberley, this ancient monument to life had been transformed by Nature's artistic hand into a number of remarkable gorges.

Geikie Gorge, known as Darngku to Aboriginal people, was one such place: the Fitzroy River having carved an impressive limestone gorge just as it had with its quartzite creations upstream. Unfortunately, similar to other places on the Fitzroy River, introduced species had thrived all too well tainting the environment with a debased homogeneity much like we see in Western society today with its processed foods, toxic healthcare, and lowbrow 'entertainment'. It was a stark reminder of how many other magnificent places across the Australian continent had also succumbed to the mediocrity of introduced plants and animals, and the aesthetic and commercial value destroyed by those mistakes.

The fact this reality equally applied to Indigenous Australians and their culture, in their own land, was not lost on me either!

Windjana Gorge, carved by the Lennard River through the Napier Range, was the last gorge I visited on the Gibb River Road. While its geology was fascinating, with the remnants of its ancient aquatic life clearly visible, it was the flora that softened the gorge's hard, chiselled form. Eucalyptus trees, sweet smelling vines, and wiry grasses provided an appreciated sanctuary from the increasing heat and humidity of the rapidly approaching Wet. The eucalyptus trees, in particular, threw a welcomed, dappled shade that enticed me from the treeless, spinifex-clad plains. The scrub through the gorge was unusually thick as a number of introduced plants had responded all too well in this ancient oasis, much as they unfortunately also had in several other Fitzroy River gorges.

Not only was the flora in the gorge quite a change to the surrounding plains, so too was the fauna. Windjana Gorge is a bastion for freshwater crocodiles. The long, narrow forms lining the edges of most billabongs through the gorge showed this was not really a place to swim despite how much I had been looking forward to one since leaving Bell Gorge several days previously. I was surprised at how many crocodiles were there as the dry creek beds downstream suggested they would not come this far inland. Nevertheless, in wetter times they had, and, at the largest waterhole, there were at least 30. Who I suspect were looking forward to the summer rains to flush the river system thereby giving them a chance to find a less populated waterhole to enjoy.

Napier Range was also unique in that it exhibited a beguiling plethora of colours, unlike other ranges experienced, with the grey weathered limestone tinged a deep ochre-red where iron oxide from the surrounding sands had leached into its porous top and sides. The range had a sharp, chiselled, and uneven surface, formed as the limestone slowly dissolved over time. Only the bottom third of the range was the white seen in coral reefs today, the result of recent flooding that had scrubbed the gorge walls clean. The jagged form of the gorge, silhouetted against the sapphire-blue Kimberley sky and the ochre-red desert sands, created a quite beguiling vista at most times of the day.

The dusk vista was particularly spectacular. The range seemed to ignite as the top glowed a deep red while the lower chalk-white walls reflected the sun's rays in their more subtle pastel hues. The view outside the gorge was no less glorious as the western sky smouldered with angled streaks of pink, indigo, and violet, silhouetting the range's chiselled form against the empty desert landscape, as the sun slowly sank below the horizon. Not only was the dusk a work of art; it was also a welcome break from the heat as Nature compassionately lowered its cool curtain of relief at the end of another hot summer day. As I sat watching that sunset over Windjana Gorge, its waters and red-grey gorge walls igniting into a fiery orange glow, the spiritual riches flowing from the natural world were magnificent indeed.

And, as if to further beguile me with its capacity for authenticity, the reverse of colours the following morning was equally spectacular. As Napier Range materialised in the cool of dawn, the coloured pastels from the eastern sky silhouetting the range's chiselled form, it gave the range a softness I had not noticed when seen in the setting sun. A softness that was slowly lost as the sun returned to its blazing strength during the day, and I returned to the cool sanctuary only found inside the gorge itself.

Windjana Gorge was my last camp on the Gibb River Road. On leaving its cool, shady embrace, the track returned to the open, grassy plains and my drive through to the oasis of Broome on the coast. Unfortunately, before too long, the dull, monotonous feel of the bitumen replaced the jarring, jolting track that had facilitated such an intimate connection and conversation with the land travelled through. I felt sad leaving the magnificent ranges and gorges of the Kimberley for their chiselled features and embracing waters were places of natural extravagance I would likely not experience again for some time. Their diversity pure and uncompromising: their visions serene and inspiring.

That is what I remember most about the Kimberley. Everywhere I travelled, Nature had created spectacular vistas that were as breathtaking in their wildness as they were beguiling in their elegance. The Gibb River Road showed the Kimberley in all its glory, through its many different forms and its many different moods. It was a place where I completely connected with its magnificence, all day, every day. It was a place where I learnt how important that connection is. It taught me how important Nature is and how important its teaching will be to my life. I was one with Nature. It was one with me.

On the majestic frontier of the Kimberley, alone in the vastness of one of the most pristine and remote regions on Earth, it is an understanding that not only becomes part of you. It is an understanding that comes to define you.

12

Spinifex and Sand

'I lie at night and watch her
As she sails across the sky
With the hidden joys and sorrows
That we know not, you and I;
And I watch her drifting onward
Over crag and dale and dune,
And I wish that I could hearken
To the secrets of the Moon.'

Will Ogilvie – The Secrets of the Moon

While the deserts, ranges, and gorges of the Australian Outback are places of rugged beauty, they are but a small part of the continent's geographic totality. While much of my time was spent enjoying these places in Nature's inland realm, my path occasionally took me to inspiring sandy vistas framed by the ocean's invigorating luxury. Although my forays to the coastal regions were infrequent, how I savoured the ocean's enticing scenery and bathing in the coolness of its waters and breezes at these times. As if to remind me of the underlying character of the Australian continent, some of the remotest places on the coast were much like their inland peers with sand dunes stretching to the horizon thickly covered in prickly spinifex, spindly bushes, and stunted pines. As I travelled into the northwest corner of the continent, to explore its ocean and desert landscapes, one constant defined the underlying nature of that country. It was the interplay of spinifex and sand, the two most basic of desert elements, which created the backdrop for the abundance of natural delights that inspired and beguiled as much as any other part of the country.

Broome was a welcome oasis in the vastness of the Kimberley. Its beaches of pure white sand, the soft ground, and cooling breeze made it the perfect location to relax after months on the track. While reaching Broome was one of the more important milestones of my journey, its attainment induced mixed feelings. For, while it was the furthermost point reached on my walkabout, my departure from its tropical haven now meant each kilometre travelled was towards home in some way.

Fortunately, there was still much to see around Broome and the Kimberley that delayed my departure for the south. There were still several places I wanted to visit before the Wet unleashed its torrents across Northern Australia: places that if missed may not be seen for some time. Given the number of kilometres to backtrack, and the closing window to visit these places, I spent significantly more time behind the wheel than used to. As it turned out, this was a small price to experience the natural diversity Northern Australia still had to offer this walkabout soul.

Though Broome relaxed my mind and body, it accosted my heart and soul as the despairing state of its Aboriginal population impinged on my conscience, once again. A wander through its backstreets and parks highlighted the same tragic incongruity seen in other large Outback towns of a culture being destroyed before my eyes. In that sense, Broome was much like Alice Springs. Another despairing insight into the tragic cost incurred by the First Australians of being forcefully and violently removed from lands that had successfully sustained and supported their culture for tens of thousands of years. The stark contrast between the inspiring Aboriginal gentleman on the Gulf Track and the people who lived in the parks and along the streets of Broome reinforced my angst at what they were now forced to endure.

Watching this ancient people as they attempted to make a life on the fringes of society filled me with a profound sense of sadness. A sadness that made me aware of my own complicit acceptance of the status quo and my previously ignorant contribution to the tragedy unfolding before me. It was another stark reminder of the significant work required by Australian society to ensure Indigenous Australians are treated in a respectful, meaningful, and fair manner in their own land. Reconciliation, it appears, still has a long way to go if Broome was any guide!

Despite this pronounced inner feeling of conflict, I appreciated my time in Broome though it was brief. Following a week's break restocking my supplies and relaxing on the beach, I returned to the road with the town soon nothing more than a receding vision in the rear-view mirror. It was time to head north into the wilds of coastal Australia. It was time to leave the vastness of the Outback sands behind to experience the majesty of their coastal peers.

The Dampier Peninsula, north of Broome, is an exquisite contrast to the inland off which it extends. With its sparkling waters every hue of blue and its sands sublimely balanced between pure white and ochre-red, this nuanced, pristine environment inspired and invigorated as much as the rugged inland. The land was rich in Aboriginal and European history. A natural, social, and cultural potpourri where Nature presented its treasures in the most enticing of colours. It was a revealing insight into Nature's different moods from its serene, reflective presence during the halcyon days of spring to the powerful, destructive force it becomes when a cyclone wheels in off the Timor Sea during the hot, humid days of summer. It was another place to reflect on Nature's bounty and to connect with its cleansing presence on all levels. And there was no better place to do that than Cape Leveque: a turquoise and azure jewel banded by gleaming white and ochre-red sands.

The road to Cape Leveque quickly revealed its underlying character once I turned off the bitumen. For the track to the beach, corrugated for much of its length, was more like a rough path through a gorge of dirty-green. On getting closer to the coast, Nature slowly revealed the luxuriant vistas it had previously hidden behind its thick wall of scrub. I was completely enthralled, for, along the coast of the Indian Ocean, places of serene majesty existed that inspired and calmed my whole being. This country was beguiling and relaxing in a way that was new to my senses, and very much appreciated after coming out of the hot, dusty, and increasingly humid vastness of the inland.

Middle Lagoon was one such place. After hours of dust, thick scrub, and countless corrugations, it appeared before me like an unexpected mirage. Its azure waters, flat and calm in the lagoon yet rippled in the expanse of ocean further out, stretched to the azure-blue sky at the horizon: the lagoon and sky seemingly one. It was almost impossible to tell where the ocean ended and the sky began with only the ripples far out to sea giving the precise meeting point away.

Its sandy beaches, two broad, white arms embracing the lagoon, pure and gleaming in the midday sun, shone with a reflection from the purest china. The dunes, dotted with clumps of casuarina pines and stunted eucalyptus trees, offered shade and respite from the hot day. It was an enchanting scene, another ideal time and place to immerse myself in the depths of Nature's bounty.

The lagoon itself was an exquisite location to savour the ocean's unique delights. The water was crystal clear with its cool and soothing caress the perfect antidote to the aches and pains incurred from long hours jolting and jarring my way along the rough bush track to this paradise. I felt mesmerised by its gentle calmness and serenity in the cool breeze of the afternoon as I swam in the salty water; its uniquely curing touch a sensation not found in an inland gorge or waterhole. Lying back within its soothing embrace, with only the occasional cry of a seagull heard overhead, I revelled in another of the gentling experiences Nature consciously and lovingly provides to all its creations.

Middle Lagoon had a timeless feel, its rhythms completely natural. Whether it was the rise and fall of the tide, the ceaseless sound of the wind through the trees, or the calls of seagulls wheeling overhead, everything pointed to the importance of the rhythms of the natural world. The Western concept of time had no place here. I ate when hungry. I swam when hot. I fell asleep when tired while listening to the sound of waves breaking on the shore. Everything about Middle Lagoon spoke to the natural order of life, to the importance of resonating in harmony with Nature's intrinsic balance. While I had initially planned to spend only a day here, that idea was quickly forgotten once I discovered its serene and deserted feel. For it was just the respite I had been looking for.

Camping next to the ocean was very different to camping in the inland's vastness. Especially in summer as the soothing ocean breeze cooled my body with a most welcoming caress relative to the sweat-stained slumber experienced inland. The breeze also provided another appreciated benefit for its caress was equally unappealing to the mosquitoes. In my ocean camp, with its light breeze, there was no need for the pale sheen of the mosquito net and its obstructive view of the magnificent Southern Hemisphere night sky.

Lying on my swag that night, bathed in the light of the moon and stars, the brilliance of the Outback sky inspired and fascinated with its sea of pulsating lights from a time when the Earth may not have even been born. Who knew where these lights came from? Who knew when they first set out on their walkabout across the unimaginable vastness of the Universe to one day be appreciated by a lone soul on his walkabout across the vastness of an ancient continent?

The majesty of the night sky never lost its appeal, not even for an instant. Waiting for the moon to appear, seeing its friendly form low or high in the night sky, was to see an old friend from childhood. An old friend whose light had followed my meandering track across Australia with as much interest as I followed its dedicated path across the night sky.

An old friend whose changing shape, as it waxed and waned, mirrored similar changes in my whole being as I underwent my own awakening under Nature's expert tutelage. An old friend whose face I had come to know as well as those of my own family given how often its silvery glow smiled a warm greeting in the inky vastness of the desert at night. An old friend whose sight, even today, still takes me back to the many places of walkabout we enjoyed together under its soothing silver hues.

From Middle Lagoon, several days later, I headed north on the same dusty, corrugated track to Cape Leveque where Nature displayed more of its enchanting ocean vistas. The beach at Cape Leveque was one of the most stunning vistas I have ever seen. It was almost impossible to believe such beauty could exist, even from Nature's hand.

The beach was the main element of the magnificent vista that first caught my eye: its pure white, shimmering presence a narrow strip to the horizon melding into the ocean whose waters reflected hues of blue never previously seen. From darker tinges further out to turquoise and azure shadows closer in, the ocean appeared to register every possible hue of blue across its watery canvas.

Yet Nature had not finished revealing its remarkable talent for using all the colours spread across its palette. For, behind the beaches of gleaming white sand, salmon-pink cliffs, a mixture of ochre-red desert and white coastal sand, rose high into the dazzling azure-blue Australian sky. Every part of this mesmerising vista was calibrated to perfection, further highlighting Nature's perpetual ability to inspire and awe in the most unexpected places.

As in other parts of Australia, I felt Nature was testing me during the day. With the glare off the white sand magnifying the rays of the sun, the day heated up very quickly once its first light appeared over the eastern horizon. Even submerged within the ocean, I felt the sun's careening rays no matter how deep I went. To swim within these cleansing waters, to feel the hot sun purify my body like steel in a furnace, was to feel the energy of the natural world in all its forms. Despite the pleasures of the ocean, however, it was not the sort of country to avoid the shade during the hottest time of the day. Yet, when the sun started its long descent to the western horizon, and Nature lowered its cool curtain of relief in the evening, there was no more enchanting place to be.

As the day evolved into dusk, the ocean underwent a captivating transformation as it evolved through every hue of blue before settling on an exotic turquoise-blue tint with a hint of green. Framed by the salmon-pink cliffs and the changing ocean colours across the watery canvas, I sat on the beach for hours just watching this spellbinding ballet of colour and light until the dusk darkened into night. Just watching as the land and ocean evolved through an array of stunning visual delights: the transformation of the natural world far more enticing and beguiling than any of humanity's artistic achievements.

It was another of those special times when Nature called to the depths of my soul, reinforcing how much I belonged within its realm now I increasingly understood its teaching and had finally awoken to its wisdom.

Following several days savouring the ocean's delights and the softness of its beaches, it was soon time to turn inland once again. As the humidity continued to build during the day, it was clear the Wet was on its way. With a quick roll of my swag and a return to the dust and corrugations, I left the enchantment of the Dampier Peninsula for the majesty of the untamed Kimberley and its exquisite natural jewels awaiting discovery.

Passing over the Fitzroy River, whose broad waters had carved Geikie, Dimond, and Sir John Gorges upstream, I headed east along the bitumen; its path to the horizon a welcome relief to the jolting, jarring drive that otherwise defined my travels through this country. My destination was now the Bungle Bungle Range, a unique geological structure found nowhere else on Earth. However, as I started down the track into the range, I heard a distinct knocking sound from the front suspension. A quick look revealed one of the shock absorbers was broken. I had no alternative but a quick 800-kilometre round trip to Kununurra to get it fixed. Fortunately, I did, for a check of the others later that day showed they too needed replacing.

As it turned out, this was not the only reason it made sense to take this unplanned detour. The tourist season in the northwest was quickly winding down for another year so there would have been no opportunity to see the wonder of the Ord River if I had visited later. Accordingly, as my vehicle took a well-earned break high on the hoist as its shock absorbers were replaced, I took the opportunity for a gorge-viewing boat trip along the Ord River.

There is only one way to see the Ord River today and that is by boat. The long, tree-lined waterway, carved through uplifted and faulted quartzite ranges, made for one rugged vista after another. Although the Kimberley landmass initially bonded with the nascent North Australian Craton around 1.8 billion years ago, many subsequent tectonic events occurred as it coalesced with the Western Craton and the Gawler Craton over the next 900 million years that either compressed or stretched the land. The impact of these ancient geological events is today seen in the country through which the Ord River flows: the ranges uplifted and tilted at 20 to 30 degrees from the horizontal. There was even one section squeezed so tightly the ancient strata rested perpendicular to the waters of the river, much like the strata of Uluru rested perpendicular to the sands of the desert, so prolonged and powerful had those forces been.

The Ord River, dammed in 1963 and 1972 to provide water to support an intensive agricultural industry, is now responsible for the awe-inspiring Lake Argyle behind the Main Dam. Before the dam's construction, the river was similar to most other Kimberley rivers: a brown, gushing, churning torrent during the Wet and a slow trickle in the Dry when only a few of its deeper gorges held water. It was the Main Dam, and the lower Diversion Dam, which created the waterway seen today. Like many other places in the East Kimberley, Lake Argyle's name reflects the Duracks' role in this land – from Argyle Downs, the cattle station they established in 1882, much of which now lies submerged beneath the waters of the dam.

The other fascinating aspect to the Ord River was the surrounding country. Most of it was dry and gaunt at that time of the year as it awaited the life-giving rains of the Wet. Except at water level, that is, where the spinifex-covered ranges had been transformed into a slender ribbon of green that meandered through the otherwise rough-hewn, ochre-red landscape.

The river beneath the Main Dam was as varied as the surrounding country. At some points, especially where its course narrowed, it became a fast flowing, turbulent torrent whose rushing waters ravenously carved away the sandy banks deposited at a slower time in the river's existence. At other places, the river had a more relaxed pace. More like that of a walkabout spirit seeking a path of which only it knew the right direction.

The river brimmed with wildlife: the grasses and waterlilies forging a life-sustaining mat where birds and insects hurried about their daily life as we do ours, only our cities are bitumen, glass, and concrete. The soothing breeze and the sweet, enveloping perfume from the many plants lining the water's edge created a heady cocktail of natural pleasure, further enhanced by the humidity-filled air. Along the river's edge, Nature's bounty exploded in a cornucopia of life. It appeared as though every plant, insect, and bird had chosen that moment to come down to the river's edge to drink from its life-giving waters. Above that ribbon, the stark, dry ranges appeared devoid of life. A green oasis or spinifex, it seemed, were Nature's only two choices when gentling this land.

Awed by the artistry of Nature's geological work and the intensity of life on the river, I felt enraptured by the natural abundance all around. It inspired and it amazed. It kept my attention far more so than many of the debased forms of 'entertainment' society has to offer today.

And still Nature was not finished with its performance. For, in the setting sun, the Ord River became a reflective wonder as Nature's geological creations were transposed onto its watery canvas by the light of dusk. The land's character was captured without a blemish despite the slight ripples across the river's surface as a gentle breeze provided an appreciated respite from the humidity. The purple-pink streaks of the dusk sky, framing the folded, fractured, and faulted ochre-red gorge walls, were reflected as if from a mirror. It was a scene of unadulterated bliss, as only Nature is capable of creating, with the blaze of dusk colours a resplendent backdrop to the river's reflective soul.

Moreover, as the boat travelled around a bend in the river, another vista slowly revealed itself. It appeared a necklace of Nature's jewels lay before us, strung together by the silken green thread of the Ord River itself. Everything experienced, whether the calmness of the river at dusk, the crafted splendour of the surrounding ranges, or the multitude of colours and reflections, encouraged me to be one with Nature, to connect with its beauty, and to find the harmony I sought in my life through its teaching and wisdom. The Ord River does that to you, as do many other equally beguiling locations across the vast, rugged continent that is Australia. And when it does, there is no forgetting that connection no matter where on Earth you finally return home.

The Bungle Bungle Range, known as Purnululu to Aboriginal people, is a particularly unique Australian creation. It rises like a multitude of ancient sculptured mounds from the vastness of the flat desert floor. In fact, nowhere else on Earth is such a breathtaking and exquisite creation to be found: its inspiring grandeur another reminder of Nature's innate ability to create great works of art with the most basic of elements over geological time.

The road into the Bungle Bungles was as rough as the country was exquisite. The further I drove down the rocky, jarring, and twisting path, the more grateful I became for the demise of the shock absorber before I took the track in. It would have been miserable navigating that country in a lame vehicle, especially in more than just one wheel! And it was hot, very hot, with not even the hint of a breeze to cool its inhabitants as the country shimmered under the ferocity of the baking summer sun. All the creeks were dry. It was a complete contrast to the abundance of Ord River delights experienced only several days before.

The track seemed to follow the route of a snake, the easiest possible path across the hard, rocky ridges and dry, sandy creek beds. The journey was very slow as I gently navigated the abrupt washouts and limitless corrugations that gave me a raw insight into the hard, rugged nature of this land. Like so many other places visited across Australia, it was the geology, once again, that defined the character of the country.

The geology here was fascinating and illuminating. From the volcanic and metamorphic rocks comprising its base to the sedimentary layers subsequently deposited and carved into the range of today, the country was a window into the timeless evolution of the Australian continent. The rocks reflected the impact of ancient glaciers, around 750 million years ago, which left the residual till now found baking on an open plain. They reflected a time when this region was covered in a lush tropical forest. They even reflected the start of the breakup of Australia's ancestral continent, Gondwana, with the rift valley, into which the sedimentary layers settled, created as parts of Southeast Asia broke away from the Kimberley on their journey north around 400 million years ago.

The Bungle Bungle Range, comprised of alternating sandstone and conglomerate layers, evolved in much the same manner as Uluru and Kata Tjuta: the eroded sediments of even more ancient ranges deposited, buried, and uplifted to form a new structure that Nature subsequently sculptured in a uniquely Australian way. The first thing I noticed was the unusual banding across the range with the alternate layers of light and dark rock. The darker bands were algae growing in the more porous layers of rock while the lighter, redder bands reflected less porous rock stained with iron oxide.

And reflecting Nature's relentless destruction of anything that dares rise above the Earth's flat parapet, the range has been slowly eroded over the last 25 million years to create the marvel of today.

Walking through the Bungle Bungles, it was easy to discern whether the underlying rock was sandstone or conglomerate. Where it was sandstone, my walk was a slog through deep sand. Where it was conglomerate, my walk was instead over rounded pebbles and small boulders.

Everywhere I walked provided clues as to how this massif was created and how quickly it was being laid waste by Nature's hand. Surprisingly, despite the impression of grandeur from afar, the range is actually quite fragile with the sandstone crumbling to the touch. It is this fragility, facilitating the crafting of its unique form, which is the primary reason for such a magnificent, though ultimately short-lived, creation.

One place I particularly remember was Cathedral Gorge: a magnificently carved natural amphitheatre whose walls stretched upwards for hundreds of metres with just a hint of the sky peeking into its cool, shady realm. The fault lines, visible in its walls, provided insights into how the gorge had evolved from a solid piece of sandstone into the hallowed space of today: a place of weakness transformed by swirling waters and grinding rocks over millions of years into a place of magnificence. I could understand if its First Australian inhabitants regarded it as very special, if not sacred, given its majesty. Whether it was the glowing walls in the midday sun, the cool of its sanctuary, or the serenity it offered from the heat outside, the gorge was a natural cathedral in every sense of the word.

While Cathedral Gorge was the most inspiring gorge visually, several other gorges encouraged me to reflect more on the sheer scope of geological time and events that had gone into the creation of this magnificent natural masterpiece. For, in this ancient land, there was evidence of the most unexpected kinds. Evidence of a time when a meteorite influenced the evolution of the land, when glaciers carved their path through the country, and when it was a lush paradise.

Piccaninny Gorge was carved from the impact zone of a meteorite, which struck around 250 million years ago. Mini Palms appeared a Kimberley version of Palm Valley, a reminder of a time long past when parts of Australia were covered by a lush tropical forest. Echidna Chasm was carved from ancient glacial till in much the same manner as Tillite Gorge in the Flinders Ranges. Perhaps reflecting its ancestral form, Echidna Chasm was the coolest and most appreciated of all the gorges I visited as the sun turned the country into a baking furnace. As I rested in the coolness of its shade, the evidence of its evolution lay all around: a mass of rounded pebbles and small boulders on its floor and rounded pebbles sticking out of its smoothly polished walls. Eroding waters had sliced a deep gorge that became narrower as I walked further into its sanctuary. With its walls towering above me for over a hundred metres and only the occasional hint of the sun-filled sky, it was the perfect place to rest during the hottest time of the day.

After several days spent enjoying its many gorges, revelling in their cool embrace, it was soon time to leave for the road still called. However, the Bungle Bungle Range had one last lesson to teach me. It was a lesson I will never forget. It was a lesson that provided another insight into the feelings of Aboriginal Australians as they continue to wrestle with the loss of their culture and the destruction of their land.

Being late in the season, the campsite I stayed was empty with most travellers making sure they were well south before the heat and humidity of November arrived. I had just finished dinner, several cups of water were all I needed, and was lying in a small pool of sweat on my swag, when a number of vehicles pulled up in a cloud of dust. It was too late to wander over and introduce myself so I lay back on my swag to appreciate the dusk orchestra and slowly increasing starlit bounty of the night sky.

Everybody who arrived was German and, until the quiet of night finally settled several hours later, all I could hear were thick guttural accents from seemingly all points of the compass. It was initially funny, in such a remote place, being surrounded by German tourists. I was impressed they had come to the Bungle Bungles at a tough time of year. Nevertheless, as their voices continued into the evening, loud and obscure, it made me reflect on how the original Aboriginal inhabitants must have felt when their paradise was first intruded upon only 20 years before.

Before the 1980s, the Bungle Bungle Range was primarily known to Aboriginal people. It was their land. It was their home and sanctuary. As it had been my sanctuary until it became home to a people whose language and customs I did not understand. Even though I was also an interloper to this land, in a sense, it was still my home. It was where I felt my strongest resonance with life. Yet, in an instant, I found myself as a minority in a land that meant everything to me. Even though the impact was nothing like the brutal, soul-destroying times experienced by Aboriginal people, it became easier to put myself in their shoes. It became easier to understand why they saw the European settlement of Australia as such a calamity, and why it remains such a traumatic event for them 215 years later.

Lying under the moon and stars that night, the bush silhouetted in a silvery glow, I found it difficult to sleep. Perhaps it was the humidity covering me in its warm layer of sweat. Or perhaps it was something far more fundamental to the land. A quiet whisper, a gentle reminder, to a fellow walkabout soul of the great wrongs wrought on the most inspiring of nature-based peoples. Wrongs that need righting for the Australia of today to become what it could truly be. It was another reminder the plight of Australia's indigenous citizens affects us all and needs to be resolved for the past to truly give way to the future.

Either way, sleep did not come easily that night as I continued to reflect on how important reconciliation remains for Aboriginal Australians. Although, I suspect, it remains even more important for the rest of us to be truly part of the Great South Land. It was therefore with a welcome relief the dawn's first light appeared over the eastern horizon and the land's quiet whisper finally and appreciatively left me in peace. After a quick cup of water for breakfast, I returned to the track and followed the same rocky path out of the range for the short drive to the Tanami Track and the long desert journey back to Alice Springs.

The Tanami Track is another of those fascinating desert tracks whose course takes you through the remote empty vastness of the Australian interior. It runs for 1,000 kilometres of bone jarring and gentle corrugations through the rock, sand, spinifex, and mulga of the Tanami Desert. It passes through some of the remotest, hottest, and driest parts of the Australian continent: its beauty stark and beguiling as the desert so often is. And, as with much of this part of Australia, it was also Aboriginal land for the length of my journey.

Driving the Tanami Track was important for me personally. For it enabled me to cross the tracks of Augustus Gregory and Nat Buchanan, once again, which was not surprising given how prolific their exploration of the Australian continent had been. Augustus Gregory was the first European to set foot in this part of Australia. He followed Sturt Creek through the Tanami Desert to its westerly point at Lake Gregory during the initial stages of his exploration from the Victoria River in 1855. Nat Buchanan was the first European to cross the Tanami Desert, from east to west, in 1896. What makes his feat even more impressive is that he accomplished it at the age of 70 with only the help of a young Aboriginal guide!

While the Tanami Track today only crosses Gregory's track and passes to the west of Buchanan's track, it highlights the same featureless and waterless country they both had to traverse. The allure and harshness of the country remains much the same as when first seen by those two explorers all those years ago. Driving the Tanami Track was similar to being at sea: the vista to all points of the compass changing only occasionally. The track started out in the rocky country of the Southern Kimberley before evolving into the softer sands of the desert until the familiar shape of the West MacDonnell Ranges finally appeared on the horizon as a purple-blue smudge several days later.

Until arriving in Alice Springs, the vista through the dirty haze of my windscreen was sand in one way or another; sand and the desert plants of spinifex and mulga whose tough exteriors were far more effective at protecting their precious water supplies than the pale skin of many of the track's modern-day travellers. I really appreciated the benefits the sand offered compared to the hard, rocky ground that is much of the ancient Australian continent. It took the sting out of the corrugations, as my vehicle seemed to float over them instead, thereby softening the jarring, jolting drive typically enjoyed and sometimes just endured. Yet, every now and then, Nature threw up another of its subsurface insights to gently remind me the desert's sands merely blanketed the underlying metamorphic and granitic base underlying much of Central Australia.

The Granites was one such place: its igneous outcrop an understated hint into the rocky base underlying the sand blanket slowly draped over much of Central Australia during the previous five million years as the continent slowly desiccated. As I passed, just for a moment, the size of the outcrop imposed itself starkly on the otherwise flat, empty vista to the horizon. And, as previous jump-ups and small ranges passed in the desert had also done, it too quickly shrank until just another speck surrounded by the sea of spinifex and sand that defined this country to all points of the compass.

After two long days of driving, with an overnight camp off the track at Rabbit Flat, the West MacDonnell Ranges appeared on the horizon with all the majesty I had come to appreciate. At first, they were nothing more than a small, purple-blue smudge peeking over the southern horizon that barely hinted at their magnificence. As I drove closer, so they grew before me: their broad ramparts slowly rising from the desert sands with all the grandeur and strength I had come to truly admire. Appreciatively, this vista prefaced the welcome sight of John McDouall Stuart's legacy, the Stuart Highway, and its shimmering path back to Alice Springs and the charms of that inland oasis once again.

From Alice Springs I headed west, back to the cool, refreshing waters of Ormiston Gorge to wash off the dirt, sweat, and smoke from weeks on dusty tracks, and to reinvigorate my whole being. To slip into its embracing waters, to feel their cool touch against my skin, to taste their sweetness and smell their freshness made all my senses come alive after the constant jarring and exhausting glare off the country I had endured since leaving Broome. As befitting Nature's Cathedral, I felt recharged after only a few days spent within its sanctuary and looked forward to the return journey back to Broome. It was another time Nature gently reminded me how critical the touch of the natural world can be to the quality of our lives.

Heading north several days later, the clouds slowly building during the heat of the day, the humidity hanging in the air now felt like a wet blanket. It would not be very long before the Wet brought its invigorating rains back to the country expectedly awaiting that relief. And while Edith Falls was a welcome respite from the heat and humidity, its cooling waters now felt more like a lukewarm bath proving there was no escape from the humidity until the Wet had run its course once again.

That night as I unrolled my swag, however, I had no idea the Wet was about to finally make its dramatic entrance. The rain started as relatively light but persistent. As it got heavier, I pulled the top of my swag over my head confident it would prove resilient to whatever Nature had in store. That confidence lasted until the first downpour hit. As the lightning flashed and the thunder roared, a torrential wall of water came rolling out of the scrub as if the falls themselves had burst.

As the rain got heavier, my swag began to leak: the long months of use now evident where the waterproofing was gone. Shortly into the storm, I felt the first cool, wet dribbles running down my body. Whether it was sweat from being wrapped in a canvas ball on a hot, humid night or the first successful breaches by the rain, it was not clear. Either way, it did not matter. The water could not be stopped and it was not long until my swag and I were completely saturated as the lightning vividly slashed the night sky and the thunder rolled in like an ever-rising tide.

To complicate matters, I had unwittingly unrolled my swag in a slight depression that quickly filled with water. Unsurprisingly, before too long, I felt utterly miserable. With the wind howling and the rain blowing, the only protection available was the small kiosk with its verandah roofed over with tin. Everybody else that night had the same idea, except most had taken cover just as the storm broke. Which meant, at the height of the storm, the kiosk was full. There was nothing else to do but roll out my swag on the periphery of bedraggled bodies and swags trying to stay somewhat dry until the first weak rays of light pierced the misty dawn. As the day slowly broke, only one job was required – stringing up a line, hanging everything up, and waiting for the warmth of the sun to do its job.

It was surprising how quickly everything dried for it only took a few hours before my swag was rolled once again, appreciatively a little cleaner and a lot fresher smelling! With that last act, I returned to the bitumen and the several day drive back to Broome. While the Wet was not successful in catching me again, it certainly made its presence felt most days through the rising humidity and the dark, heavy bank of cloud that slowly built to the north.

After several days of driving west, passing through torrential squalls that lashed the road with a watery fury so fierce I could barely see, I was soon back in the Kimberley with only a day's drive left before Broome once again appeared on the horizon. I had completed my journey across Northern Australia just in time.

Yet the Kimberley had one last gift to bestow before I left its delightful realm. It was on this final run back to Broome I met the second of two travellers whose memory will always bring a smile to my face. A gentleman as different from Lars as can be imagined.

Takashita, or Taka as he politely asked me to call him, was a diminutive but resilient Japanese student cycling around Australia on a break from university. He had none of the wiry toughness of Lars, just a determination he was not going to be stopped. I met Taka under the much-appreciated shade of the large-boughed eucalyptus trees of the Mary Pool Camp on the Margaret River, just off the bitumen.

As I prepared my camp that evening, throwing my swag onto the ground, I noticed a cyclist setting up his camp a short distance away. Having bought a watermelon earlier that day, I was set to indulge in its refreshing luxury. Looking over to the cyclist, however, I suspected he would appreciate a fresh piece of watermelon far more than I would ever know. Accordingly, I cut a chunk off and wandered over. A squatting figure was crouched over a small stove preparing a meal of noodles and canned vegetables. When I offered Taka a piece of watermelon, his smile radiated pure gratitude. Feeling he would appreciate it more than I would, I offered him another piece that he politely refused. Given the heat of the day, I wondered if he would wander over later for that final piece.

By the time Taka did wander over, the watermelon was gone. It was barely a memory, though a very enjoyable one. Taka asked if there was any left. A quick gesture of stomach rubbing sign language indicated he was too late. He laughed and that was the start of a great evening. As the sun appreciatively set, and the day started to cool, the respect of one human being for another left an indelible mark on my memory.

The thing I remember most from that night was how differently we approached the same tasks. As I organised the fire, Taka asked if he could help. Almost reverently, he placed small twigs on the fire, one at a time. My approach was to lay a large dead branch across the fire letting the flames do the work of whittling it into smaller pieces, before pushing them into the flames. Taka sat cross-legged next to the fire's edge while I lay on my rolled swag, both of us relishing the hardness of the ground in our own way. I pulled out my quart-pot and asked Taka if he would like some tea. The fact it was green tea brought a surprised smile to his face. With that, he went over to his bike and came back with a small packet of biscuits. Seeing this, I delved into my tucker bag for my biscuits.

And there we rested and chatted, respectively and respectfully, under the starlit bounty of the night sky with just the glow of the fire for light, sharing everything we had. We talked until quite late that night, until the fire died down and the biscuits were finished. As I discovered with Lars, Taka and I were far more similar in who we were as human beings than we had initially thought. We had both undertaken business degrees at university, both worked in the United States, and both left our former lives behind for the benefit of time on the track. In many ways, we were on the same life path at that moment.

That was one of the most inspiring aspects of my Australian walkabout. The people I met from around the world, of all ages and nationalities, with completely different life philosophies, were among the most generous, inspiring, and happy souls I have ever met. Accordingly, it will be Taka and Lars, and the other adventurous, aware, and awakened souls like them I was fortunate to cross paths with, who I will most remember from those delightful, fascinating, carefree days.

While Broome's appearance on the horizon represented another stage of my journey's progress, it now represented something else. It represented the beginning of my journey's completion. There would be little northerly or westerly travel from now on. Most would be towards the south and the east, pointing my vehicle in some way towards home. It was the first time I had contemplated the end of my journey. It was a sobering thought to realise that by Christmas my walkabout would be just a memory.

Christmas had once been a time to excitedly look forward to whether as a time of enjoyment for a child or as a time for an expatriate Australian to leave the snow and cold of a New York winter for the pleasures of an Australian summer. But now it represented something different. It represented the end of my walkabout. It represented the end of a journey that had, most-appreciatively, invigorated and inspired, enthralled and educated, heartened and humbled since first leaving Sydney almost two years before.

Fortunately, Broome held one more surprise that somewhat mitigated my concern. An important and welcome reminder my walkabout experience would continue to evolve where I stayed true to its spirit and intent. Like other similar experiences, the catalyst was a spur of the moment decision by a small group of travellers, including my cousin and her husband who were undertaking a similar journey around Australia. We decided to spend the evening together enjoying dinner on one of the long stretches of pristine, white sand that makes Broome the unexpected paradise for travellers it so often is.

That night, on a remote part of Cable Beach in the company of this small group, was another I will never forget. As the sun slowly sank into the Indian Ocean, its rays lighting up the breaking waves and sand, a golden blaze embraced us all. Swimming in the waves, I could almost climb Nature's lighted path into its embrace as had been similarly possible at Manning Gorge all those months ago. The evening was perfect with the humidity in the air cooled by the soothing breeze off the ocean: its welcomed touch most appreciated compared to the heat and humidity of most other campsites enjoyed over the preceding months.

Sitting on the beach that night, the stars a glorious canopy overhead as the wind gently blew a thin film of sand and salt over all, there was no other place I would rather have been. As we each shared our small contributions to the table, pulled from the bottom of our respective tucker bags, to create a delicious banquet, the friendship and happiness glowed like a small fire lighting the faces of everybody through the excited and laughing conversations we enjoyed.

Our only concern that night was the tide which rose quickly and quietly. Shortly after dinner, the sound of breaking waves indicated our concern was justified. For a scan with the torch revealed the waves quickly encroaching on our small slice of paradise. With a deft packing job and drive back along the beach, we retreated to the dry security of the caravan park where I relished a most relaxing night's sleep on my swag; the cool wind off the water making it the perfect place to savour Nature's nightly embrace. There was no humidity, no mosquitoes, and no bush flies at dawn. It made Broome an even greater paradise than when I first drove out of the Kimberley all those months ago.

Looking over the ocean the following morning, its sparkling waters a mosaic of blue hues, my connection to Nature felt as strong as it had ever been. Nature alone was responsible for the benefits I had reaped from the simple act of immersion into its bountiful realm: its teaching largely undoing the damage incurred on being part of modern-day society.

Experiencing the life-changing benefits that had come from simply taking the risk of leaving the workforce for walkabout was the biggest insight of all. In hindsight, the biggest risk would have been not following my heart and taking the road less travelled, not embracing the inspiring words and life philosophy articulated by Charles Bean, and not exposing my life to the winds of change and the vicissitudes of fate.

It was through Nature's teaching alone that I rediscovered the life of health, happiness, and adventure I had long sought. Now I understood how critical Nature's teaching was to my whole being, I knew I could never return to the self-inflicted dis-ease that had been my previous reality. No longer would I base my life choices on the shrill, deceitful, and self-destructive messages dictated by an all-consuming, materialistic Western society. For only by listening to Nature, when all was said and done, could I accept full responsibility for what happened in my life. Only in that way could I rest secure in the knowledge I had lived my life on my own terms. Which is probably about as good as it gets until it is time to return to Nature's welcoming embrace for the very last time, for all time.

13

Beginning of Time

'Before the engine's throb and thrust,
Before the humming of the wires,
This overlander, swathed in dust,
Across the last dim range retires.
Yet those who know shall not forget
That North and Westward, rod by rod,
He saw the conquering camp-fires set
And broke the track an Empire trod.'

Will Ogilvie – The Maker of Empire

The Pilbara is one of the oldest landforms on Earth. Its creation over 3.5 billion years ago provides a fascinating insight into the true genesis of our world. Not only do its ancient iron, basalt, and granite hills contain some of the oldest rocks on the planet, they also contain insights into the earliest life on Earth. And while the Pilbara is an ancient place, 500 kilometres to the southwest, in the Jack Hills of Western Australia, the discovery of an even more tantalising hint pushes the age of Australia's oldest rocks back almost a billion years. That hint is a 4.4 billion-year-old zircon crystal from the Western Gneiss Terrain, an ancient sliver of crust now part of the Yilgarn Craton, whose existence is the first insight we have into the true genesis of the Earth. Not only do these ancient landforms represent the beginning of the Earth, they also represent the beginning of Australia. For it was the Pilbara Craton joining with the adjacent Yilgarn Craton, to form the Western Craton around 2 billion years ago, which forged the core from which the Australian continent was to ultimately evolve. Travelling through the Pilbara not only reinforced my connection to the majesty of the Great South Land and its transformational life path; it was another reminder of the power of the natural world and, accordingly, the importance of its teaching to my life.

Heading south from Broome, the country reflected the dryness of the land before the Wet arrived. Short stunted trees, clumps of spinifex, and yellow-brown grassy tussocks spread randomly across the sandy waves of an ancient coastal plain; the blur of ochre-red only matched by the blur of sapphire-blue overhead. It was a pleasant change to be following the bitumen, once again, with the resolute hum of the engine and the tyres' soft rumbling a soothing melody as the kilometres quickly passed. The country here was flat and wide with the rippled, soft red sand of the Great Sandy Desert stretching to all points of the compass: its western edge only stopping at the warm, azure waters of the Indian Ocean.

My objective was the small mining town of Marble Bar, a town whose sole reason for existence was defined by Nature's hand. Marble Bar gets its name from the stunning jasper outcrop found just outside the town, a rock originally thought to be marble hence the town's name. It was a metamorphic rock first laid down as sediment on an ancient sea floor before being buried, heated, uplifted, and tilted almost to the vertical of today's outcrop. The rocks today show their sedimentary origin with the blacks, reds, whites, pinks, and greys banded together in the manner of an

Aboriginal painting memorialising the colours of the Outback. Within the gaudy beauty of these ancient rocks lay an emerald-green pool whose waters sparkled in the hot, dry wind. A pool of cool water that made for a most appreciated swim as the scorching Pilbara sun drained every drop of liquid from my body.

Fascinatingly, the jasper outcrop at Marble Bar, a nondescript rock in a tired, worn land, reflects the critical moment for the birth of life on Earth. Inconceivably, the nuanced iron-red staining in the 3.5 billion-year-old sediments comprising the outcrop today reveal the first hint of oxygen on Earth. For it was around this time cyanobacteria perfected the photosynthesis process as the chlorophyll molecule evolved. This allowed them to extract hydrogen from water to meet their increasing energy needs: an 18 times more efficient energy extraction process than other bacteria used. Incredibly, one consequence of this ancient evolutionary step changed the world forever.

For the act of photosynthesis produced free molecules of oxygen, what was then a waste gas, as the metabolic process consumed the hydrogen atoms only. As the volume of free molecules of oxygen in the oceans increased, facilitating vast algal blooms and even greater oxygen releases, the soluble iron in the oceans rusted thereby precipitating a cleansing process that lasted for over a billion years from that first moment. Ultimately, the free oxygen from the act of photosynthesis, a process now used by 99.9 percent of all life on Earth, created the atmosphere and life we know today. Who could ever imagine a remote outcrop in the baking Pilbara sun contained hints of life's first tentative steps?

Travelling through this ancient land, revelling in its geological bounty, the road into Marble Bar quickly brought me back to reality as the rocky country worked the suspension of my vehicle the way only Australian dirt roads can. Geology defined this country and its homogenous vistas to the horizon. Small, eroded ranges and jump-ups dominated the skyline: their jumbled rocky form sometimes hiding a small gorge whose waters offered a welcome respite from the heat of the Pilbara summer and the dust of the track.

These gorges also provided a hint into the powerful geological forces that created and then shaped this region. Folded, tilted iron-red rocks, twisted like a contorted snake trying to escape its rocky lair, defined the landscape. There were rocks everywhere; the remnants of ancient ranges slowly raised then razed as this country was created and recreated over several billion years.

Like other parts of this ancient, fascinating continent where significant geological forces impacted the land, small pockets of mineral riches awaited those who could unlock their metallurgical secrets. Randomly scattered smokestacks rising from among the rocky hills were evidence of where those riches lay and humanity's attempts to extract them. Yet it was not the mineral riches that called to me on this journey. It was instead the physical and spiritual riches that came from simply discovering the allure of the land and the natural treasures the Pilbara held.

Glen Herring Gorge was one such place: the twisting track into the gorge mirroring the twists and turns of the folded, uplifted strata. The gorge started out simply enough – a small creek whose path meandered through the ranges in no particular direction. Slowly following its rock-strewn course, it transformed into an inspiring vista whose refreshingly cool waters provided a welcome respite from the intense heat now defining each day. The gently waving reeds along its banks, the rippling emerald-green waterhole, and the worn, layered gorge walls all appeared in complete harmony as though a very specific but perfect natural formula governed the creation of this place.

Completing Nature's beguiling scene, the sapphire-blue Australian sky contrasted exquisitely with the iron-red hues of its rugged domain. In early summer, the gorge was almost empty of water for the rains of the Wet were yet to cleanse its rocky waterholes with their precious gift of life.

To see this gorge after the Wet, once the rains have washed its dusty heart and cleansed its rocky soul, must be a wonderful experience. For, even in the driest of times, Nature had created a magnificent vista. And, as I quickly learnt out here, where I found one gorge, I would almost certainly find another. This reality defined my Pilbara experience until it too was another receding vision in the rear-view mirror. Especially in the majestic and inspiring grandeur of the ancient Hamersley Range in Karijini National Park.

The Hamersley Range has a fascinating geological history from almost the beginning of the Earth's creation. Initially formed from iron sediments deposited off the southern edge of the ancient Pilbara Craton, it was subsequently uplifted as the Pilbara Craton joined with the Yilgarn Craton during the Ophthalmia and Glenburgh Orogenies around 2 billion years ago: the ranges of today an understated hint into 3.5 billion years of geological history. The ranges defined the spectacular Southern Pilbara region with the narrow, chiselled gorges through the banded, iron-red ramparts among the most inspiring natural creations I saw across the Australian Outback.

Here on this ancient craton, a land from the beginning of time, Nature had created an endless panorama of sculptured magnificence that enraptured and beguiled from the moment I entered its domain. Incredibly, the Hamersley Range reflects an environmental change not matched until that imposed on Earth by the coming of man. In fact, this country literally highlights the most important stage in the creation of life on Earth.

As life first started down its evolutionary path around 3.5 billion years ago, the atmosphere was very different to the one we know today. At that time, the Earth was surrounded by a cocktail of poisonous vapours and bombarded by the sun's direct, lethal radiation. Quite simply, the atmosphere responsible for the magnificent sapphire-blue sky of the Pilbara I had come to love did not exist. It was not until the generation of sufficient oxygen through photosynthesis, which started in earnest around 2.8 billion years ago, did the atmosphere commence its slow evolution into the majesty we enjoy and require today.

As the level of oxygen increased, the iron-laden oceans increasingly rusted with iron oxide sediments falling to the ocean bottom in a continual rain primarily from 1.8-2.5 billion years ago. Having swept the water clean of iron, oxygen molecules then seeped from the oceans to create the atmosphere of today. It was this process, whose initial start is seen in the jasper outcrop at Marble Bar, which created the sediments forming the ranges of the Pilbara today. Yet it did not just create the ranges. It also created the sapphire-blue sky stretching over them and the plant life living throughout them. Literally, everything seen and experienced in the Pilbara today, and likewise across the Australian continent and the Earth, can trace its beginning back to the processes first seen on this ancient, unassuming land.

It was in these ancient ranges, a throwback to the beginning of time, I found jewels of inspiring, humbling, and beguiling beauty scattered across the rugged, majestic landscape. Dales Gorge was one of these magnificent natural gems; its glistening emerald-green waters a welcoming oasis after days on the dusty track. I reached this gorge at dusk just as the low hills glowed with a fierce redness in the setting sun: the high iron content of the rocks inducing the fiery effect. Even though it was dusk, the opportunity to wash the dirt and smoke of several days travelling from my body was one not to be missed. Especially in a waterhole as magnificent as what I saw from the top of the gorge.

However, this was not going to be as easy as other gorges I had enjoyed for Dales Gorge was deeply set with almost vertical sides and there was only one path down. Along a narrow, winding track to the oasis below. The track into the gorge was fascinating for it wound its way slowly down through hundreds of millions of years of geological history; the banded, fractured formation creating the impression the same laconic builder from Jim Jim Falls had also built this place brick by brick in the ancient past. As the pine trees sighed in the evening breeze, their fragrance contrasting exquisitely with the smoky-honey smell of the spinifex, Nature reminded me yet again how it can create the most inspiring of natural jewels with the most basic of elements in the most unexpected places.

The turquoise-green pool at the bottom of the gorge was an enchanting place, especially in the cool of dusk with not another soul around.

As the water cascaded down the steep rock face of Fortescue Falls into the pool, the rock worn smooth from countless millennia of flow, I was seduced by the wonder of this ancient land. The sound of water gurgling and splashing, gently reverberating off the gorge walls, was a natural symphony that relaxed my tired mind and exhausted body. As I lowered myself into its refreshing realm, a feeling of total bliss washed over me. It was a most welcome gift, even more appreciated for its role in banishing the smoke, dust, and sweat from my body back to the land from which it came.

The water was crystal clear, cool, and sweet: its succouring touch connecting me to the land in a most subtle way. Swimming in its welcome embrace completely alone, the purple-blue sky darkening as the dusk turned to night, my feeling of love and gratitude to the natural world was overwhelming. It washed away any feelings of fear or concern that occasionally bubbled up as my walkabout slowly, but inevitably, neared its completion. Nature has created a delightful and mesmerising sanctuary within Dales Gorge, one I appreciated even more the next day as I followed the creek deeper into the gorge.

Coming from the dry and spinifex-covered ranges, where I camped the previous night, the abundance of wealth from the natural world throughout the gorge captivated me. Eucalyptus, pine, and paperbark trees thickly lined its banks while a gently gurgling creek created an oasis for all living things. In some places, it was almost impossible to make my way through given the vegetation's thickness. The air was alive with the sounds of insects and birds with their pulsating chant, as if from a didgeridoo, a constant reminder of their joy at living on such a permanent source of water in such a dry land.

The ground could have been an Aboriginal painting so well marked was it with the tracks of kangaroos, goannas, echidnas, and snakes where they had come to drink the previous night. The tempo of life in the gorge was very different to that on the waterless ridges and plains, just a short distance away, where only spinifex, galahs, and small lizards appeared to thrive.

In addition to the pool at the base of Fortescue Falls, another much longer, more exotic waterhole was found downstream: a reach of water stretching for several hundred metres. Although I had seen it from the top of the gorge, I had no idea how appreciated it would become. It was the perfect temperature being cool enough to keep the heat of the day at bay but warm enough that its caress never left me with the desire to seek the rocks heated by the sun. Further downstream, the creek opened into a cascade of small falls: their gurgling and splashing providing a harmonising, symphonic backdrop to the bountiful vista spread out before me. It was another gentle reminder of the physical, emotional, and spiritual balm Nature provides and its true worth to our lives.

Kalamina Gorge was another majestic Pilbara gorge that literally took my breath away. Its shade and sanctuary on a hot summer day made it a welcome contrast to the dry, rocky ridges that distinctly defined much of the surrounding country. Walking into its welcoming sanctuary, deep within the ranges during the heat of the midday sun, the splendour of Nature's work astounded me as the gorge transformed itself into a most captivating yet serene place.

The gorge walls, worn smooth from the countless millennia of running water that carved this sacred place, stretched out like two strong arms before me carefully embracing a precious treasure much as a mother cradles a child. Clasped between these two strong arms was a shallow pool whose clear waters faithfully reflected the changing iron-red hues of the gorge as the light changed over the course of the day. The end of the gorge was a tangle of trees and grasses, their reflection off the water a faithful representation in all respects. I could see the bottom of the gorge as small fish darted about as a flash of silver in the otherwise iron-red landscape. The rocks, though hard to lie on, were a cool and welcome change to the furnace-like feel of the open ground.

It was another idyllic place to just sit and watch how the feel and mood of the land changed over the course of the day. It was enough to be part of Nature's sanctuary, in this rugged and inspiring land, with nothing more than an open heart and a gentled soul.

While Dales Gorge and Kalamina Gorge were inspiring places in their own right, they barely prepared me for the most spectacular sight in the Pilbara and certainly one of the most breathtaking panoramas across the Australian Outback: Oxer Lookout, the meeting point of four magnificent, converging gorges.

Weano Gorge, Hancock Gorge, Red Gorge, and Joffre Gorge are each spectacular gorges in their own right. They first appeared as vivid slashes across the spinifex-covered landscape: ancient points of weakness transformed into magnificent gorges by the most basic of elements over geological time. To see them converge at one location left me in awe and astonishment of what Nature was truly capable. From the top of the lookout to the bottom of the junction was a vertical drop of about 130 metres; the gorges' depth and size magnified by the sheer-sided walls that seemed to plummet forever.

Yet, this was just a tantalising hint of the depth of the Pilbara's iron sediments. For it is estimated that over 2.5 kilometres were ultimately deposited as the ancient seas were cleansed of their iron content. Peering down into these ancient gorges connected me to the earliest days of Earth and the natural magnificence subsequently created from that moment. It represented another opportunity to understand Nature's omnipotence, the power of its elements, their ability to create vistas that continually inspired and awed me on every level as a human being, and the importance of that creative capacity to the quality of my life.

To explore these gorges, I followed Hancock Gorge down to the junction first seen from Oxer Lookout. Half walking, half sliding into the iron-red depths was another of the many geological self-teaching experiences I relished across the Australian continent. The layered sediments, known as a banded iron formation, were polished and rounded from the sharp, rectangular form typically seen in the ranges thereby creating a smoothly shaped pathway. Following the rippled surface as I moved deeper into the gorge, I felt I was in an ancient sluice box though fortunately without the rocking! It was often difficult to find a good handhold or foothold as I slowly scrambled down along the gorge floor over or around any obstacle barring my way.

Kermit's Pool was one such place. From a distance, it was another emerald-green jewel bound strongly to the Earth. Up close, it was an exotic rock pool carved out by grinding, tumbling rocks during times of fast-flowing water, and a quite unexpected treat as I made my way down into the gorge. The pool was held fast within the gorge walls, their wrinkled sides and smooth surface cool to the touch. To swim within its embalming waters, with the sound of a small, lazy waterfall at its head echoing through the chamber, and a sliver of the sapphire-blue sky visible overhead, I felt pampered by Nature's caress in a very special way. It was another of those unforgettable places, and moments, when Nature gently reminded me of its predilection to create great works of natural art in the most unexpected places.

Following the gorge down, the walls narrowed to a small opening on the other side of which lay the waterhole that first drew me from the top of the gorge like a moth to a flame. The opening was barely wide enough for two people to stand side by side. It was through this opening the waters flowed from Hancock Gorge to combine with those of the three other gorges. On climbing through the narrow opening, I reached the waterhole first seen from the top of Oxer Lookout. It was a lot bigger than the miniaturised version seen from above.

The waterhole was a quiet, idyllic location with its stand of tall, broad-boughed eucalyptus trees providing a dappled, welcomed shade. Swimming in the quietness of such a unique place while looking up to the top of the gorge, it was only then I realised how far down I had come. Slipping across a sandy beach, into the waterholes of the other gorges, I made sure to spend time in each of them separately to understand and appreciate their unique beauty and feel. Their depth and vertical walls not only reinforced my awe for the country; they ensured my swim was of a most bracing kind as the sun's rays only warmed these waterholes for several hours each day.

Although, in the middle of summer, with temperatures north of 40 degrees Celsius waiting back in the ranges, it was one of the most relaxing places in the Pilbara to be!

It was not just the Pilbara gorges that provided an objective lesson into Nature's power. On one unexpected occasion, it was actually the weather. And like the cleansing feel of a swim through one of its gorges, a drive through one of its storms was equally insightful though in a quite different manner.

Driving towards the mining town of Tom Price, after my time at Oxer Lookout, I was fascinated to watch a storm sweep in from the horizon. So quickly did it gather, the sky changed from sapphire-blue to dark grey and black in a couple of minutes. The grey, threatening clouds, tinged an angry orange by the rays of the setting sun, briefly registered their individual existence before combining into a sea of dark grey intimidation sweeping across the land.

From the horizon, a wall of water roared across the plains directly towards me: its tell-tale vertical torrent of grey dropping straight to the ground a brief insight into its intensity. Reinforcing the seriousness of my situation, lightning increasingly flashed vigorously around me searing the darkness with bright, jagged spears. As the storm appeared to be moving quite slowly, however, the situation did not appear too alarming. That was until I came over a ridge and saw there were actually several storms moving across the horizon. Furthermore, they were all converging across the one road into Tom Price. There was nowhere to go but into the storm.

It became quite scary, quite quickly. There was nowhere to take cover and, with the sky an inky black, the only light apart from the beam of my headlights were the flashes of lightning quickly followed by loud claps of thunder. Driving into the heart of the storm, the thunder and lightning came increasingly quickly and increasingly loudly. As the storm blew overhead, a jagged shaft of light split the darkness next to my vehicle. The roar of thunder that broke next to me was deafening. The wind was so intense it pushed my vehicle across the track. I had to fight with the steering wheel to keep my 4WD pointed somewhat in the right direction. With bolts of lightning searing the night sky all around, I felt each one was aimed directly at me.

It seemed as though a certain deity of my Nordic ancestors was looking to make a very succinct point with everything around a mad rush of rain and dust, lightning and thunder. That deity could only be Odin, with his eight-legged charger Sleipnir, galloping across the Pilbara sky as he had similarly done across the Nordic sky for my ancestors centuries before. Why would he do that? Maybe his presence at this stage of my walkabout was a stirring reminder that, as I neared the end of my journey, I still had much to learn. Maybe it was an important reminder that seeking Nature's wisdom would be a lifelong quest for me, as it had been for him, and not necessarily an easy one.

Perhaps it was instead an overt sign of respect from my walkabout talisman for my commitment to the quest of seeking Nature's wisdom just as he had also done on similar journeys. Or perhaps it was sign from Odin that his role in my walkabout was now finished, and a memorable farewell until our paths crossed again once more. Which, in all likelihood, will be when it is time to return to a wandering journey through the natural world to, once again, repair the damage incurred from Western society's increasingly destructive beliefs and behaviours.

Passing through the storm was also very insightful. Seeing the absolute power of Nature reinforced my respect for each of its many moods, not just those I found inspiring or beguiling. Everything Nature designed and created, I realised, was a thing of beauty and deserving of our respect and appreciation even though society may deem it otherwise based on some abstract cultural or religious belief.

Even though the storm initially disturbed me, it came to beguile me with its beauty and power. To me, Nature's basic elements, earth and fire, wind and water, were simply converted into a dynamic work of art just as they had equally been at Uluru and Ormiston Gorge, except in this case the elements were combined in a different way. I realised that floods, droughts, earthquakes, volcanoes, fires, and other natural events are also just that. A unique expression through which Nature combines its elements into the form necessary for its life-giving role. I realised that many natural events humanity does not appreciate, which reinforce our self-imposed segregation from the life-creating mystery of the natural world, are actually critical parts of the dynamic lifecycle we require to survive on Earth.

Humanity's overriding conviction that it is somehow the superior species, that we should not be impacted by the lifecycle of the Earth in a negative way, that we are entitled to use the Earth entirely for our own benefit at the expense of its other species, became a philosophy now impossible to reconcile with Nature's teaching. To assume humanity's existence is the sole purpose of the Earth, to assume our needs outweigh those of all other beings, to assume we can take what we want from the Earth without any concern for the damaging affect, is probably the biggest problem we face today. It is one that will certainly remain a fundamental cause of our greatest challenges, and problems, until we recalibrate our relationship with the Earth: our ultimate creator.

To respect Nature, to be appreciative of how much its teaching enhances our health and happiness, to find beauty in all the cycles of the Earth, defined my new life philosophy. For where we ignore the wisdom of the natural world, where we fail to respect each stage of its lifecycle and see them as part of its natural functioning, where we instead impose our beliefs of how the Earth should function for humanity, how can we expect to connect with the life force that actually supports us? We do not control Nature. It is not there for our exclusive benefit. We are part of Nature. It is part of us. And when we break that sacred bond with the natural world, when our so-called rights to consume and irresponsibly take overwhelm our responsibilities to moderation and self-respect, we alone are responsible for the self-inflicted consequences we ultimately bear.

Well, it certainly seemed that way to me on walkabout across the soulful vastness of the Australian Outback surrounded and nurtured by the natural world alone!

Following my Odinic experience within the storm, it was with significant relief Tom Price finally came into view. The storm had blown through leaving only the sweet fragrance of rain on the breeze and a smattering of leaves and small branches across the ground. Yet it was not the illusion of the safety of civilisation that gave me relief. It was instead the opportunity to indulge in a long awaited hot shower, for the first time in several weeks, to wash the dust, sweat, and smoke from my body that was such a natural part of living in the bush.

Unexpectedly, this was not to be the only attraction as I soon discovered. In fact, it was not even to be the primary attraction. For Nature was to indulge my interest in my favourite bird with a unique show in the caravan park where I stayed.

The following day, my campsite appeared to be hosting a galah corroboree. They were everywhere; their pink, white, and grey plumage distinctly contrasting against the deep iron-red of the land and the sapphire-blue sky. A small flock had settled into the trees, under which I lay my swag, and here they played for several hours providing the most amusing entertainment. They were fascinating to watch, appearing to have lost their fear of humanity which made them easier to observe than when out in the bush. They flew into several trees as a flock and this was the only time they were not individuals.

As they took up residence in their chosen tree, each galah focused on very specific tasks that were undertaken with great attention to detail. Whether it was stripping small leaves off the trees and tossing them around, much like a horse will do with its food, or preening themselves with the fastidious attention of a teenager, they were hilarious to watch. Every now and then, one launched itself into the sapphire-blue sky, wheeling and careening through the trees, twisting and turning like a fighter plane. They revelled in their acrobatics, with their loud, energetic squawks echoing around the caravan park another reminder of the importance of play to a happy, healthy life.

It was impossible not to laugh at their antics that were undertaken with a great degree of humour on their part judging from the shrillness of their calls. Then they flew back to a tree to pick more leaves and to preen one another before more acrobatics. Their curiosity allowed me to become part their playful world for a short time. They seemed as interested in me as I was in them. As I rested under a tree, sitting on my swag, several slowly inched towards me along a branch, their heads cocked to one side peering at me from their small black eyes. Once they satisfied their curiosity, about what I will never know, they slowly moved their way back or launched themselves into the air with a shrill squawk and flapping of wings to, once again, indulge their acrobatic skills among the trees.

Interestingly, as Nature would have it, the curiosity of Australia's wildlife in me was not only limited to galahs. In fact, the most inquisitive animal I came across during my entire journey was met here – a large kangaroo no less. And this was no normal visit!

Each night, I unrolled my swag under the mosquito net. And each night, sleep came quickly until woken by the sun's dazzling rays or the raucous calls of galahs. This particular night, however, I was amazed and a bit shocked to wake in the dark and find a kangaroo pawing at the mosquito net trying to get into my swag. It took a little time to understand what was happening after waking out of a deep sleep. I was not quite sure what he had on his mind, but he seemed quite convinced that I was part of it.

To discourage him, I tried pushing him away with my hand. All this did was make him more aggressive as he sat upright on both feet clawing at the air. Lying on my swag, covered by the mosquito net, with an agitated kangaroo looking down on me, I decided that valour was the better part of discretion in this case. I pushed him away several more times before he lost interest in his pursuit and hopped off into the dark. Needless to say, I did not get much sleep for the rest of the night.

Returning to Tom Price was also important for a very personal reason. My first memory had been here, of looking out into the bush over 30 years before and first hearing Nature's siren call. I had always wanted to revisit this place, to understand if the connection I felt all those years ago was still there. Finding my old home was not difficult for its shape and location ensured those who sought it a high probability of success. And with a slow walk back along the street of my first memory, to the concreted cul-de-sac, another surprise awaited me. The view was just as I remembered it all those years ago. It had not been touched for subsequent building had all occurred in other parts of town.

I sat on the curb for some time just absorbing the landscape remembered from my first memory, and reflecting on how its siren call had influenced my life since that moment. It is not often we have the opportunity to revisit the wellspring from which our own life evolves. Despite the passing years, I still felt very connected to that place. I felt it was part of me and I was part of it. I felt increasingly grateful I had listened to its call not only on being 'liberated' two years previously, but also from my earliest days. For it was living with respect for that call, and the wisdom it had taught me through the years, that brought an abundance of experiences into my life I would never have otherwise enjoyed.

Sitting on the kerb, the same feeling I experienced in the horse yard at Mellaluka my last night bubbled to the surface. The natural world and its teaching would always be my guide, and Outback Australia would always be my home. That was just the simple and endearing reality of it all.

I spent my last night here enjoying the delights of Hamersley Gorge, one of the few Pilbara gorges whose simple horizontal geometry had been somewhat disfigured. The rocks here were folded and uplifted; the gorge walls a scientific and artistic tribute to the tectonic forces behind its creation. Given its allure, and remoteness, it was also another perfect location to spend the night with only my fire's warming glow and the starlit bounty of the night sky for company.

The sunset that evening was stunning: its burning orange radiance lighting up the western sky and plains as if a roaring conflagration was sweeping down from the range. Deep in the gorge, the ancient layered and folded sediments glowed red, pink, and purple with such an intensity it seemed the gorge would burst into flames. As the sun slowly sank below the horizon, as dusk turned to night and the conflagration slowly petered out in a purple-blue haze, the majesty of the star-jewelled crown overhead tantalisingly revealed itself. With no moon, the landscape was increasingly lost to view except for the small circle of light around my fire and the dark, hulking shape of the range silhouetted by the starlit night sky.

Lying on my swag, looking into the night sky, I could have been the last person on Earth. Given the pristine nature of the environment down in the gorge and on the plains, I could also have been the first. It was a reminder of the importance of living in the wild places Nature has created for our benefit. Tucked into my swag later that night, the glow of the late-rising moon and stars bathed the country in a balming, silver sheen as the coals of my fire gently pulsated with a deep, red glow. It was another of those times I felt especially grateful for everything the natural world had made possible from the moment of its siren call over 30 years before. Moreover, it was a call I had no doubt I would gladly follow for the rest of my life.

As much as I would have appreciated spending more time exploring the magnificence of Karijini National Park, the road still called. There was still much to see in the Pilbara before taking the road south towards Perth, and then east across the continent towards home. On leaving Hamersley Gorge, my swag tossed into the 4WD after a quick breakfast of water, I headed northwest into Millstream-Chichester National Park to enjoy its gorges. Their cool, deep luxury was just the respite I needed from driving the hot, dusty roads that define the Pilbara in summer.

Deepreach Pool, a waterhole on the Fortescue River, was particularly appreciated. Several kilometres long and quite wide, surrounded by vegetation on all sides, it was actually a gorge carved through an aquifer whose waters keep it filled to the brim thereby making it the perfect place to enjoy several relaxing hours in the late afternoon sun.

Crossing Pool, a waterhole downstream from Deepreach Pool, was the ideal place to spend the night: its tree-lined oasis the perfect respite from the rigours of travelling the rocky, jarring roads. Following a quick swim, as dusk approached, dinner was a meal of whatever cans of food remained washed down with a cup of red wine. Lying on my swag later that night under the mesmerising starlit night sky unfolding above, as the tangy smell of eucalyptus appreciatively wafted up from the waterhole, I had everything in life I could possibly need. Alone in the majesty of the vast Outback, surrounded by the magnificence of the natural world, there was nowhere else I would rather have been!

The following morning, it was the local avian community who woke me from my sweat-stained slumber. Their raucous calls, echoing along the waterhole, were a delightful chorus that always brought a wry smile to my face. With a day of driving through hot, dry country to the coast, a quick swim was in order before returning to the track. Slipping into the cool, clear water of Crossing Pool in the early morning light, surrounded by fish swimming almost within reach, Nature pampered me with its luxuriant touch. Looking up from deep within its watery embrace, the sun's rays playfully danced across the surface as random flashes of light like a healthy smattering of small diamonds gently cast across the river.

Embalmed by the cool, sweet waters and the all-pervading smell of eucalyptus, harmonised by Nature in the most Australian of ways, I never wanted to leave. On the other hand, perhaps it was knowing what lay in front of me that made that particular early morning swim a little more difficult to finish. Either way, the road still called. With my swag the last item swung into the back of the vehicle, it was soon time to leave. While it had become a little more difficult each day to return to the track, as my journey neared its completion, it was at places like Crossing Pool after a delightful early morning swim it became especially difficult.

To the west of the Pilbara, another of Nature's mesmerising oceanic jewels can be found. Here, at Ningaloo Reef, Australia's largest fringing reef, Nature's DNA has created a most enchanting location along the western edge of the North West Cape. Ningaloo Reef is one of the most exquisite reefs in the world: its waters a plethora of sparkling blue hues gently lapping a gleaming white, sandy beach that dazzled brilliantly during the day and glowed a fiery orange-purple in the dusk. Close to shore, the ocean teemed with fish while the sands were alive with fauna that left their multi-toed prints and paw marks across its soft bedding awaiting discovery in the early morning light.

As if to remind me of Nature's propensity for change, Ningaloo Reef has an ancient land-based peer located nearby – a limestone reef reflecting a time when an ancient sea covered this land. This ancient reef is now a majestic limestone range; its ramparts carved by Yardi Creek into an exquisite gorge just as Windjana Gorge was carved from Napier Range. The water in Yardi Creek Gorge was brackish, its taste unappealing compared to the sweet, refreshing waters of its inland peers. However, in every other sense, it perfectly reflected the majesty and opulence I had come to appreciate from other gorges enjoyed across the vastness of the Australian continent.

One of the unexpected items found on the North West Cape today, in Cape Range National Park, is an abandoned oil well. This wellhead is the only remnant of one of the more exciting times in the Australian energy industry. For, in 1953, Australia's first 'gusher' was drilled here. Fortunately, for the local Ningaloo Reef environment, it turned out to be uneconomic after only a short time.

However, while onshore exploration for oil and gas proved unsuccessful, it was a very different story offshore. For just off the coast lies the Northwest Shelf, one of the most sought after hydrocarbon provinces in the world today. Such that, to the north, south, and west of that humble wellhead baking in the ranges, globally significant volumes of natural gas are now being produced and shipped around the world. With an increasing demand for cleaner energy driving further development in the region, the fear is that areas surrounding Ningaloo Reef may be developed and lost forever.

Looking across the mosaic of reefs submerged beneath the gently breaking waves, the water dappled by the most beguiling hues of blue, it was difficult to imagine any evolved society could ever seriously contemplate putting such natural splendour at risk. It was simply too precious, too unique, and too rare to consider doing so. With so few wild and pristine places remaining on Earth, Ningaloo Reef is surely one of those few remaining natural jewels that deserves our protection at all costs.

From Ningaloo Reef, I followed the coast south to Shark Bay. This part of the coast was fascinating, particularly its stromatolite population. Stromatolites today, mainly found as fossils of which the oldest is over 3.5 billion years old, represent one of the earliest forms of life on Earth. In fact, the cyanobacteria that played a role in their creation were the same bacteria that first exhaled oxygen as a waste gas, ultimately giving rise to the world of today. At Shark Bay, these simple yet life-creating organisms have survived an incomprehensible passage of time with little change to their ancient compatriots.

Fascinatingly, back to the northeast, where the first hint of oxygen in the oceans was seen in the jasper outcrop at Marble Bar, 2.8 billion-year-old fossilised stromatolites remain attached to the very land that gave them life. It just goes to show how ancient the western portion of the Australian continent really is. Especially one of its founding pieces: the Pilbara Craton.

Shark Bay was also remarkable for another reason. For it was here, at Monkey Mia, I experienced an interaction of the most precious kind. Monkey Mia is one of the few places on Earth wild dolphins interact directly with people. It was heartwarming to watch these cheeky, muscled creatures swim up and down the beach early one morning. Several of them came almost onto the beach, rolling over onto their backs while watching me with very intelligent eyes. They appeared to appreciate when I made eye contact with them and acknowledged my probably confusing attempts to communicate. They were certainly gregarious, with lots of high-pitched squeals and teeth clicking, as they played in the surf just a metre or so from where I stood.

The opportunity to watch these dolphins swim and play, to be part of their world for a short time, took me back to my experiences with galahs and horses, and how critical play was to their lives. It was another important reminder, for me at least, of how much we can intrinsically learn from our four-footed, feathered, and sea faring friends about what is truly important in life!

From Monkey Mia, the road continued south to Kalbarri National Park and the Murchison River: a river carved through ancient multi-coloured, layered sediments first eroded from the adjacent Yilgarn Craton around 400 million years ago. Resting in the slow moving, appreciatively cool waters, as the sun's rays quickly heated up the day, I enjoyed another intimate connection to this most ancient of lands. Reaching the Murchison River was important for another reason, however. It represented my final connection with two inspiring explorers whose paths I had actively sought, and whose lives I had respectfully connected with, during my walkabout.

The Murchison River represented the beginning of Augustus Gregory's exploration success and the end of Nat Buchanan's droving exploits. In many ways, it bookended the most interesting times and personalities from Australia's exploration and pastoral history. Gregory reached this river in 1848 on one of his first expeditions into the unknown western portion of the continent. It was the success he achieved on this expedition that placed him at the forefront of candidates to lead the North Australian Expedition to the Victoria River less than a decade later.

And while the Murchison River represented the beginning of Gregory's exploration feats, it also represented the end of Nat Buchanan's unique pioneering achievements. For it was to the banks of this river, aged 66, he drove a mob of cattle 2,000 kilometres from the Kimberley in 1892. This was his last effort at pioneering another droving track across some of the most remote and challenging country Australia has to offer.

As I reflected on the enormity of their respective achievements, and those of the other explorers and pioneers who opened up the inland, I also thought of the packhorses who supported their expeditions. For it was primarily their strength, patience, persistence, and endurance that facilitated the exploration and pioneering successes achieved. Given their outsized contribution to these successes, it is a shame there are so few memorials in Australia to those wonderful animals and the key role they played in opening up the vast, rugged interior of this most challenging of continents.

To that end, the verse at the beginning of this chapter serves as a recognition of, and a lasting memorial to, their unflinching and inspiring service across the daunting vastness of the Australian Outback. It also serves as a memorial to the 180,000 horses Australia sent overseas to support its troops in both the Boer and First World Wars, of which only one ever returned to Australia. Those horses deserve at least as much recognition as those whose lives are woven throughout these pages.

Looking over the cool waters of the Murchison River, in the summer of 2003, it seemed appropriate they now marked the slowly approaching completion of my journey. For, while the road still beckoned, its call was now increasingly less alluring. Not only would my connection to the country travelled through be limited by following the bitumen, humanity would increasingly impose its so-called civilised imprint on what had once been a plethora of striking natural vistas. From the banks of the Murchison River, much of the rugged and untamed wildness I had previously connected with was unfortunately to be in memory only.

Driving south towards Perth, it was with an increasing sense of sadness I watched the country slowly become more urbanised, more shackled, as the wild, untamed lands of Outback Australia were lost to view. The inspiring vastness of the Australian continent, the magnificence that provided the intellectual, physical, emotional, and spiritual succour and freedom I had long sought, which ignited my desire to rediscover a life of health, happiness, and adventure, was increasingly lost to the unfortunate propensity of humanity to fence, control, and destroy the environment. Nature's opulence and spirit were now limited to an occasional, tantalising hint of what had existed before the caging of its soul and the plunder of its bounty over the previous 150 years.

While the road home would provide a few more opportunities to appreciate and savour Nature's grandeur across its Australian Outback canvas, they would be limited and restricted. However, the road still called as it had since first leaving Sydney almost two years before. Fortuitously, it had all worked out well so far. I just had to trust it would continue to do so.

14

Journey's End

'She has hidden each footprint of mine
With a swirl of her drifting sand;
My camp-fires leave no sign
And nowhere my tent-pegs stand;
On her tracks I have left no trace,
Yet my heart to her heart shall cling;
I shall remember her face
To the end of remembering.'

Will Ogilvie – Australia

After two years of happily living out of a dusty swag, of exploring Australia's diverse and breathtaking vastness, of seeing the inspiring natural brilliance that is the Great South Land, my journey now approached its completion. For much of my wandering, there had been no real time pressure. I moved on when it felt right to move on and stayed when it felt right to stay. The concept of time only influenced my life through the amount of light each day. With Christmas on the horizon, however, my journey now became a logical progression versus the random walkabout it had previously been as mileage goals became part of my travelling calculus. It was a difficult habit to re-establish having delighted in the energising resonance of Nature's circadian rhythms during my walkabout. But that is life, circumstances change, and it is up to us to make the most of those changes whether we like them or not. After being 'liberated' from my career, I could have become disillusioned and frustrated. Instead, I took advantage of the opportunity to experience the adventure of a lifetime with all the blessings and lessons such a journey entailed. I just had to trust the end of my walkabout would facilitate the same opportunities for growth and wisdom its unexpected beginning certainly had.

While Perth represented the beginning of my journey's completion, it also represented a return to civilisation and its appreciated culinary treats. For someone who had spent much of the previous two years living almost exclusively on muesli, long-life milk, canned fruit, canned tuna, four bean mix, green tea, and the odd cup of red wine, it was an epicurean delight.

Perth was to my body what the gorges had been to my soul. Tantalising seafood, fresh salad, delicious summer fruits, and the chilled exotic beverage of the grape made for one sybaritic indulgence after another. My palate reinvigorated itself when foods such as these replaced the months of bland, constant fare previously enjoyed, then just endured! With the cool breeze off the ocean replacing the humidity, heat, and dust of the inland, each sense came alive with an anticipation that enhanced every experience. Swimming in the cool, clear azure waters of the Indian Ocean added another appreciated layer to the pampering feel of Perth, making me appreciate its charms even more.

Like other travellers who reach Perth across the sands of the desert, it felt like a veritable oasis. The feeling of attraction to the city becomes quite strong encouraging many people to settle and stay for some time. Fortunately, or unfortunately, the road called a little more loudly than the charms of Perth. Accordingly, before long, it too was nothing more than a shrinking image in the rear-view mirror as the last stage of my walkabout got underway.

Driving south towards Albany, into some of the most bucolic parts of the country, vineyards and pristine sandy beaches stretched into the lazy azure hues of the ocean and sky beguiling me with their sensuous pleasures. While Nature's geological DNA had played the primary role in creating the wonder of the Australian Outback, here on the coast it was almost the opposite. And as the climate became milder, so the magnificence of the flora increased as forests of giant Karri trees towered over the narrow bitumen road with their immense trunks and broad branches seeming to hold up the sky. The diversity of plant life was astounding compared to the meagre portions served up across the desert. It gave the land a very different feel.

Yet, while the diversity of shade and colour made for unique vistas, I felt they lacked the vitality of the more rugged and remote regions that most inspired me. The raw natural energy was gone here: the balance between life and death had moved away from the edge it rested on further out. Despite broad views over the ocean from windswept headlands and patches of thick, almost impenetrable, scrub, the land did not inspire or excite as much as the vistas from remoter regions previously had. The agricultural manicuring of the country further reinforced my feeling that Nature had been made subservient to the whims of humanity irrespective of what it truly wanted to show.

Returning to the more civilised, benign parts of the continent, culture shock now set in. Confronted by Nature's subservient role to the ways of the modern world, I had a difficult time accepting this unfortunate reality having spent much of my journey admiring and respecting its unadulterated wildness and connecting with its untameable energy. I felt that something critical to our own physical, emotional, and spiritual being had been lost through the mindless destruction of the environment and our decreasing connection to Nature itself. Fortunately, I now understood there were many other ways to remain part of the natural world which made that loss a little easier to bear.

Albany is a town that played a significant role in Australia's Anzac heritage. It was here, in late 1914, troopships from the six states of the newly formed Australian Commonwealth first gathered before sailing as a fleet towards the Middle East and the Western Front. It was the wooded hillsides and rounded granite islands of King George Sound that were to be the last glimpse of Australia for most of the men on board those ships. Over three quarters of the soldiers who left on that fleet were destined to remain in the hallowed acres of Anzac Cove, the fields of France and Flanders, or the deserts of Palestine. It would be almost five years before the survivors of that terrible conflict returned home to the smell of eucalyptus and the sound of galahs, once again.

Overlooking the harbour today are several memorials to those 'greathearted men' as Charles Bean reverently described them. One of these is the Light Horse Memorial (known as the Desert Mounted Corps Memorial) which was consecrated in Cairo in 1932 in memory of the Australian and New Zealand troopers who died in Palestine and the Middle East. Following its destruction during the Suez Crisis in 1956, its remains were shipped to Australia where the brassy gaze of the Australian and New Zealand Light Horse troopers now extends over the very harbour from which their comrades first left Australia almost a century before.

It is one of the most poignant First World War memorials in Australia given the tragic reality of the panorama over which it looks, and how important the memory of that land was to the men who would never see it again.

Having walked the hallowed acres of Gallipoli and the fields of France and Flanders, past thousands of gravestones into which the 'Rising Sun' badge of the First Australian Imperial Force was carved, I now felt honoured to be back at the point their journey commenced. Understanding the great deeds they achieved and the role they played on the world stage in that terrible conflict made the sacrifice of so many of those men a little more bearable – but only a little. And if you listen closely today, you can almost hear the laughter and cheers of those same men lining the rails of their troopships all those years ago. The same wind that caught their slouch hats and tunics yesterday, much as it does our hats and coats today, still carrying their voices for all of tomorrow.

Enhancing the poignancy of the Light Horse Memorial are the individual plaques lining the road leading up to the memorial. Remembrances for men that cry out against the cruel waste of war; cries that sound eerily similar to that of the seagulls gently hovering overhead. Men who never imagined their final view of Australia would be the wooded hillsides whose disappearance over the horizon marked the start of their great adventure. Among the many individual plaques lining the road leading to the memorial, one final resting place frequently shown is Gallipoli with one battle in particular most remembered: the charge at the Nek.

The charge of the 10th Australian Light Horse Regiment at the Nek was one of the most tragic actions of the whole Gallipoli campaign. In fact, Bean remarked that, in his final analysis of the war, there was no finer example of reckless obedience than this action. Over the course of only 10 minutes, 300 men knowingly charged into oblivion believing their certain sacrifice would ultimately be to the benefit of their comrades fighting other battles that day. This just after they had watched a similar number of men from the 8th Australian Light Horse Regiment brutally cut down in front of them.

The 10th Australian Light Horse Regiment was raised entirely in Western Australia, a state with a small rural population. Given the devastation of the regiment, it was said that almost every pastoral family in the state lost at least one of its own that day, with many families losing two or more members. Respectfully, almost a century later, that action remains a key part of the Australian identity from its remembrance on memorials in Perth, Canberra, and at Anzac Cove to its gently rippling influence across society today.

And should you follow the path to the Light Horse Memorial atop Mount Clarence, you will find another memorial to those men. It is a bench, with a small plaque in memory of the 10th Australian Light Horse Regiment, which encourages you to sit and reflect on what happened so many lifetimes ago. Sitting on that bench in early December 2003, my thoughts returned to a small cemetery at Anzac Cove, the Nek Cemetery, where most of the young men whose memorials surround you actually lie.

Reflecting the brutality of that battle, almost all of those men have no known grave. Instead, their remains were buried together where they fell, after the Armistice, in 1919. It was a heartrending moment as I appreciated how their sacrifice had enabled me to live in a country where freedom on all fronts, for most, was a given.

Resting beneath the memorial, with not another soul around, the quiet allowed my mind to wander back through the pages of Australian Light Horse history to those long gone days and the men who comprised its regiments. Many, a significant majority in fact, had been born in the bush, had learnt its ways, had been toughened and strengthened by its trials and tribulations, and had unwittingly been prepared for the crucible of modern warfare. They endured through those hellish times creating a legacy that remains admired and respected by their country's citizens down through the generations.

At the core of their ability was the lessons they learnt in the Australian bush. It was the natural world that played the primary role in developing the mettle and capability they showed. It was the bush that facilitated the skills and insights that made them one of the most respected fighting forces of the First World War. It was for this reason I found the Light Horse Memorial in Albany a telling tribute to the troopers and their horses, and an important reminder of Nature's fundamental role in the creation of those most inspiring regiments of men. It was another reminder of how much Australians owe the bush as a people, and how much we can benefit from learning its wisdom and including its teaching in our lives, even today.

As the going down of the sun that day, its glowing rays lighting up the magnificent memorial to horse and man, it was with a sense of sadness, respect, and gratitude I left that sacred place with the shouts and cheers of the men still dancing about in the wind as they first had almost a hundred years before.

Heading east from Albany, as the climate got drier, the country slowly changed, reverting to its more marginal nature and seemingly giving it more of a chance to breathe. Scrubby country became the norm until reaching the empty vastness of an ancient sea floor plain just outside the mining town of Norseman: a town whose name uniquely commemorates the horse of the prospector who discovered its gold-bearing reefs, Hardy Norseman. Not surprisingly, Lawrence Sinclair, the prospector, was born in the Shetland Islands. I drank a quiet beer in Norseman as I thought of Odin, my Scottish and Nordic ancestors, and how that nondescript Scottish-Norse island in the depths of the North Sea had bred a people who always seemed to end up on the frontier in one way or another!

From Norseman, stretching out before me for almost 1,100 kilometres to the east was the Nullarbor Plain: its ancient limestone floor covered with a mixture of saltbush and sand until the agricultural regions of South Australia were finally reached. Reflecting its vast waterless spaces and scant lack of vegetation, it was never seriously considered as a pastoral region until the more economically attractive regions of the country were first developed. Accordingly, the most exciting part of its history revolves around the early European exploration to discover a suitable crossing between the established settlements in South Australia and the newly evolving settlements in the West. With chiselled, steep cliffs preventing access to the ocean for much of any crossing, expeditions were required to be self-sufficient for most of the journey across what is essentially a waterless plain.

Only one man was initially willing to attempt such a task. A man who realised it was highly likely he may leave his bones in the desert, but who took the chance anyway. He was the last of the 12 mentors whose tracks I wanted to cross. Not only did he successfully traverse the Nullarbor Plain, he was also the first explorer to undertake expeditions into the deserts of South Australia, discovering Lake Eyre in 1840. That man was John Eyre.

John Eyre set out with several companions, and an Aboriginal guide Wylie, in an attempt to reach Albany, then known as King George

Sound, in February 1841. He was one of the first Australian explorers who used horses in this way, who saw that a fast moving expedition had a much greater chance of success than one loaded with the accoutrement of other expeditions. As he foresaw, however, finding water on that dry, flat, desolate plain was his most difficult problem almost costing him his life several times. Despite the effort he put into organising his expedition, he barely survived reflecting not only the challenging nature of the country crossed but also a series of unexpected misfortunes. Not only was his friend killed by several Aboriginals accompanying his expedition, most of the supplies were subsequently stolen leaving Eyre and Wylie, with only several packhorses, some food, a little water, and their wits, to find their way out of that waterless vastness.

Based on Wylie's bush survival expertise, both men were able to push their way to a point where serendipity played a key role in their ultimate success. On one of the few accessible beaches, they spotted a schooner offshore whose attention they were able to attract. This proved the turning point for their gruelling journey. With their food and water supplies replenished, they reached Albany several weeks later in July 1841. Yet, had it not been for this unexpected encounter, the expedition may very well have foundered on that desolate plain. Had they arrived eight hours earlier, or later, their story may have been more akin to that of Burke and Wills.

It was another reminder of how fine a line many an explorer trod, and the key role fate could play in both their successes and tragedies.

Driving east across the Nullarbor Plain, 162 years after John Eyre's expedition for which he received the Founder's Medal from the Royal Geographical Society, I followed the narrow stretch of bitumen to the horizon: its narrow path the only hint of humanity in an otherwise mesmerising vista of saltbush or stunted scrub to all points of the compass. While the road across the Nullarbor Plain did not parallel the coast, its path did pass the edge of the Great Australian Bight where, on several occasions, my reward was a spectacular view over the Great Southern Ocean.

The water here was another beguiling patchwork of blue hues as the waves and currents splashed across Nature's ocean canvas, dashing against the continent in a white ribbon of foam that ran parallel to the line of cliffs for as far as the eye could see. Standing at the edge of the Nullarbor Plain, the cliffs plunging a hundred metres into the ocean below, the natural inclination of the continent to rest above the ocean floor was starkly exhibited even though the reality played out on the edge of the continental shelf some distance over the horizon.

Apart from these few sporadic but appreciated distractions, the Nullarbor Plain passed by in a blur of azure-blue above and dirty brown below, meeting at the horizon, much as the Barkly Tableland had also done. Fortunately, this part of my journey was punctuated by several delightful campsites along its route and various seafood delights from occasional small towns passed. After several days driving, Port Augusta was finally reached after which, heading north, the purple-blue smudge of the Flinders Ranges appeared on the horizon: an important landmark for my return to Central Australia. This represented an opportunity for a last visit to the magnificence of the West MacDonnell Ranges, and Nature's Cathedral at Ormiston Gorge, for one last stay within its welcoming embrace, before the final stage of my journey back to Sydney commenced.

On returning to Ormiston Gorge, my feeling of connection was as strong as when I first entered its realm 18 months before; my delight at being back within its domain as heady as the tangy eucalyptus smell wrapping the land in its invisible swathe. Returning to this natural cathedral, the feeling of belonging was as unwavering as any other time I had visited this sacred place. Everything about the gorge was just as I remembered, particularly the magnificent, ancient eucalyptus tree spreading its branches across the waterhole as the hot summer air throbbed with the deeply resonating tones of a cicada symphony.

The sand was hot to the touch, its glare blinding. I felt I was slowly roasting when walking across the sand and rocks as the sun's reflection gave me a double dose of its considerable kick. The waterhole was lower than I remembered as its life-giving waters had slowly evaporated under the intense glare of the desert's summer sun. The gorge glowed a deep ochre-red, its walls stretching high into the cobalt-blue sky creating the synthesis of colour that remains my favourite memory of Central Australia. I had to wait for dusk for Nature to reveal the broader, softer palette of colours I had come to enjoy most of all.

I spent several days relaxing in Ormiston Gorge, heading into its sanctuary in the early morning light, with only a book and my thoughts, and not emerging until the starlit night sky had made its welcome return late in the evening. Each day, as the gorge lived and breathed, it inspired and beguiled with its beauty and charm. Each day, the gorge showed me another side to its being that astounded me yet again.

A painter's palette could never have captured the subtleties of colour reflected in the majesty of its walls and the enormity of the sky over the course of the day. A religious text could never have provided the spiritual insights that came from simply sitting within the realm of this ancient, natural cathedral. An opera's drama could never have captured the inspiring story of its creation and the dramatic conversations among its many elements since the dawn of time.

The quietness of the gorge gave me time to think about such things, to reflect on the important questions of life. The grandeur of the gorge inspired me to believe in an adventurous life and the importance of time and patience to its accomplishment. It helped me to appreciate the great gift I had received from my 'liberation' and the opportunity it represented to redirect my life down a more fulfilling path. Everything about Ormiston Gorge inspired and intrigued as it had from the first moment I entered its domain. Sitting on the rocks that last evening, looking towards the shining beacon of Mount Giles in the distance, I felt uplifted and inspired. As I prepared to return to civilisation, and down a new life path, I knew these were the times I would remember most of all.

That last night, I could not turn to leave until the sun had set. Therefore, I sat and watched as the vista over Mount Giles unfolded one last time, as mesmerised and fascinated as the first time. High in the midnight-blue sky, I caught a glimpse of the first evening star. Soon the shy twinkle of that first star was answered by the twinkle of another and then another: the sky slowly lighting with the energy of the Universe. As the stars grew in number, so the dusk slowly spread its shadow across the land until even the light on Mount Giles was finally extinguished. Only then was it time to leave this sacred place, one that had enchanted and inspired from the moment of my first connection.

Walking back through the gorge to the waterhole, the increasing darkness cool and comforting, there was total silence except for the soft sound of an occasional wallaby bounding away over the rocks. The towering gorge walls, their inky blackness silhouetted by an increasing number of stars, ensured only a sliver of the night sky was visible. As the hard, rocky floor petered out into soft sand, and the faint dusk light on the horizon increased as the gorge opened up, the waterhole came into view. Not wanting to leave, I sat on the sand for some time just watching and listening as the waterhole's native wildlife around me slowly came to life that evening. I wonder if they know how fortunate they are to call a place like Ormiston Gorge, home.

My last act of connection with this sacred place was swimming in its waterhole the following morning. With the relentless sun beating down, its furnace-like feel draining my body from the moment I walked out of the shade, the cool depths of the waterhole were a welcome respite from the heat of the day. Caressed by its pristine waters, the natural world's enchantment lay all around with its abundance of colours enhanced and magnified by the simple purity of the landscape. The deep ochre-red gorge walls with their quartz veins, towering grandly over the gently rippling waterhole, contrasted exquisitely with the white brilliance of the sandy beach and the cobalt-blue sky.

Not only were my senses inspired visually, they were inspired harmonically as the cicadas started their chant. A pulsating, didgeridoo-like hum that mirrored the heat waves' resonance as they gently pounded me through the morning.

Immersing myself into the waterhole for the last time, I felt pampered by the bounty of Nature's realm. I felt completely revitalised as my whole being was finally cleansed of the residual dis-ease from my former life. It was in this moment I finally felt ready for the new life that awaited once my walkabout was completed.

Swimming across that nurturing waterhole for the last time, I felt free. I felt completely alive. I felt enveloped by the resonance all around. I felt connected with the soul of the natural world, the life force of my whole being. I felt part of Nature. It felt part of me. Life was truly that simple. Nothing else was required to be healthy and happy. It was this enlivening feeling of intellectual, physical, emotional, and spiritual freedom, as rediscovered in Ormiston Gorge, which I will never forget.

Travelling south, the heat and dry of early summer continued to make its presence felt. Dancing mirages appeared on the horizon: the outlandish shapes conjured up by Nature's hand a pleasant distraction to the spinifex and saltbush vista covering the ancient sea floor to all points of the compass. It almost looked like the surface of the moon so completely sparse and homogenous was its cover. Then, as if to make me question whether in fact I was on the moon, the town of Coober Pedy came into view.

Coober Pedy's fame lies in the geological bounty painstakingly won today from that ancient sea floor: its surface pitted with what appeared to be hundreds of small meteorite craters. Yet it was not treasures from the Universe that created this moonscape. It was instead geological treasures unique to the Australian continent. Opals, the fiery rocks of captured rainbows from Nature's hand, were its lifeblood. There are some tough mining towns in Australia but probably none tougher than Coober Pedy given the heat, the dry, the isolation, and the desolation!

Reaching Coober Pedy was important for a very special reason. For it was here I found the items required for a last bush supper, a last meal under the magnificence of the Southern Cross and night sky deep within Nature's Outback realm. For this was to be my last night in the Outback before civilisation would, once again, impose its unrequited influence on my life.

To the south of Coober Pedy lie a number of salt lakes: their white, pristine surface the perfect natural canvas to savour Nature's visual harmony as a sunrise or sunset unfolds across the horizon. Lake Hart was one such place with the contrast of its white, pristine vastness against the soft, ochre-red sands of the desert particularly beguiling. It was hot on arriving in the late afternoon and a bit uncomfortable as the amorous bush flies crawled into every open part of my body looking for that all-important drop of moisture. Their presence was something I would not miss when my walkabout was over!

Perhaps because it was my last Outback camp, or perhaps because it was my final night in the desert, I remember that evening's sunset as particularly captivating, especially as its colours started their slow dance across the salt lake and sky. Several small sand dunes next to my camp, their rippled, nuanced shadows constantly changing as the sunset slowly turned to dusk, reminded me how much the natural world is a dynamic, living creation. As the orange rays vertically streaked the last of the dusk sky, turning the white salt lake into a mirror of gold, and the rails from the Indian Pacific transcontinental railway skirting my camp glowed as if straight from a furnace, the first stars twinkled their welcome return.

As the sun set that evening, and the flies ended their hitherto unceasing assault, the cool, refreshing curtain of relief I always looked forward to in the desert started its slow descent. Its subtle caress was an appreciated reminder of Nature's ability to succour and sustain me once I had proved my mettle through the draining heat of the day.

Sitting on my swag in the dust, lathered in sweat and smoke from several days of living on the track, I once again realised how my happiness came from simply connecting with the surrounding delights of the natural world. I required nothing more to be happy with my place, and role, in the world. It was another of the valuable insights I took away from the many remote bush campsites enjoyed on my walkabout.

My routine that night was the same as it had been since first commencing my walkabout two years before. On choosing a campsite, I tossed my swag onto the ground near where I intended to build the fire. Following a quick walk through the surrounding sand dunes to collect firewood, I started the small fire needed for cooking my last bush supper. As the fire crackled and hissed, slowly transforming the small pile of branches into the hot coals required, the tangy smell of burning eucalyptus leaves appreciatively marked the transition of the dusty smell of day into the sweet fragrance of night.

Watching the fire come alive, its flames dancing their way back and forth across the stage of broken branches, was to see another of Nature's ballets. Whether it is the creation or destruction of a continent over the eons, the changing environment over the course of the seasons, or the splash of light and colour over the course of a day, Nature exists in a perpetual state of dance. A dance we can choose to be part of, which will always be to our benefit, or a dance we can ignore at our peril.

As the fire slowly transformed the branches into a pile of pulsating, red coals, so the night sky slowly evolved into a multitude of pulsating, white coals. Stars spread their message of inspiration and hope across the desert landscape providing the only source of entertainment I now needed. The stars were my constant companions and had been so for the many months on the track. They were a source of excitement and wonderment. They painted the bush in colours and shapes that inspired me to understand how tender and inspiring the natural world can be.

That is one of the things I will miss most about the bush – the opportunity to lie at night on the cool canvas of my swag with nothing but the moon and stars above to entice and inspire me with their visual delights. Nothing more was needed once the night sky held me deeply within its thrall.

As Nature's ballet of light across the western horizon slowly came to a close, and the flames of my fire converged into a pulsating pile of glowing coals, it was soon time to focus on the task at hand. The cooking of my last bush supper. This feast, an epicurean delight, was a most appreciated change from the previous meals of canned tuna and four bean mix I had eaten for most of my recent journey. This time, I savoured saltbush-raised lamb and roasted vegetables cooked on the coals, washed down with the dregs of the small cask of red wine that had bounced across the Outback in my 4WD since leaving Broome quite some time ago. It was a meal worthy of celebrating the completion of my walkabout following the quite unexpected nature of my 'liberation' over two years before.

It was a meal whose tantalising sights, flavours, and aromas brought back countless memories of other remote bush campsites previously enjoyed. Whether it was my first campsite at Combo Waterhole, where I likewise savoured a meal of saltbush-raised lamb and roasted vegetables cooked on the coals, or the hundreds of other campsites also enjoyed, each taste brought back a different time and a different place. And, as the flames returned to life as I gently stoked the fire, so the faces and voices of the many people I met during my journey also came back to life.

I could see the Aboriginal gentleman I crossed paths with in the Gulf, one of the finest human beings I have ever met. I could see Robert and his family working their cattle, content in a strenuous life that keeps them close to Nature's embrace. I could see the Swiss Family as we laughed and joked around the fire at Sandy Billabong or Edith Falls, with the other accents from that time creating their own delightful melody. I could see Lars and Taka on their bikes, happy in the time they too were spending alone in the vastness of the Australian Outback. I could see the faces, and hear the laughing voices, of the many new friends whose generosity and goodwill made my walkabout such a wonderful, inspiring, and enlightening experience.

In many ways, sitting on my swag in the dust by the fire, it was hard to believe my journey was ending. It was hard to believe there would be an end. Maybe not an end but a change of direction that would bring my carefree time on the track to a close. It was hard to believe, sitting on my swag next to the fire that evening, this night would soon be just a memory. It would be a time in the past, spoken of in the present, wistfully hoping it would apply to the future.

Looking into the fire, I thought of my 12 mentors, the desert philosophers and guides, whose achievements had encouraged a bush child to live with the same sense of adventure they had. Seeing the continent as John McDouall Stuart, Ernest Giles, Burke and Wills, Charles Sturt, Patsy Durack, Nat Buchanan, Augustus Gregory, and John Eyre had first seen it connected with that part of my soul that had called since my first memory to discover the magnificence and wisdom of the Australian bush. Crossing the tracks of Essington Lewis, Charles Bean, and Hubert Wilkins connected with the importance of using my mind as much as my body in following an adventurous life path. Reading the bountiful poetry of Will Ogilvie facilitated my connection with Nature in a most heartfelt way having now experienced the teaching and wisdom about which he had so intuitively and lovingly written.

Sitting with my mentors in the sands of the desert that last evening, I more fully appreciated the enormity of their respective achievements and why their lives were such a beacon of inspiration. They had discovered what I had been seeking on my walkabout. The knowledge that following the life path that calls, irrespective of the obstacles placed in our way, is the key to making the most of our time on Earth. Despite being alone in the desert that last evening, it was impossible to feel lonely connected to their lives and spirits as I was.

Sitting by my fire, I realised that, while my mentors played a significant role in my journey and the insights gained, the most important lessons had come from the land itself. It was the Australian continent, and my time spent within its nurturing embrace, which had the biggest impact of all. It was the land, for me, as it had been for the First Australians, that most influenced my understanding of the wisdom required for a life well lived and the teaching necessary for its accomplishment. In that moment, I intrinsically understood how much I was shaped by the land, and how it would always influence how I saw the world and my role in it.

I also understood how the land had significantly influenced and determined the nature of the Australian identity. How it influenced the music and movies created, the sports developed, and the painting styles Australians bring to the world. How it influenced thought processes and the energy of ideas in a manner unique to the continent itself. And how it influenced how we see problems and opportunities, and the approaches taken to those dynamic changes.

I now understood how the land has an energy different to that of other lands; an energy that does not always synchronise with that of other continents hence the discordance sometimes incurred from the wholesale importing of mindsets from other cultures. Particularly in how Australians have increasingly rejected their egalitarian ideals, induced by the land itself, and have increasingly taken on self-limiting, outdated mindsets from other continents instead.

Most importantly of all, I realised that as Australians try to understand their place in a rapidly changing world, it is only by getting to intimately know the land that created us will we ever understand who we truly are and what our role and contribution should be. I also realised the more we ignore the innate wisdom of the First Australians, and the importance of their connection to the land, the more we actively desecrate this inspiring, beguiling, and magnificent continent, and ourselves. A behaviour, with its associated consequences, for which we alone are solely responsible.

As the fire slowly died, my only earthly light was the slow, dull pulse of the coals: their red glow impervious to the darkness that enveloped the land. Above, the night sky gently resonated with light as the stars and moon cast their soft, silvery touch that soothed the landscape in a most beguiling way. It was another perfect night to roll out my swag: its cool canvas providing the ideal bed to be embraced by the light from the night sky. It was the type of evening I remembered as a child, of not wanting to fall asleep in case something special was missed; the type of evening whose memory still ignites the same feeling of emotion when reflected upon many years later. It was also the type of evening, with a good meal and a couple of cups of red wine under my belt, I had about as much chance of staying awake as turning back the Wet!

The only time I woke was when the Indian Pacific train snorted through my camp in the early hours of the morning. Apart from that unexpected occurrence, my camp was otherwise perfect and worth the risk of an unscheduled waking if it came to pass. With the roar of the engines and the endless rattle of its carriages passing by, the train played its role to perfection. For with my waking came another chance to enjoy the magic of the Southern Hemisphere night sky until sleep, slowly, returned once again.

The next morning, it was not the train that provided Nature's alarm but rather the flies. They were clearly early risers in this part of Australia. There is nothing quite as difficult as trying to sleep with the sound of a dozen flies buzzing in each ear. As I rolled my swag for the last time, tightening its two leather straps and tucking each end under their buckle, I thought back to Combo Waterhole when I had first unrolled my swag at the start of my journey. I could not quite believe, given the hundreds of times I had gone through this morning ritual, this was the last time I would do so on this journey. I could not quite believe my walkabout was almost at an end.

Not without some regret, I tossed my swag gently into the back of the 4WD for the last time; the thin film of dust wafting up adding yet another layer of ochre-red to the inside of the vehicle. Looking around the campsite that morning, the only hint of my stay was a small pile of ashes from the fire, flattened ground where my swag was unrolled, and boot marks connecting the two. And almost immediately, as the wind gently blew the ancient desert sand down off the dunes, my campsite began to revert to the unadulterated paradise it had been from the beginning of time. Fittingly, after the next rainfall, there would be nothing to show anybody had ever enjoyed the delightful, inspiring, and serene beauty of that nondescript place in the desert.

That is how it should always be. That is how we will ensure humanity always has places to explore and feel the sense of exhilaration that only comes from experiencing Nature in its untrammelled and natural state. It had been difficult leaving Ormiston Gorge that last time. It was equally difficult leaving this nondescript place to the winds of the desert that would shape and reshape it until the end of time.

Driving away from that campsite, I could not quite believe by evening the Outback would be just a memory. Its expansive and rugged domain no longer all around but far to the north and far to the west. It was with a feeling of sadness I pulled out onto the bitumen for this was also my last chance to follow in the tracks of John McDouall Stuart, the man whose legacy had enabled and supported so much of the journey undertaken. It seemed fitting the end of my walkabout occur on his path given his tracks were the first I crossed at the start of my journey. His path had been my path for only a short time, yet he now felt like a close friend given how much I had come to understand and truly appreciate the scope of his magnificent achievement.

Even though my walkabout was almost completed, it was important to remember it was just another step in the longer journey of life. Moreover, other opportunities would likely arise to, once again, roll my swag and follow another track to learn Nature's life-changing wisdom. The important thing to remember was to bring the right philosophy to these expected and unexpected changes in my life. They would not always be easy, these necessary lessons of life, but where I stayed true to the path of walkabout, where I followed Nature's teaching and conscientiously applied it every day, there would be no limit to what could be achieved and how much pleasure that would bring.

Following the Stuart Highway to Port Augusta, where I left the sands of the desert for the last time, the road home hugged the coast through Adelaide, Melbourne, and finally, to Sydney. Importantly, as I had promised Mum, I arrived home late in the afternoon of Christmas Eve. Nature had rolled out the welcome mat once again; the bush alive in all its Christmas glory as the cicadas hummed their appreciated welcome and the galahs and kookaburras loudly and excitedly conversed with me as they had across innumerable bush camps. The tangy smell of eucalyptus, mixed with the lightly-salted balm wafting in from the Pacific Ocean, weighed down with humidity as it had been across much of Northern Australia, was the final, definitive sign I was now back in Sydney.

Yet, while a loving family welcomed me back, I knew deep inside I was not entirely home. In fact, I could never come home as I once had. For home was not where I happened to live. Home was where I had just come from. Home was every campsite I had unrolled my swag whether under the stunning opulence of a Central Australian night sky, in the spinifex and rocks of the ancient Western Australian Pilbara, in the beguiling diversity of Northern Australia, or next to the many gorges, rivers, and creeks enjoyed. Places whose resonance, allure, harmony, and peace would remain part of my being always. In essence, home was now the Australian continent; the wild, rugged, enchanting beauty of the Great South Land as it had always been. Only now, I knew for sure.

As the engine gently idled, I could not quite bring myself to finally turn it off. It was almost impossible to believe my walkabout had reached its conclusion. In many ways, it had been a lifetime since being 'liberated' over two years previously. Yet, in many other ways, it felt like only yesterday when I first rolled my swag, first started the engine, and first looked into the azure-blue sky through the windscreen as the continent gently beckoned with its promise to recharge an exhausted mind, strengthen a weakened body, expand a numbed heart, and inspire a dejected soul.

In that moment, before turning the engine off for the last time, my walkabout came alive one final time as a thousand memories of Outback Australia rolled across the dirty haze of my windscreen. The smiling faces of many new friends flashed before me just as they had when we first met. The splendour of countless unforgettable vistas ignited in my memory with the emotion and connection to each of those places as strong as when first inspired by their allure on the track. Edith Falls, Kakadu National Park, the Devils Marbles, the MacDonnell Ranges, Ormiston Gorge, Uluru, Kata Tjuta, Chambers Pillar, the Flinders Ranges, Cape York, Lawn Hill, the Kimberley, the Pilbara, Lake Hart, and a hundred other places, many remote and rarely seen, each a jewel of such refinement as to make a mockery of the baubles humanity spends much of its life unnecessarily chasing.

It was in that moment the Australian bush fully revealed its soul and its wisdom, teaching, and whispered messages all became one.

It was in that moment I understood each part of the puzzle and how to piece them together to reveal the wisdom of the natural world.

It was in that moment I connected with the Australian continent, its rocks, plants, and animals, such that I would never be lonely again.

It was in that moment I understood how important it was to live in harmony with the land that created me, not based on transplanted ideas from other continents.

It was in that moment I understood the critical life lessons taught by my mentors and the importance of my connection to the places of their greatest triumphs.

It was in that moment I understood anything was possible, nothing was impossible, and my life path was now back in my own hands.

It was in that moment I understood the past and an opaque future became clear and focused.

It was in that moment I understood why it had been so important to follow Nature's siren call back to the Australian Outback to reconnect with my soul's home.

As my mind slowed, almost to a stop, I thought back to the moment I first rolled my swag as my walkabout commenced. I thought back to that moment and felt the circle finally close. After the events in New York that precipitated my 'liberation', and my initial confusion about what it all meant, everything now made complete sense. In that moment, there was an absolute quiet. I had accomplished everything required of me. It finally felt right to turn the engine off. My walkabout was over.

There was no regret and no sadness. Just a realisation that everything has a time and a place, and a journey has a beginning and an end. Even though my journey was now completed, it was an experience to be remembered to the end of remembering. For, with Nature's wisdom learnt and its teaching understood, it would remain a fundamental part of my whole being. Nature's wisdom was the key I had been searching for; the critical elements of meditation, exercise, diet, and sleep the core insights I had been seeking. It was ultimately Nature's tender soul that facilitated my connection with the teaching so critical to a life well lived.

For that, I will always remain incredibly grateful. For that, I will never forget.

Thank you, Nature, for sharing your beauty and wisdom with me.

Epilogue

In late 2004, I returned to New York and my investment banking career. After my three years away, it was a pleasure to return to the intellectual challenges enjoyed though now supported by a healthier, more balanced perspective. And, for the next four years, I focused on my career working with natural resources companies across the United States and around the world as I had before the first act of 'liberation'.

Yet, just when I finally felt my career was back on track, the Global Financial Crisis rolled around. As happened in late 2001, I was 'liberated' once again, in late 2008, as the destructive forces of Western society set yet another tragedy in motion much like the humanitarian disaster facilitated seven years previously with its ignorant and foolhardy response to the September 11 attacks. What else could I do but laugh at the absurdity of the situation and Western society's perpetual inability to learn from the self-inflicted problems it continually brings on itself through the same unthinking behaviours?

Moreover, just like my experience in 2001, it was the healthy and adventurous who were 'liberated' while the greedy, irresponsible, selfish, and political kept their jobs. Initially frustrated and disappointed at what had transpired, I soon realised how lucky I was to, once again, have an opportunity to follow the path that called, though in a manner I would never have otherwise expected.

Accordingly, I returned to what I know best – a walkabout. This time, I decided to enhance my professional skill set within the natural resources industry and, accordingly, swapped the wilds of Australia for the wilds of South Kensington, London, where I undertook a Master of Science degree at Imperial College. Instead of light-filled Australian days resplendent with horses and polocrosse, galahs and gorges, this second act of 'liberation' revolved around dark-filled London days replete with geology and engineering, management and finance. It was fascinating to be back at university learning more about geology, with field trips to Southern England and South Africa the highlights of the course.

This experience also provided the ideal opportunity to delve further into the awe-inspiring geological history of the Australian continent, and the inconceivable manner of its creation, as I had long sought to do. Although not living in Australia at this time, my studies further enhanced my whole body connection to the continent as I increasingly understood and appreciated the fascinating story of its birth and evolution.

After finishing at Imperial College, and seeking an opportunity to apply my skill set more broadly, I decided to walk the entrepreneurial path. Accordingly, I returned to work in 2012 with a private energy company focused on the plethora of challenges such a role entails. For six years, I indulged my fascination for strategy, operations, and finance across the upstream and midstream sectors of the energy value chain, all the while utilising Nature's appreciated insights from my walkabout to maintain my health and happiness through my connection with the natural world.

Yet, as on walkabout 15 years previously, what has a beginning also has an end. Intrinsically believing Nature requires as many voices as possible in its defence at this time, I 'self-liberated' in 2018 to publish this book thereby completing the final, yet unfinished, obligation of my walkabout. To show my heartfelt gratitude to that magnificent continent that so unexpectedly and generously gave me so much. In essence, to give the Australian bush, and the environment globally, a voice deserving of the value of its wisdom and the importance of its teaching.

Remarkably, as I finish this book, it feels like only yesterday when my time in the Australian Outback was my everyday reality. Propitiously, the tantalising smell of smoke from my fire, the sweet taste of water from an inland gorge, the delightful calls of a flock of acrobatic galahs, the lowering of the cool curtain of dusk, and the night sky casting its silvery glow across the landscape are all memories that return with an appreciated regularity.

It has been 15 years since my Australian walkabout ended and I last unrolled my swag in the vastness and quiet of the Australian Outback, under its magnificent sky, within its nurturing embrace. It has been 15 years since Nature, and Odin, released their gentle but firm grip on my soul with the call to walkabout answered for the time being at least. It has been 15 years since I appreciatively reconnected with Nature's siren call and the wisdom it generously imparted to achieve the life of health, happiness, and adventure sought.

Today, the bush continues to call, as it has from my earliest childhood days, and I will respond to that call until no longer able. When that day comes, when it is time to return to Nature's earthly, appreciated embrace one last time, for all time, it will not be to a grave in a fenced-in cemetery. It will instead be to the splendour of Ormiston Gorge, under its ochre-red ramparts overlooking Mount Giles in the distance, where my ashes will be scattered onto the waters of Ormiston Creek. In the timeless rhythms of that land, they will slowly travel into the Finke River and out into the sands of the desert one last time.

They will travel to where I will always call home. The majestic brilliance of Nature's inspiring realm in the Australian Outback.

Glossary

Acacia – A common species of tree in Australia of which there are over 1,000 varieties.

Akubra – A broad-brimmed hat made from rabbit fur, manufactured in Australia.

Anzac – A First World War abbreviation used to describe the Australian and New Zealand Army Corps.

Billabong – An Aboriginal Australian word for a waterhole in a river channel or creek that only flows after heavy rain.

Bitumen – A type of road surface built using tar and gravel.

Brigalow – A type of Acacia found through Central Queensland and into Northeast New South Wales.

Bush – Those parts of Australia outside the settled areas.

Bushranger – An Australian outlaw or highwayman operating in the bush.

Cleanskin – A term used to describe an unbranded beast, typically a calf, in the cattle industry.

Country – An expression that refers either to the whole continent or to a smaller region within the continent.

Didgeridoo – A wind instrument used by Aboriginal Australians created from a hollow tree or branch.

Drover – A person who moves stock over long distances primarily through the Outback.

Eucalyptus – A common species of tree in Australia of which there are over 700 varieties.

Gidgee – A species of Acacia that provides the hard wood used in many cattle yards and burns with great heat making its coals ideal for cooking.

Jump-up – An abrupt rise in flat country or a point where a track rises abruptly to another level.

Line of Lode – The location and direction of the Broken Hill orebody, which was shaped like a boomerang with only the middle exposed at the surface as the 'broken hill'.

Matilda – A swag or blanket bedroll typically carried by a swagman via a strap over their shoulder.

Mess Tin – A personal cooking pan and plate used by British and Commonwealth soldiers in the First World War.

Moleskins – A pair of jeans made from a heavy cotton fabric that is soft on the inside and protects your legs while riding.

On The Wallaby – To travel the Wallaby Track.

Outback – The sparsely settled regions of inland Australia.

Polocrosse – An Australian horse sport played with a cane racquet and soft, rubber ball.

Quart-pot – A steel container holding a quart of water, with an enclosed cup, typically used by ringers, stockmen, and drovers to boil a cup of tea.

Ringer – A name given to those who work in the cattle industry on large cattle properties or stations but are not qualified as stockmen or stockwomen.

Sapling – A young tree with a diameter of 10 centimetres or less.

Station – An Australian pastoral property, raising cattle or sheep, which is of a large size for the region located.

Stockman/Stockwoman – A person experienced in handling stock on a station.

Swag – A roll of blankets and pillow enclosed in a waterproof canvas wrap to protect against both the ground conditions and the weather.

Swagman – A person who carries a swag while travelling through the Australian bush.

Tucker Bag – A cloth or canvas bag carried by a swagman for food or other supplies.

Walkabout – An Aboriginal Australian word used to describe a ritual journey of discovery and connection through, and with, the Australian bush.

Wallaby Track – A track through the Australian bush used by itinerant and rural workers to move from one job to another.

Waltzing Matilda – To carry your swag. Also known as 'humping the bluey' with the word 'bluey' coming from the colour of the blankets.

Bibliography

Bailey, J., *Mr. Stuart's Track*, Pan Macmillan Australia (2007).

Bean, C.E.W., *Anzac to Amiens*, Penguin Books Australia (1946).

Bean, C.E.W., *Official History of Australia in The War of 1914-18, Volume 1, The Story of Anzac*, Angus & Robertson Ltd (1921).

Bean, C.E.W., *Official History of Australia in The War of 1914-18, Volume 2, The Story of Anzac*, Angus & Robertson Ltd (1924).

Birman, W., *Gregory of Rainworth: A Man in his Time*, University of Western Australia Press (1979).

Blainey, G., *The Rise of Broken Hill*, Macmillion of Australia (1968).

Blainey, G., *The Steel Master: A Life of Essington Lewis*, Melbourne University Press (1995).

Buchanan, B., *In the Tracks of Old Bluey*, Central Queensland University Press (1997).

Buchanan, G., *Packhorse & Waterhole*, Hesperian Press (1984).

Cane, S., *First Footprints: The epic story of the First Australians*, Allen & Unwin (2013).

Coulthart, R., *Charles Bean*, HarperCollins Publishers (2014).

Durack, M., *Kings in Grass Castles*, Transworld Publishers Australia (1959).

Durack, M., *Sons in the Saddle*, Transworld Publishers Australia (1983).

Eyre, J.E., *Journals of Expeditions of Discovery into Central Australia and Overland from Adelaide to King George's Sound in the Years 1840-41, Volumes 1 & 2*, Dodo Press (1845).

Flannery, T., *The Future Eaters: An ecological history of the Australasian lands and people*, Reed New Holland (1994).

Gammage, B., *The Broken Years: Australian soldiers in the Great War*, Penguin Books Australia (1974).

Gammage, B., *The Biggest Estate on Earth: How Aborigines made Australia*, Allen & Unwin (2011).

Giles, E., *Australia Twice Traversed*, Dodo Press (1889).

Gregory, A.C. & Gregory, F.T., *Journals of Australian Explorations*, BibliBazaar (1884).

Johnson, D., *The Geology of Australia*, Cambridge University Press (2009).

Lewis, D., *Beyond the Big Run*, University of Queensland Press (1995).

Lewis, D., *The Murranji Track*, Central Queensland University Press (2007).

Maynard, J., *The Unseen Anzac*, Scribe Publications (2015).

McDouall Stuart, J., *Explorations in Australia*, Kessinger Publishing (1864).

McLaren, G., *Beyond Leichhardt: Bushcraft and the exploration of Australia*, Fremantle Arts Centre Press (1996).

McLaren, G., *Big Mobs: The Story of Australian Cattlemen*, Fremantle Arts Centre Press (2000).

McMullin, R., *Farewell Dear People*, Scribe Publications (2012).

Morrison, R., *Australia: Land Beyond Time*, New Holland Publishers (2002).

Murgatroyd, S., *The Dig Tree: The Story of Burke and Wills*, Text Publishing Australia (2002).

Nasht, S., *The Last Explorer: Hubert Wilkins – Australia's Unknown Hero*, Hachette Australia (2005).

Ogilvie, W., *Saddle For a Throne*, Openbook Publishers (1996).

Pascoe, B., *Dark Emu: Aboriginal Australia and the birth of agriculture*, Scribe Publications (2018).

Sawrey, H. et al., *The Stockman*, Lansdowne (1984).

Sturt, C., *Expedition Into Central Australia*, Kessinger Publishing (1848).

Thomas, L., *Sir Hubert Wilkins: His World of Adventure*, Charles Birchall & Sons (1961-62).

Wilkins, Captain Sir G.H., *Undiscovered Australia*, G.P. Putnam's Sons (1920).

CPSIA information can be obtained
at www.ICGtesting.com
Printed in the USA
BVHW021215270519
549082BV00005B/6/P

9 780648 329220